SINS OF NEW YORK

AS "EXPOSED" BY THE POLICE GAZETTE

SINS OF NEW YORK

AS "EXPOSED" BY THE POLICE GAZETTE

By EDWARD VAN EVERY

Author of "Muldoon: The Solid Man of Sport"

With an Introduction by
FRANKLIN P. ADAMS
(F. P. A.)

A NEW WONDER OF THE METROPOLIS

With 120 Reproductions of the Original
Woodcut Illustrations

FREDERICK A. STOKES COMPANY
NEW YORK   MCMXXX

Published, October 23, 1930
Second Printing (before publication) October 15, 1930

INTRODUCTION

"WHITHER are we drifting?" ask the hodiernal tabloids.

"We are on the crest of the crime wave!" said the journals of the mid-Nineties, whose noisy yellowness of that day is now only the inaudible yellowness of age. "The city is rampant with crime," said the Rome *Tribune*. "SIN SWEEPS SODOM, SAYS LOT," was probably the headline of the Gomorrah *Mirror*.

Which is by way of saying that the history of a people is shown in the record of its vices and crimes and sins. Shown as accurately—and to the most of us more interestingly—as in its political history. And when these vice-and-crime records are at once more and less than the facts—that is, when they are the records of a prejudiced reporter rather than the log of a police blotter—they become more fascinating. For the years have corroded the prejudice away, and the scream of yesterday that froze the blood is the absurd squeak of to-day that arouses—if it can be heard at all—laughter.

To most of us the *Police Gazette* was something that we saw in barber-shops of the Eighties and Nineties. One of the first jokes I ever heard (at Sam T. Jack's Madison Street Opera House, Chicago) was "Seen the Police Gazette?" "No, I shave myself." Of course, the names of *Puck* and *Judge* sometimes were substituted, but that wasn't funny to me, because we used to have *Puck* and *Judge* every week at home. But I never saw a copy of the *Police Gazette* outside of Frank's barber-shop, which was on the south side of 35th Street, between Indiana and Michigan Avenues. It was, as World's Fair Chicagoans will recall, across the street from Hoteling's Bicycle Repair Shop, and half a block from the drugstore of Thos. H. McInerney and the residence of the growing boy who is now S. W. Straus, but who was then Art's big brother, Simon.

The *Police Gazette* was fascinating to us boys whose faces never needed Frank's razor oftener than once a week.

But I remember little of what I read or saw in the *Gazette,* though the little is vivid and accurate. I remember a feeling of disappointment when the picture of a pugilist appeared on the front page; for the pugilistic world was not my interest, even as it bores me now. But Women and Crime—that magic front-page partnership, dear to the heart of every circulation manager past, present, and future—interested and thrilled me. That is, pictorially, for I never read anything but the description of the picture—and I would gaze at the picture a long time.

Usually it was the picture of a woman, or of many women. Sometimes they were pursuers, sometimes pursued. Occasionally somebody had a revolver, later known to headline writers as a gun or gat. But it was ankles and legs that really got me. Those were the days when a woman's shoe-top was considered, as you might say, uptown. And these pictures showed some women's skirts—thousands of skirts—in abandoned disarray. Women were running, and were ostentatiously careless whether they displayed their legs almost to the knee. Yes, I used to stare at those pictures, and so did all the boys that I knew. Some of those boys have attained distinction in one field or another; but none has yet served a jail sentence or a term in the poorhouse. And while this proves nothing, I submit, to the censors who talk of Harm to Youth, that all these things—the amorous movies, the pornographic tabloids, the so-called obscene books—do no harm whatever. I am not controversial enough to try to prove that they do good. For either Wisdom or Age—or the mixture—tells me that nothing does youth much harm. Or good.

I do remember some of the advertisements that the *Old Police Gazette* carried, and I think that they were harmful and insidious. It seems to me that the *Gazette,* with the various crusades against umbrageous advertising, must have had litigious difficulties in its day, for it published dozens of "cures" for all manner of venereal diseases, remedies for impotence in appeals to "weak men and women, 'Pleasure Promoter,' tells how 'twas done to Helen," " 'How a Married Woman Goes to Bed,' 10 full-page illustrations, with comic reading, 10c," and hundreds of that sort.

Of the influences of the *Police Gazette—The National Police Gazette, the Leading Illustrated Sporting Journal in the World*—on the sporting life, especially on boxing, Mr. Van Every has written exhaustively in this book.

His book shows, uniquely and fascinatingly, a great part of the history of the American people, their tastes, their violences, their recreations. I would rather read a file of the *Police Gazette* than a file of the *Century Magazine,* or even of *Harper's Weekly.* And I'd rather read Van Every's report and interpretation of those files than read the files.

He tells me that in its heyday, long before the tabloids beat the *P. G.* at its own game, its circulation was about 400,000, and on big fistic occasions like the Sullivan-Kilrain fight it went as big as half a million. To-day the circulation, I am told, is below 50,000; and what with the daily newspapers printing pictures that make even the old *Gazette* seem conservative, and tabloids out-sensationing the *P. G.* at its pinkest period, the once popular weekly is in what the boys call a Tough Spot. Its zippiest picture (June 7, 1930) is its front page one of Clara Bow, a further cry from the nude than you can see in the movies. Its "hottest" advertisements in that issue were such as "If you want a 'rich' and pretty sweetheart, write Grace Dotson, South Euclid, Ohio," and "The 'Stuff' You Want for Men Only. 20 French style pictures. 9 original, all different, daring and spicy French stories. Momart Importing Co., Brooklyn."

I feel old, writing about the *Police Gazette*. I feel almost like answering one of those advertisements to assure me that I could regain my Vanished Virility for a dime, ten cents, the tenth of a dollar. But what makes me feel old is the certainty that before long my two-year-old son, getting his 10,000,000 circulation newspaper over the television radio, will be writing an introduction to Van Every's grandson's history of the 1931 tabloids, and how we Old Gentlemen used to get a kick out of those outworn one-hoss shays of journalism.

But he'll need this book for reference, the little upstart!

F. P. A.

CONTENTS

CONTENTS

ILLUSTRATIONS

ILLUSTRATIONS

ILLUSTRATIONS

[xiii]

ILLUSTRATIONS

FOREWORD

THE POLICE GAZETTE!

Against the background of American newsprint, this oldest of illustrated periodicals stands out a scarlet silhouette. While it flourished in other generations, the name, POLICE GAZETTE, still intrigues as a cherished though bawdy souvenir of the bygone. Even if our impressions as to what the *Gazette* once stood for, be merely something that has been handed down to us, we are yet alive to the fact that this glamorous roué of journalism was conceived and thrived on sins.

In fitting this epitome of sin between book covers I have carried my researches only to the end of the gaslit era. Even so, it has meant delving into five decades; decades that embrace the middle Forties to the early Eighties; decades that picture a New York suffering from growing pains, obstreperous adolescence and other ills a young and eager nation falls naturally heir to. My task has been to select out of this overgenerous wealth of material, what I may be permitted to describe as the *Gazette's* best worst features. I have chosen liberally from "Lives of the Felons," "Glimpses of Gotham," "Tales of the Tombs," "Deadly Dives," "Vice's Varieties," and similar popular serials and departments peculiar to the *Gazette,* together with generous excerpts from its accounts of big murders, misdemeanors and mysteries.

In the selection of the pictures, this has been done with an eye to giving as diversified an example of the workmanship of the *Gazette* artists as possible, even at the expense of any attempt toward having some conform overclosely to the text. And among the reproductions of these woodcuts (ranging from eighty-odd to a half century old) will be found some of the finest work of its kind, and with the original captions retained in practically every instance.

Against the fact that the *Police Gazette* esteemed itself a national weekly, and was so known, I have confined myself to the sinning that went on in New York. For did not New York, even in those halcyon days, set the pace?

A survey of these sins brings realization that the monster sins which the city of New York combated were Poverty and Politics. The fight against political corruption, of which New York had more than its share, has been ably and extensively dealt with in recent books, such as the history of Tammany Hall and others which single out the Tweed and Fernando Wood régimes. For this and various reasons, I have gone but lightly, if at all, into such momentous happenings as the Draft and Police Riots, the Fisk killing, the raid of the ghouls on the Stewart tomb, as well as some other historical occurrences. And the following still remains a fairly comprehensive survey of the sins of the times. What is more, most of the foregoing transpired when the fortunes of the *Gazette* were at a low ebb, or when the paper was a tool of corrupt powers, and when its handling of the sins we have neglected was nowise noteworthy.

In the matter of such famous cases as the Nathan and Richardson murders, both extraordinary crimes when the Sixties were giving way to the Seventies, the *Gazette* was quite its vigorous self. These cases, which show a different side of the *Gazette,* were touched upon by both the original and the modern *Gazette.* As years went by and persons who had played a prominent part in these affairs were brought to public attention through death or some other cause, these murders were always reviewed anew and additional matter brought to light. It is of interest, particularly in the Richardson affair, to note the change in attitude that came over the *Gazette* with advancing years. A distinctly new tone is evident in the ultimate treatment as compared with its handling of the first important murder case that engaged its outraged attention, the tragic deaths for which Polly Bodine was thrice tried.

The *Police Gazette* came into existence in 1845, and so dates back beyond such contemporaries as *Harper's Weekly, Frank Leslie's Weekly* and *Robert Bonner's Ledger,* eminent publications in their respective days, and in competition with which the *Gazette* shone in its own special fashion, and all of whom the *Gazette* outlived, being still in existence. There were two distinct *Gazettes,* the first, strangely enough, being a crusading journal. Then, in the Seventies, Richard K. Fox took it over and made it into the pink periodical of sensations and sports, and of which most of us still retain vivid recollections. Its heyday, under Fox, extended beyond the Nifty Nineties, when it began to take on the complexion of a more sophisticated newspaper; one more reason why I have not extended these delvings beyond the gaslit era. The *Gazette* ceased to be funny when it started to take itself as a joke.

E. V. E.

SINS OF NEW YORK

AS "EXPOSED" BY THE POLICE GAZETTE

PART I

THE ORIGINAL POLICE GAZETTE

(1845)

NATIONAL POLICE GAZETTE.

VOL. 1. NEW-YORK, SATURDAY, OCTOBER 18, 1845. No. 6.

THE NATIONAL POLICE GAZETTE,
CIRCULATION, 9,200 *COPIES*,

Will be published, for the present, once a week, or oftener, if necessity demands, at the low rate of $2 per annum, to mail subscribers, payable invariably in advance.

Agents forwarding $5, will be entitled to three copies sent to their order, and in proportion for more.

An extra will be published at any time, either by day or night, if desired, containing descriptions of recently stolen money, drafts or goods, and the thieves suspected, which will be instantly forwarded to our numerous correspondents throughout the Union.

Advertisements published on reasonable terms.

☞ All letters, to insure prompt attention, must be *post paid*, and addressed to CAMP & WILKES, Editors and Publishers, 27 Centre street.

Entered according to Act of Congress in the year 1845, by Enoch E. Camp and George Wilkes, in the Clerk's Office of the District Court of the United States for the Southern District of New-York.

LIVES OF THE FELONS.

NO. II.—CONTINUED.

ROBERT SUTTON,

ALIAS "BOB THE WHEELER."

The clouds kept lowering over Redmond, and it appeared as if some malicious genius was contriving circumstances to conspire to his destruction. A few days after his cruel and gloomy incarceration, a hack-driver, living in Brooklyn, named Robert Howard, big with a circumstance which seemed to weigh momentously in the balance of the prisoner's guilt, called upon John Low, the President of the Union Bank, and communicated a fact which appeared to set doubt completely at defiance. He informed that gentleman that on the day after the presentation of the forged checks by Redmond, a person named Robertson engaged him to drive him to the "Narrows,"—that he acted singularly throughout the ride, and in addition to asking many simple questions, displayed immense amounts of money in bank notes, which he stuffed now and then carelessly in different pockets about his person; that on their arrival at the hotel at the place of their destination, the stranger took a large handful of the bills, with a lot of letters, and a key, and folding them all up together in an envelope, directed it to Redmond; then telling witness it contained $2,700, requested him to hand it to Redmond, and directed him, if he put it into the post-office, instead of delivering it in person, to be sure and seal the parcel before doing so. He obeyed the direction by handing it to Redmond in person, who received it without surprize, and only remarked on taking it, that it was "all right." Here was an incident that included every element of strong corroboration, and the prosecutors pressed the complaint against the unfortunate accused anew, and with a good heart. The man Robertson, who had not been heard of since, was regarded as the fugitive accomplice named by Ware, and every feature of the story now seemed complete.

Impressed with the straightforward story of Ware, and overwhelmed with the positive testimony of the cashiers and the mass of corroborative testimony, the Grand Jury of the Oyer and Terminer unhesitatingly found two bills of indictment on the 1st December against "Timothy B. Redmond, impleaded with John Reed and David Ware"—one being for burglary and the other for forgery.

Immediately upon this result, Redmond, by the advice of his counsel, commenced a suit against Daniel Ebbetts, of the Union Bank, for false imprisonment, and laid his damages at $20,000. This, however, though the natural recourse of wronged and injured innocence, was only regarded by the public as a *ruse*, and was generally laughed at as a remarkable specimen of daring and audacious effrontery.

On the 13th December, he was arraigned in the Court of Sessions for trial, but the proceedings were quashed by his counsel (who were obliged to fight his doubtful case on technicalities) on the ground of the indictments having been found in a higher Court. Upon this defeat, the prosecution immediately sent in the papers of the case to the Grand Jury of the Sessions, and so ready were they to further the proceeding that indictments were also found by them at once. The trial was then set down for the following term, and on the 15th, the dread ordeal commenced. Pale, nervous, and fearful, Redmond was brought into the densely crowded Court and placed in the felon's dock. Confinement and ignominy had told with terrible effect upon him. The bloom had faded from his cheeks; the flowing curvatures of untroubled health which had abounded in his form, had given place to sharp and attenuated angles, and his bold, cheerful, careless eye glared cavernous and haggard, deep in the recesses of his head. He gazed for a moment furtively around in search for a sympathizing glance, but chilled to death by the walls on walls of cold and eager eyes that peered unmoved upon his misery, he abandoned the effort in despair. Where was that "consciousness of innocence" to bear him up which vain and superficial moralists are so fond of vaunting as the consolation of the guiltless? Contrast its effects with the unshaken confidence of the crime-stained and pampered fiend who sat calmly by the county prosecutor's side to accuse him, and we find an answer: an answer that tells us that coarse, hardened, indurated guilt is incapable of that refined and piercing agony which strikes so deep into the pure and penetrable soul. Infamy, the sharpest weapon of avenging Justice, makes no impression upon one, while it stabs the other to the very heart. Talk not of the consolation of innocence! Hell can invent no torture so refined as this, to the condemned who cannot make it known.

SUTTON'S "DARBY & JOAN," 24 ROSEVELT STREET, NEW-YORK.

The broken energies of Redmond were capable of one more effort. He beckoned to his counsel and faintly begged that he might be permitted to leave that ignominious box and be seated by their side. The Court listened to the motion and graciously assented to it.

Ware was the first witness called. Without a tremor, without the slightest trepidation, he ascended the stand and again refastened perjury upon his soul. We subjoin his testimony, as furnished by the reports, without addition or comment, as it was drawn from him by direct and cross-examination.

WARE.—I know Timothy B. Redmond. I first became acquainted with him at his hotel in Pearl street, on the 15th of September last, and was introduced to him at that time by a man named John Reed, then calling himself William Patten. After this I was frequently in the habit of seeing Redmond at his hotel, but as we had some things in preparation, he advised me not to come there so often, as it might occasion suspicion. He, Reed and I, used frequently to go out at night together for roguish purposes. One night previous to the burglary we went together to the Bowery Theatre, and while there Reed cut off a gentleman's pocket. It contained a pocket book with eighty-six dollars in it. This we divided in going home. It was shared equally. I got for my portion *thirty-three dollars*.* I had not been doing any business in particular for some time. I used frequently to pass counterfeit money which Reed would furnish me. The plan for robbing Howlands' store was concocted one evening while we were all three walking from the American Hotel (where we frequently met after Redmond cautioned me not to come to his place,) down to Church street. When we had fixed every thing right, we all went down to South street about midnight on the 29th September. Redmond and Reed went in while I stayed outside *to watch the watchman*—(A laugh.) After they had stayed in for some time they brought out a bundle of papers. Howland's check was filled in by Reed, in the Exchange, with ink which he took out of a little bottle that he carried in his pocket, and which he had procured for the purpose at Howland's store. On the 15th October they gave me a check to draw on the Merchants' Bank for $3,500. Redmond, who handed it to me, waited on the corner of Nassau and Wall streets till I came back. I offered the check to the Cashier, but on his turning to examine the books, I got frightened and ran off. I then went back and gave the check to Redmond, who, on taking it, called me a fool, and went himself to the Union Bank and cashed the check for $7,760, and put the money in his coat-tail pocket. He got in payment one $5000 post note, two $1000's, one $50 and one $10. He had on at the time an oldish black hat and a dark greenish coat. We then went down to the North River, through Dey street, to the steamboat "Congress," and divided the money in the privy. Redmond then gave me *three thousand dollars*† of the money as my share, and offered me one of the $1000's to present the other check. I then went to the Franklin Bank with Reed, who went in and changed $1800. We all met again about an hour afterwards at the United States Bank and changed the $5000 note there. I will not tell where Reed is now, because I do not wish to get him into the scrape, but I was induced to bear evidence against Redmond, as I thought if I did not he would get the start and blow on me. I believe he and Reed used often to get the best of me in our operations and take me in, but in the end I have taken them all in. The last time I saw Redmond previous to being confronted with him at the police, was at the American Hotel. I believe if he is pressed hard he will confess his guilt. I have no expectation of getting clear by this testimony, but give it because Redmond has injured me and led me into scrapes."

When Ware left the stand a rustle of relief went round the Court, and again all eyes were turned upon the prisoner to scrutinize the effect of these revealments of his guilt. He betrayed no sign, however, except a deep depression, and during the testimony only evinced his agonizing pangs by an occasional shudder which shook his whole frame.

Edward A. Nichol, the paying teller of the Merchants' Bank, was next called, and testified that Redmond was the man who presented Aspinwall's check to him on the 15th October. He insisted that he could not be mistaken, as he had noticed the prisoner very closely at the time and perceived that he was slightly pock-marked.

J. Leggett, the first teller of the Franklin Bank, recollected distinctly the fact of a person having changed a $500 note of the Union Bank at his counter on the 15th October. The man who brought it was Redmond. He could not be mistaken, as he had visited him subsequently in prison. Shortly after changing the $500 note, another man had came in, whom he now recognized to be Ware, and saw $1500 on the Bank of America changed for him.

Daniel Ebbetts, the paying teller of the Union Bank, "believed Redmond to be the man who presented the $7,760 check to him, but did not feel willing to swear positively to him, as he considered it a very delicate thing to swear positively against any man, who had previously borne a good character. His impressions, however, were very strong, and he hardly thought he could be mistaken." This extreme caution on the part of Ebbetts was doubtless induced by a dread of the consequences of the suit for damages which had already been commenced against him by Redmond.

Howland and Aspinwall next testified to the falsity of the checks, and Ralph Watson, the keeper of the reading room at the American Hotel, mentioned by Ware as the place of rendezvous, testified to having seen Ware and Redmond there about the middle of September, though he did not recollect ever having seen them together.

Ten witnesses were then introduced from among the employees in Redmond's household, who testified to his having been confined at home the whole of the 15th of October with a slight derangement of the bowels, though sight of him had been lost at intervals on his retiring to his room. The *alibi*, therefore, was no more perfect than Holdgate's would have been upon a similar investigation.

Three witnesses, D. Munro, Charles Cox, and Charles Matthews, were next introduced by the defence to prove the prisoner's previous good character. These gentlemen testified to having known him some years previous in Petersburg, Virginia, where he had for a long time kept the first hotel in the place. The latter had known him as early as 1815, when he was a Quartermaster in the Army and stationed at Norfolk. In Petersburg his standing was very good, though it had been rumored he had burnt his house

* This defective arithmetic was not overlooked by Redmond's astute counsel.

† Here the perjurer's arithmetic trips up his statement, and he also makes a more unfortunate mistake in trying to work a round amount of $3000 out of an unchanged $5000 note.

THE MORALIZING MUCKRAKER

I

"In this Christian age,
'Tis strange, you'll engage,
When everything's doing high crimes to assuage,
That the direst offenses continue to rage;
That fibbing and fobbing,
And thieving and robbing,
The foulest maltreating,
And forging and lifting,
And wickedly shifting
The goods that belong to another away,
Are the dark misdemeanors of every day."

Dark and sinful, indeed, were the ways of the city of New York in the Forties. The poet of the period from whom we have just quoted had much material for his nimble fancy, which touched on doings even more fell and varied than those referred to in his next two lines:

"And then, too, the scrapes of seductions and rapes,
And foulest of crimes in the foulest of shapes."

Only shortly before this rhythmic catalogue of crime had been accorded the majesty of print by the *National Police Gazette,* the new Halls of Justice, which soon came to be known as the Tombs Prison, had raised their somber heights. The gibbet had already been erected for the third time in the prison yard, and the cells had been the scene of a combined marriage, honeymoon and tragic suicide; an incident enthralling in drama and romance. The world, indeed, had not yet ceased talking of the final hours upon this earth, of John C. Colt, brother of the inventor of the revolver, who, after a long legal battle that carried through one court after another and a lavish expenditure of money, had been sentenced to pay the penalty for the murder of Samuel Adams.

Caroline Henshaw, although not married to Colt, was during his incarceration, a constant visitor to the Tombs. It was the doomed man's desire to marry her before he was hanged, and the marriage ceremony

SUPPER FOR HER OLD MAN

TOMBS SHYSTER AND SHOPLIFTER: NO MONEY, THEN GIVE ME YOUR JEWELRY.

DEATH WATCH ON MURDERERS' ROW

THE BURGLARS' FAITHFUL MISTRESS.

A MURDERER GUSHER

IN THE YARD WHERE THE HANGINGS TAKE PLACE

A PRISONER WITH DELIRIUM TREMENS BEING TRANSFERRED TO BELLEVUE

THE NEW YORK TOMBS.
SCENES AND INCIDENTS IN THE AMERICAN NEWGATE.—[SKETCHED BY SPECIAL ARTISTS FOR THE POLICE GAZETTE.

was performed at noon of the fatal day, the time of execution having been fixed for four hours later.

The bride was accompanied by Colt's brother and inappropriately enough by John Howard Payne, author and composer of "Home Sweet Home." The Rev. Mr. Anthon performed the ceremony. By law the mistress became the wife just in time to become the widow. The marriage took place in the presence of David Graham, Robert Emmett, Justice Merritt, John Howard Payne, and the brother of the doomed man. After it was over the bride and groom were allowed to be alone one hour. And after this brief honeymoon the wife departed and Colt requested to be alone.

Just as the sheriff was about to intrude upon the prisoner's privacy to summon him to the gibbet an alarm of fire was raised. The cupola of the prison was ablaze. The hanging was forgotten in the excitement; but once the blaze was extinguished the sheriff remembered his job and sought his prisoner.

Upon his bed in the cell John C. Colt was stretched, with his hands composedly crossed upon his bosom and a knife buried in his heart.

There were those, the *Police Gazette* included, who hinted that the body found was not that of Colt but a corpse prepared for the occasion, and that the supposed suicide escaped either to Texas or California. The coroner, it was charged, was aware of the deception, and his jurymen were selected for their ignorance of Colt's appearance. New York was a lawless city, as had been proved in the mysterious murder of Mary Rogers, a recent happening, and one that was ever to remain a crime unsolved. It was high time a new organized police had come to take the place of the old police, better known as Leatherheads, who had guarded the city previous to 1844. They prowled the town at night in camlet cloaks, carried huge lanterns and cried the hour. Their leather caps were varnished twice a year and became like iron.

But we are now come to the year of Our Lord, 1845. Only a few months before, in the Polk-Clay presidential campaign, political excitement had been running precariously high. During one of the mass meetings, among the out-of-town delegations that marched down Park Row, were the Mill Boys, one thousand strong. A joyous free fight had developed during which knives, swords, pistols, clubs and fists were brought into play, six were killed and many dangerously wounded.

At this time, what was known as the "lamp district" did not extend above Fourteenth Street. The corrupt administration of Mayor Robert H. Morris had already felt the resentment of angry taxpayers at the public polls. Civic indignation was expressed over the fact that a city with a population of 400,000 persons should have a police department only eight hundred strong, and there was bitter protest against these men being compelled to work more than twelve hours a day. The Committee of Streets had reported in favor of employing Professor Morse to

A GIRL LAMPLIGHTER.

construct the new magnetic telegraph so as to communicate with all police stations in town. The City Corporation had engaged Mr. Ackerman, the sign painter on Nassau Street, to affix the names of the streets on the gas-lamps. The "unregenerate and unscrupulous vermin of the Five Points was for a time confined to its own breeding ground, which, in its debasements of crime and filth had been found to rival even the Whitechapel district of London, from which it had inherited many

Entered according to Act of Congress, in the Year 1879, by the Publisher of THE NATIONAL POLICE GAZETTE, in the Office of the Librarian of Congress at Washington.

Vol. XXXIV.---No. 96. NEW YORK, SATURDAY, JULY 26, 1879 Price Ten Cents.

A MASHER MASHED—HOW A CHICAGO YOUTH, OF THE "TOO-AWFULLY-SWEET-FOR-ANYTHING" VARIETY, WHILE ESSAYING THE ROLE OF A LADY-KILLER, WAS TAKEN IN AND DONE FOR, LIKE THE VERIEST COUNTRYMAN, BY A BRACE OF SHARP DAMSELS AND THEIR MALE ACCOMPLICE. SEE PAGE 7.

of its denizens." Not that the old town had been relegated to a tame place, confesses the *Gazette* some time later:

> . . . for the devotees of Melody, Bacchus and Cupid there were many celebrated sporting haunts flourishing in the neighborhood of Broadway Church and Walker Streets and along Park Row.
>
> The most famous probably was the Cooper House, corner Anthony (later Worth) Street and Broadway. And The Senate, in Church Street, was generally well thronged with women rich in raiment and poor in chastity. Sandy Lawrence's hostelry, famed for its "square meals," was only a few minutes' walk from this resort. Mike Murphy (the celebrated Irish pugilist) had his sporting drum on Broadway, corner Leonard

PICKPOCKET ON THE BATTERY.

Street. "Butter-Cake" Dick's coffee-and-cake saloon under the *Tribune* building was a respectable though popular hang-out. For those who liked politics with their refreshments, on Elm Street was The Ivy Green, headquarters of the Empire (afterwards the Americus) Club, then the Democratic stronghold of the State. It was presided over by John Clancy, later a member of the State Legislature. Tom Hyer, first champion pugilist of America, was at 26 Park Row, which was the headquarters for the Unionists, the Whig organization. There was strong rivalry between the two headquarters and the flagstones of Park Row were often thumped mercilessly with the brawny carcasses of the combatants.

Notwithstanding claims that, through new reforms, New York had suddenly become the best regulated city in the world, violations against law, morality and public welfare were still so much in evidence in 1845 that two of its more or less consequential citizens deemed it a fitting time to provide a new method of combating the evil-doer. And in this way there came into being the first of the American illustrated newspapers. It was named the *National Police Gazette* and the name has never been changed.

To the memory of not a few of the present generation, but in the main that of its fathers and grandfathers, the attractions of the *Gazette's* pink pages and what its pictures and printed content stood for, is still fairly fresh. But of the *Gazette* of three-quarters of a century and more ago, and its interesting history, little is now known. Its purposes and intent can best be explained by referring to its prospectus, which is reprinted in part, herewith.

> The necessity of such an instrument as the *National Police Gazette* to assist the operations of the Police department, and to perform the species of service which does not lie within the scope of the present system, will make itself felt at a glance. Our city, and indeed the whole country, swarms with hordes of English and other thieves, burglars, pickpockets, and swindlers, whose daily and nightly exploits give continual employment to our officers, and whose course through the land, whatever direction they may take, may be traced by their depredations. These offenders, though known to our most experienced members of the police, are protected from the scrutiny of the community at large; and the natural result is, that the unconscious public are in continual contact with miscreants who date their last stationary residence from the walls of Newgate, the shores of Botany Bay, or who have but recently left the confines of our own State Prison.
>
> It is of first importance that these vagabonds should be notoriously known. The success of the felon depends mainly upon the ignorance of the community as to his character, and until a system be adopted which will effectually hold him up to public shame and irrevocable exposure, the public will remain at the mercy of his depredations and nine-tenths of his fraternity go scot-free of any punishment.
>
> Suffering under the continually increasing evils which the immunity thus enjoyed by large classes of offenders has encouraged, plan after plan has been devised, and system after system to reform and remedy, projected. The throes of years, and the undiscouraged travail of a thousand brains, instead of resulting in the adoption of new, bold and original measures, has merely eventuated in the remodelling of a department. The press— the mightiest conservator of social welfare—has been left from the category of appliances, while every other branch of civil polity feels the force of its protective surveillance.

The success of felons depends mainly, as we said before, upon the public ignorance of their persons and pursuits. It will be our object, therefore, to strip them of the advantages of a professional incognito, by publishing a minute description of their names, aliases, and persons; a succinct history of their previous career, their place of residence at the time of writing, and a current account of their movements from time to time. By this means the most dangerous offenders, the knowledge of whose infamy has slept for years in the bosoms of a few tenacious officers, will be spotted from one end of the Union to the other, and every community throughout its length and breadth be put upon its guard against them. The peculiar stock in trade of the officers will be made the common property of the public; and the felon, branded with his shame, will be pointed

GEORGE WILKES,

THE FOUNDER OF THE "POLICE GAZETTE" AND OTHER JOURNALS, LATELY DECEASED.

out on all sides, and be stripped of the social impunity which mainly emboldened him to offense. The result of an active adoption of this course must therefore necessarily be to drive all resident rogues to a more safe and congenial meridian, and to deter all floating tribes of vagabond adventurers from embarking to a region where an untiring and ubiquitous minister of public justice stands ready to hold them to the public gaze until they become powerless from the notoriety of their debasement.

II

It happened like this: George Wilkes, a journalistic genius of his day, and Enoch Camp, who had turned from journalism to the law and then combined both

callings, were the founders of the original *Gazette*. The first-mentioned, just previous to this venture, had been the editor of a four-paged publication dubbed
The Subterranean, which was devoted in the main to the exposé of the source of
various political incomes, and how these were derived from inelegant vices. Wilkes
exposed to such purpose that he was set on by gangsters numerous times and was
even shot at twice. In addition, he was arrested no less than six times. The final
arrest, though followed by the demise of *The Subterranean,* had an unpleasant
aftermath for the administration of the city of New York. The editor's reports
made up from what he had seen and heard during his residence at the Tombs made

GEORGE W. MATSELL, Esq., Chief of New York City Police.

itself felt in the ensuing election by Mayor Robert H. Morris all the way down to
the warden of the Tombs.

Camp made an ideal partner for Wilkes. Camp handled the business and legal
end of the affairs of the concern, while Wilkes had charge of the editorial end.
After a few years Camp retired a rich man, and George W. Matsell, while yet
a Chief of Police in New York, became a part owner. This partnership lacked
the business acumen possessed by Camp, whose association with Wilkes must have
been exciting while it lasted.

If one chronicler is to be believed, the very first appearance of the new publication had fatal results. Its first number chanced to be carried to the place of call
of Jonas Burke, on Delancey Street, where the palatable blend in which he special-

ized gave his house the name of Gin and Calumus Hall. Some one took exception to an item in the *Gazette* and words wound up in a mêlée from which the proprietor emerged minus a couple of fingers and a portion of one ear, while the instigator had his nose very much disarranged, and a participant, who proved to be Croucher Collins, was carried out dead.

In the *Gazette's* initial issue, dated October 11, 1845, and under the title of "Lives of the Felons," the first of a series dealing with the notorious criminals of the period was started. No. 1, in this series, gave the opening chapter in the career of Robert Sutton, alias "Bob the Wheeler," whose exploits, to lift from the *Police Gazette,* "were they not substantiated by irrefragable proofs, they would be discarded by the most susceptible imaginations as the merest vagaries of fiction." We will deal with this villain in a separate chapter, so it may be seen that the amanuensis in question did not let his fancy or flow of English run away with him.

Before taking temporary leave of "Bob the Wheeler," it should be recorded how that personage was instrumental in putting the *Gazette* temporarily out of business, which happened every now and then. Soon after his release from jail, which was not so long after the completion of his life story in the *Gazette* columns, Bob Sutton descended on the latter's headquarters with a number of his cohorts, among them James Downer, the resurrectionist (whose grave-robbing exploits had been given attention by the *Gazette*). The roughs and the police milled all over Centre Street, and the railroad-tracks, which had not yet been laid down West Street to the Canal Street Depot of the Hudson River Railroad, were ripped up and used as weapons. Downer and two others of the Sutton forces were killed this time. Sergeant Belcher, who with Tim Mooney, the Keel Layer, were the bodyguards of Wilkes, were the only *Gazette* casualties. Mooney, who was alleged to have killed two policemen during a London riot, was only slightly injured, while Belcher suffered a broken arm. Though a mob of close to two hundred attacked the *Gazette,* the press and editorial rooms, then in the cellar of 27 Centre Street, seem to have been well barricaded.

It was quite necessary that the *Gazette* sanctum should be well barricaded, as it was in a more or less perpetual state of siege from the rage of the underworld. The most serious assault came in 1850, and this time six deaths resulted. Not only Wilkes himself and Belcher were carried to the hospital, but so was the *Gazette's* star reporter, Andrew Frost, who passed away from his wounds. Of the attacking mob, which was led by Country McCloskey, who had stood one hundred rounds with Tom Hyer, Nobby McChester and other ruffians of the Five Points, and such well-known Amazons as Lizzie the Poor Beauty, and Donkey Dora Cole, five were left dead in the streets. The plant of the paper was demolished this time.

These were perilous times for crusading tirades. Only the year before, which had opened with the excitement of the California gold rush, it had been the unfortunate duty of the militia to pour a rifle volley into a mass of rioting humanity, and twenty-two bodies had been left in Astor Place shot or trampled to death. While this horror was the outcome of jealousy between Edwin Forrest and the English tragedian, William C. Macready, there is plenty of reason for the belief that political chicanery brought about the crisis. Forrest had been coldly received in England. This was charged to Macready's envy and to the criticisms of the cuspidorial customs of the United States by Charles Dickens during a visit to this country. On May 7, 1849, both Forrest and Macready played Macbeth in New York and the latter's performance was broken up. Washington Irving and other leading citizens persuaded Macready to give another performance three nights later. On the same day handbills of an inflammatory character branding the appearance of the English actor as an insult to our Americanism were distributed through the city wherever they would do most harm. It was later proved by the *Gazette* that the handbills had been ordered by some one who had headquarters at the Empire Club, which was then led by Captain Isaiah Rynders. Where Bible House now stands was a stone-yard; also a sewer was being constructed along Fourth Avenue. Cobblestones and the contents of the yard made plentiful ammunition for the infuriated mob that descended on the Astor Place Theater to break up the Macready performance. When the militia was finally brought to the aid of the police the first round of fire was discharged above the heads of the rioters. Still they would not disperse. The fatal command then followed.

Going into the Fifties the *Gazette* was up against a twofold fight, battling not only the breakers of the law, but its guardians as a combination in addition. The municipality was sinking into such a mire of political corruption that in 1857 the city of New York was declared by the Legislature to be unfit to govern itself. There were two antagonistic police forces for a time that were more concerned in battling each other for authority than they were in fighting the enemies of public safety. As "an untiring and ubiquitous minister of public justice" the *Police Gazette* didn't have a chance. Still the weekly fired its barbs of righteous indignation, only the targets were far too numerous.

That frightful sink of human degeneracy in the forbidding heart of the Five Points, known as the Old Brewery, has been demolished several years by now. But the building, known as "the wickedest dwelling in the world" and its environs, had constituted merely the scum of human depravity and made up a quarter repellent to the normal citizen. The glittering and protected profligacy that had come into brazen existence along Broadway and Houston Street and its adjacent votaries is a far more dangerous snare.

One of the first and worst in the area is the tough concert saloon at 50 Houston Street and of which the proprietor, Charley Sturges, is well known to the entire crooked brigade of both sexes. At this place plots are hatched to break into banks, flood the country with "queer," spirit some pal out of prison, to put away some principal or witness, or to square it with the police. Here not a little counterfeit engraving is turned out by that first-class workman, "Cooley" Keyes.

This is a fair example of how the *Gazette* kept after the underworld, a tribute to its courage rather than its judgment under the existing conditions. The attack was kept up on 50 Houston Street even after "Dusty Bob" took over the place and held forth there until he was called to "do his bit in the jug" for cutting off the ears of some one who had annoyed him in a crib on Ninth Avenue.

Any number of similar places were given attention in the columns of the *Gazette*. There was Poughkeepsie Jake's at 27 Houston Street, and the House of Commons, which was right next door. And Fanny White's too well-known "palace of joy"; where her successor, Eliza Pratt, was referred to as "the madame known to widest shame in her day." Close by on Broadway was Stanwix Hall, where "Bill the Butcher" Poole was done to death shortly after his historic rough-and-tumble fight with John "Old Smoke" Morrissey. Near by was Abe Florence's famous The Corner, and a block or so away was Phil Maguire's equally notorious Lafayette Hall.

Here and hereabouts the loosest and most desperate characters of the city were wont to congregate. Not only did the felon and fancy female hold forth in this district, but likewise the so-called sporting element, which was then made up of "shoulder-hitters," dog-fighters, gamblers, actors and politicians. Here festered an appalling record of knifing, shooting, gouging, biting and manhandling affrays, and mayhem and murder. Jim Irving, who, like Morrissey, later became a member of the Legislature, and Jack Somerindyke "tasted each other's mutton." Poole beat and kicked Wally Mason so severely he never recovered, and Poole's brother-in-law, Charley Lozier, had holes blown through him by Johnny Lyng—just to cite a few of the doings with which the *Gazette* regaled its readers. Some years after the *Gazette* presented a list of the hangers-on of the Houston Street resorts who met a violent end, and enumerated half-a-hundred without much trouble. Some, like Poole and Tim Heenan, brother of John C. Heenan, of pugilistic fame, were shot to death; others, including William Farley, better known as Reddy the Blacksmith, and Jack Hilton, alias the Limerick Boy, were carved to eternity; and not a few were hanged.

The original *Gazette* started off bravely enough, but battling the criminal ranks when these were backed by the police and the politicians, was simply too much of an undertaking.

III

One of the very first exposures that exercised the indignation of the *Police Gazette* had to do with the ruinous effects of policy gambling. For a time the prize numbers were drawn from a wheel on the steps of the old City Hall in the Park, until the Legislature, in 1832, annulled the charter of the lottery company. It moved over to New Jersey, where it was drawn as late as 1850. After being driven out of New Jersey the lottery companies operated from Delaware, Maryland, Louisiana and other southern states. The operations of the drawing were revealed and one was also initiated into the mysteries of "station" and "day" numbers, "gigs," "whips" and "saddles." It was explained how "through this system of insurance" men of extensive capital were reaping a monetary harvest at the expense of the poor and at a rate of 31 per cent profit.

> The results of this are easy to be seen. Its deluded victims, unable to satisfy its exorbitant demands by their legitimate earnings, yield to its corrupting influence and commence pilfering from their employers. Step by step they wade deeper into crime, until advancing beyond the limit of precaution they are "engulfed" in ruin. The miserable victim is then consigned to the horror of a cell, and subsequently to a convict's doom, while those who are chargeable for his guilt, those who suborned him by their devilish traffic into crime, curse him for a "d——d black rascal," and riot in the avails of his plunder.

SPARKING IN TOMPKINS PARK.

A PLACE WHICH CUPID HAS MADE HIS FAVORITE STAMPING GROUND, AND WHERE THE STERN PATERFAMILIAS IS WONT TO APPEAR.

[16]

We do not hesitate to say, and we believe facts will bear us out, that nine-tenths of the crime and prostitution of the colored classes of the city are produced either directly or indirectly by policy gambling. Examine our prisons and see if the history of their inmates will not attest to this fact. [Apparently the Demon Rum did not get its just due for fell work.] Is this longer to be endured? Are the authorities of our city any longer to foster these jackals by tolerating their nefarious practices? Is the statute to be defied and the law mocked by a horde of villains who cluster like flies in every street where poverty has shrunk to its abode, and where gasping labor can be extorted of its pittance in the vain hope of casting a golden anchor in the future? What lacks, good Messieurs of the sword and scales? Cannot evenhanded Justice, who bestows her slashing strokes so liberally upon the impoverished and friendless victim, make one of her six cuts over the costards of this contemptible banditti? Do we live under laws, or is ruin and defiance licensed to grin from bow windows of five thousand dens of plunder without rebuke, while a force of eight hundred men loaf by turns on grocer's barrels, or hang about hydrants to pass soft compliments to errand serving-maids, or waste their tremendous energies upon the apprehension of wandering drunkards? Is there no one man in the country, in remembrance of his oath, bold enough to step into these nurseries of crime and cry "Forbear to violate the law!"

That is the kind of paper the original *National Police Gazette* was—at the start. As a result of the attack on the policy-gambling interests, the following letter of warning came to the offices of Messrs. Camp & Wilkes:

Some dozen of us have determined (if you persist in annoying us) to annoy you in a more disagreeable manner than the one you have so unsuccessfully aimed at us.

Yours,

THE POLICY BOYS

The *Police Gazette,* as already indicated, got quite used to this sort of thing through its years as a reform publication. And as for libel suits, they welcomed them.

We do not heed threats or libel suits. We are strong in the justice of our motives and will have out the truth at any cost whatsoever. We never dodged a challenge or evaded an investigation in our lives. Those who fear, make truce, but coercion never swerves the just and bold.

Thirty-odd years later the *Gazette* not only had room for the advertising notices of the Louisiana State Lottery Company, but gave a column to the annual listing of those who had won prizes above one thousand dollars.

THE ANNUAL RECORD.

Its Enormous Total and Wide Distribution. Caprices of Fortune.

A partial list of the prizes above One Thousand Dollars, paid by The Louisiana State Lottery Company during the year ending May, 1885, together with the names and addresses given to the Company by the holders, omitting those who have requested it.

Receipts for the amounts are on file at the offices of the Company.

DRAWING OF JUNE 17, 1884.

S. M. Rothschild, 232 Church street, New York...	25,000
Philip J. Gruber, Milwaukee, Wis.	4,000
Philip Hoffman, 1,836 Cass avenue, St. Louis, Mo.	2,500
D. Geo. Henkels, Philadelphia, Pa.	2,000
Chas. Clark, Philadelphia, Pa.	2,000
A. T. Badlam, collected through Wells, Fargo & Co.'s Bank, San Francisco, Cal.	2,000
Wm. Boyd, 3,122 School street, St. Louis, Mo.	2,000
Frank Cunningham, San Francisco, Cal.	2,000

DRAWING OF JULY 15, 1884.

Bank of Commerce, Memphis, Tenn.	15,000
N. M. Sewell, Spring Creek, Tenn.	5,000
E. B. Comstock, 295 Ninth street, Milwaukee.	5,000
W. Loud, West Oakland, Cal.	4,000
Chris. Hettinger, Memphis, Tenn.	1,200
Mrs. Emma J. Hoggard, Norfolk, Va.	1,200

DRAWING OF AUGUST 12, 1884.

Eugene Gaudins, New Orleans, La.	15,000
Louis Seymour, carpenter, Exposition Buildings, New Orleans, La.	15,000
Wm. de B. Elliott, Whitney National Bank, New Orleans, La.	6,000
T. S. Tutwiler, Sanford, Fla.	4,000
A. B. Glover, 25 S. Compton ave., St. Louis, Mo.	2,400
Lewis S. Day, New Haven, Ct.	1,200
Chas. Foote, Colchester, Ct.	1,200

DRAWING OF SEPTEMBER 9, 1884.

Mary Cunniff, 1206 Spruce street, Phila., Pa.	15,000
Louis P. Alpman, 325 Spruce street, St. Louis, Mo.	15,000
Henry W. Rahner, U. S. Towboat "Wm. Stone," St. Louis, Mo.	15,000
Drovers & Mechanics Nat. Bank, Baltimore.	15,000
J. Jacobs, 1,400 Mission street, San Francisco, Cal.	5,000
Mrs. R. S. Durst, San Francisco, Cal.	5,000
Union & Planters Bank, Memphis, Tenn.	5,000
Robert Locke, Memphis, Tenn.	5,000
F. H. Rudd, Columbus avenue, Boston, Mass.	4,000
G. A. Brown, corner Montgomery and Washington streets, San Francisco, Cal.	4,000
Bank of New Hanover, Wilmington, N. C.	2,000
Nathan Leiber, 40 Wylie avenue, Pittsburg, Pa.	1,200

DRAWING OF OCTOBER 14, 1884.

Louisiana National Bank, New Orleans, La.	75,000
Harry Smith, Greenville, Miss.	5,000
Wm. M. Kennedy, Planter, Greenville, Miss.	5,000
A. C. Bennett, 210 Sedgwick street, Chicago, Ill.	5,000
Wm. C. Briggs, Chicago, Ill.	5,000
O. C. Fox, Portage, Wis.	4,000
Sergt. James Scott, Taxing District }	
Patrolman J. Dougherty, Police Force }	1,200
Patrolman Con. Daley, Memphis, Tenn.	1,200

DRAWING OF NOVEMBER 11, 1884.

Thos. Mulhern, 2020½ Washington street, Boston, Mass.	15,000
Frank Crockett, Engine No. 12, San Francisco.	15,000
Jno. M. Moberley, Harrodsburg, Ky.	15,000
Louis J. Wild, Donaldsonville, La.	10,000
Robt. Richter, 2,541 Christian street, Phila., Pa.	5,000
Frank K. Duffey, 47 Washington street, Hartford, Conn.	5,000
D. L. Orr, Stephenville, Tex.	2,000
Hy. Brotherhood, Milwaukee, Wis.	2,000
Chas. R. Mueller, 409 Locust street, St. Louis, Mo.	1,200
First National bank, Indianapolis, Ind.	1,200
Brownson & Sibley, Bankers, Victoria, Tex.	1,200

DRAWING OF DECEMBER 16, 1884.

J. H. Kuttner, Georgetown, Ky.	30,000
Canal Bank, New Orleans, La.	30,000
First National Bank, Memphis, Tenn.	15,000
Paul Tischer, San Francisco, Cal.	15,000
Henry Levy, San Francisco, Cal.	15,000
Geo. M. Shackelford, Fireman M. & C. R. R., Memphis, Tenn.	15,000

Germania National Bank, New Orleans, La.	5,000
Albert Mass, } Employees of A. Goebel	
Lorenz Traub, } & Co., Brewers, Detroit,	
William Brommer, } Mich.	5,000
Benj. Noes,	
Gus. Phillips, Memphis, Tenn.	5,000
Mrs. Margaret Bressal, 402 Shelby street, Memphis, Tenn.	5,000
Jno. J. Mueller, 498 Hastings street, Detroit, Mich.	5,000
W. J. Hightower, Dublin, Ga.	2,000

DRAWING OF JANUARY 13, 1885.

Thomas M. Thornton, Shelbyville, Ill.	75,000
Lee Sampson, Sigourney, Ia.	5,000
Daniel Shutt, Chicago, Ill.	5,000
State National Bank, New Orleans, La.	5,000
H. E. Browne, Fairmount, Ind.	5,000
A. E. Hall, with Sanger Bros., Dallas, Texas.	2,000
Fred. Cheadle, Dallas, Texas.	2,000
Louis H. Kaichan, of Sux, Krouse & Co., Cincinnati, O.	2,000
O. J. Ferris, Cincinnati, O.	2,000
H. G. Vines, Lincoln, Neb.	1,200
Wells, Fargo & Co., San Francisco, Cal.	1,200

DRAWING OF FEBRUARY 10, 1885.

A. Vatuone, Hotel Italia, San Francisco, Cal.	75,000
Bertha Carey, Algona, Ia.	6,000
Mrs. J. B. Franz, Mansfield, O.	6,000
First Nat. Bank of Birmingham, Pittsburg, Pa.	2,000
F. Goessel, 421 I street, Washington, D. C.	2,000
Reuben Joel, 62 Monroe street, Lynn, Mass.	2,000
B. W. Bradbury, Woodland, Dak.	2,000

DRAWING OF MARCH 10, 1885.

Geo. A. Spear, Bay City, Mich.	75,000
Henry L. Schmidt, Memphis, Tenn.	5,000
Gabe Poindexter, Mason Depot, Tenn.	5,000
Hugh Neil, Mayfield, Ky.	5,000
T. R. Roach, State National Bank, New Orleans.	2,000
State National Bank, La.	2,000
Lewis Johnson & Co., Washington, D. C.	2,000
Louis Hinz, 433 Turk street, San Francisco, Cal.	2,000
Susan Fegan, 402 Hayes street, San Francisco, Cal.	1,200
L. Lalond, San Francisco, Cal.	1,200
Welbey W. Bargin, Richmond, Ky.	1,200

DRAWING OF APRIL 14, 1885.

John W. Haywood, 38 Charlton street, Savannah, Ga.	15,000
W. C. Parker, Windfall, Ind.	15,000
F. Spendrup, Donaldsonville, La.	15,000
——— Washington, D. C.	15,000
J. A. B. Putnam, Mt. Pleasant, Tex.	15,000
Frederick Maas, New York.	5,000
Henry Orban, U. S. Marine Hospital, San Francisco, Cal.	5,000
Fred. S. Beach, New York.	5,000
Bank of California, San Francisco, Cal.	5,000
Jno. M. Gies, 217 Crogham street, Detroit, Mich.	4,000
Wm. J. Collins, G street, N. W. Washington, D. C.	2,000
Dan. M. Moriarty, 96 Second avenue, New York.	2,000
Critton & Koentz, Natchez, Miss.	2,000
Ah Foo, 275 Tremont street, Boston, Mass.	1,200
H. C. Donnelly, St. Paul, Minn.	1,200
Wells, Fargo & Co., San Francisco, Cal.	1,200
Samuel Light, Montgomery, Ala.	1,200
Carson Rubey, Gainesville, Tex.	1,200

DRAWING OF MAY 12, 1885.

George Williams, Washington, D. C.	15,000
Orsini Zapp, Round Top, Tex.	15,000
Sam F. Spencer, Greensburg, Ky.	15,000
Harry Duthon, Melrose, Mass.	15,000
P. G. Sexton, Bruton, Stewart Co., Tenn.	5,000
Bank of Greenville, Greenville, Miss.	5,000
Jno. R. Jewell, Cattaraugus, N. Y.	5,000
W. W. Speers, Memphis, Tenn.	2,000
Wm. Greer, La Cygne, Kas.	2,000
Wm. Primean, Chatham, Ont.	1,200
A. Smith, 157 Cedar street, Nashville, Tenn.	1,200
W. R. Looney, Malden, Mo.	1,200
J. W. Harris, Atlanta, Ga.	1,200

—*Toledo (Ohio) Blade.*

Another objective that gave the *Gazette* considerable editorial concern in its very first days was an unusual one. It was nothing less than an argument in favor of employing females instead of males as store clerks as a remedy against theft, fraud and embezzlements in retail stores. Just get an eyeful of this:

It is an undoubted fact that one-third of the whole annual amount contributed by spendthrifts and débauchées to the support of houses of ill fame in this city, comes from the pockets of retailers' clerks; and many a shining satin and rustling silk that sweeps the pave, is extracted clandestinely from an employer's store as a return for illicit favors. If females

WILLIAM PARKINSON, THE BARGE ROBBER.

CONVICTED SATURDAY, NOVEMBER 22D, OF ROBBING THE BARGE "CLINTON" OF $34,000.

were employed in stores instead of gay young men, we should be rid of these results. The employer would find his interests in the hands of safer guardians, for women have no outside pleasures to be dishonest.

We have another motive in recommending the adoption of this system. It is said that ladies prefer to purchase of male clerks, and that the main inducement that sends many a fair one out a shopping, is the desire to be waited on by rosy-cheeked young men. We do not believe this against the sex, and on this ground we would like to see Stewart undertake the refutation of the slander.

In those early days, just to give a slight line on its activities, the *National Police Gazette* waged an interesting warfare on the prominent abortionist, Madame Restall and others; gave much unwelcome publicity to Bob Sutton; and to John A.

Murrell, the great western land pirate; Joseph I. Hare, bold robber and highwayman; James Dowling, alias Cupid, the notorious pickpocket; John Honeyman, the celebrated City Bank robber; William Parkinson, the "Barge Robber," who robbed the Albany boat, the *Clinton,* of $34,000; and numerous others. One of its exposures found John B. Gough, foremost temperance lecturer of his time, very much intoxicated in a bawdy house on Walker Street.

The following paragraph from an early number tells its own story:

We offer this week a most interesting record of horrid murders, outrageous robberies, bold forgeries, astounding burglaries, hideous rapes, vulgar seductions and recent exploits of pickpockets and hotel thieves in various parts of the country.

What more could any one ask for a nickel, and later for only four cents per copy (the *Gazette,* with rapid increase in circulation reduced its price one penny), or two dollars per annum, payable in advance?

Regular departments were given over to the crimes and misdemeanors above enumerated and to "Counterfeits," "False Pretenses," "Perjury," etc.

The *Gazette,* though opposed to capital punishment, did not share the revulsion of other contemporaries over the public execution of the first woman in the State of New York. She (Mrs. Van Volkenburgh) deserved her fate, the gallows, and thus ended the story of her execution:

The drop was then let fall, and as the rope straightened upon her neck and just as she raised from her feet, she gave a shriek and thus passed from time to eternity. Thus ended the life of a lewd and wretched woman, who had sent two husbands (perhaps unprepared) into another world.

IV

Editorially, the *National Police Gazette* at the outset may seem uncouth in its treatment of news, and its comment at times must be pronounced naïve. We find room for only a few examples:

JUST SENTENCE—Heustis, the Long Island abductor, who ran away with another man's wife some weeks ago, has been tried for the offense of stealing the clothes which the lady wore at the time of her departure, and has been found guilty of petty larceny. He was thereupon sentenced to imprisonment in the penitentiary for six months as a warning to all such villains in the future. According to this sentence, all scoundrels who meditate absconding with other men's wives will, hereafter, find it necessary to take them *e puris naturabilis* or not at all.

ATTEMPTED RAPE—A villain by the name of Martin Shays, attempted a rape upon a young lady in this town Wednesday last, but entirely without success. The lady was in bed, but fought like a tigress *in defense of her private rights.*

SHE DIDN'T LOVE HIM—Catherine Foster, a young woman of eighteen years, has been convicted of the murder of her husband, by arsenic; he was a respectable young man to whom she had been married but three weeks.

CURIOUS SEDUCTION CASE—His Honor, Judge Edwards, of the Circuit Court, delivered several decisions, one of which, on a motion for a new trial in a case of seduction, disclosed some very curious facts, highly illustrative of the morals of the up-country folks. The case was tried by Judge Edmonds, at Hudson, September, 1844, and in which John D. Cater sought to recover damages from William H. Cook, for the seduction of his stepdaughter, Sally Ann Irvin.

At the trial, Sally Ann testified that, in the summer of 1843, she was living as a maid servant in the family of Edward P. Livingston, Esq., where the defendant was a hired man. One warm night, she, Sally Ann, went to sleep with another girl in a small room in the long hall, when the girl proposed to smoke some cigars, which they did; the defendant soon after came in, put his hand on the bed, and asked who slept on the front side; a boy who was also in the bed said "Sally Ann"; he then got between the two, when she tried to get up, but the defendant lay on her clothes and she could not get away, and he tickled her so, she was out of breath, "and had to give up," and the seduction followed.

The jury gave $350. damages. A new trial was asked, on the ground that a stepfather could not maintain the action, she being in service elsewhere. The court held he stood in *loco parentis* and denied the motion.

With such goings on in the Forties, and others to which we will call attention in due time, it is evident that the *National Police Gazette* had work to do, and especially with female virtue valued as low as $350. And, possibly, incidents such as this, and others to be related, may go to prove that the *Police Gazette* did play some part toward laying the foundation for an improvement of later-day morals. For, while it is true that the sex, one time referred to as the weaker, is being caught

Copyrighted for 1883, by RICHARD K. FOX, PROPRIETOR POLICE GAZETTE PUBLISHING HOUSE, Franklin Square and Dover Street, New York.

RICHARD K. FOX,
Editor and Proprietor.

NEW YORK, SATURDAY, MARCH 17, 1883.

{ VOLUME XLI.—No. 286.
Price Ten Cents.

HOW SHE CURED HIM.

A YOUNG WIFE ASTONISHES HER ERRATIC HUSBAND BY EMULATING HIS EXAMPLE, AND CAUSES HIM TO PROMPTLY ABANDON THE VAGABOND HABITS OF HIS BACHELOR DAYS.

[22]

in ticklish positions even to-day, yet is it not worthy of note how casually mention is made of flappers of that period smoking cigars? And we criticize our modern damsels for puffing the pernicious cigarette!

By the end of its second year of existence the *Police Gazette,* which had been launched with an edition of 4,200 copies, laid claim to having more than one hundred thousand readers, and had grown from four to eight pages, tabloid size, and four columns to the page. As an advertising medium it was doing very well, ten to twelve of its thirty-two columns being given over to such paid notice. Let us have a glance at the advertisements.

Burgess, Stringer & Co., booksellers and publishers of Broadway, corner Ann Street, call attention to the very latest of Alexander Dumas, "The Count of Monte Cristo"; to J. Fenimore Cooper's brand-new novel, "The Chainbearer"; to the romances of Eugene Sue, which includes the now-forgotten "Matilda," "a first-rate domestic tale albeit by a Frenchman."

Medical advertisements were numerous. Drs. Ivans & Hawes bring to notice "a great triumph" in "Vegetable Extract" for epileptic fits, which the proprietors of the compound "have no delicacy in saying can be cured." H. Johnston, chemist, in making known his "Italian Hair Dye," advises that "it is perhaps a commendable deception to give a beautiful color to one's curls and locks if nature has not done so. It is used by hundreds of our fashionables with approbation." The same advertiser catered to the patent-leather sheiks of the Forties with his pure and highly scented "Bear's Oil," an unequaled preparation for the hair or whiskers.

Dr. Townsend's "Compound Extract of Sarsaparilla" was good for a column in not a few issues and offered testimonials which told of marvelous cures in the way of dyspepsia, scrofula, cancers and much else. The certificate of his cure from one John McGown, who, "after using a bottle or two," had his cheek cleared of a tumor, has his letter backed up by his good pastor, who writes:

"I am acquainted with Mr. McGown, and know that for several years he had a very bad face. . . ."

Another full column extolled Dr. Brandreth's Pills, which had made a certain D. Stors feels just half his fifty years after a deplorable visitation of ills, and he was so appreciative that he prayed that God would bless Dr. Brandreth, the maker of Brandreth's Pills.

McAlister's "All-Healing Ointment," which checked "insensible perspiraton,"

MISS VIOLA CLIFTON, BURLESQUE ARTISTE AND VOCALIST.

N'LLE BARTOLLETTI, PREMIERE DANSEUSE.

M'LLE ELISE, OF THE CIRQUE ET THEATRE HISTORIQUE, PARIS.

FAVORITES OF THE FOOTLIGHTS.--See Page 2.

[24]

is acknowledged to have power to "cure more diseases than any other five remedies before the world."

Very few theatrical advertisements were to be noted, though the Bowery Amphitheatre desired it known that "Dale and McFarland throw 60 somersaults each night, besides all else to be seen in this establishment."

"STOP THE VILLAIN," was the heading over a personal advertisement, which went on to tell how: "William G. Moody, formerly of Boston and New York, but recently of Jersey City, opposite New York, has run away leaving a wife and two helpless children to the tender mercies of an unpitying world and who has taken with him a valuable piano belonging to the little son of a friend who has ever been kind to him." Details as to the appearance and characteristics of the unfeeling scoundrel are set forth. "He has large whiskers extending under his chin, is a great talker, very conceited and has an awkward imitation of the French shrug of the shoulders when in conversation. He will probably pass himself off as a professor of music. His voice is very harsh and cracked in singing. . . ."

"STOP THIEF—$20. REWARD." This call and offer comes from the Protestant Episcopal Church in Mount Holly, New Jersey, from which edifice sixteen yards of carpet had been stolen.

It was in the second year of publication that the United States went to war with Mexico, and it may be significant of the weight that was already carried by the *National Police Gazette* that, "by Command of Major General Scott," the following official order came from "Head Quarters of the Army in Washington," and dated October 24, 1846;—

> It being supposed that advertising deserters in the "National Police Gazette" may have a tendency to check desertion by increasing the chances of apprehension of the offender, a large subscription has been authorized with a view to its general distribution among the troops. Accordingly, every company, military post and recruiting station will be supplied with a copy.

The Civil War, however, found the *Gazette* coming into its lean years. After hostilities between the North and the South had ceased, its popularity waned steadily and from a once lucrative property it became a dead weight and Wilkes now seemed more interested in the *Spirit of the Times,* which he had purchased

[OFFICIAL.]

A LIST AND DESCRIPTION OF DESERTERS FROM THE UNITED STATES ARMY.

PUBLISHED EXCLUSIVELY IN THIS PAPER BY ORDER OF THE ADJUTANT GENERAL OF THE U. S. ARMY.

NO.	NAME	REGIMENT AND COMPANY	AGE.	EYES.	HAIR.	COMPLEXION.	HEIGHT.	WHERE BORN.	OCCUPATION.	DATE AND PLACE OF ENLISTMENT.	DATE AND PLACE OF DESERTION.	REMARKS.
659	Thos. M. Davis	m't rifl'm A	25	blue	light	fair	5 9	Alabama	bricklayer	Oct. 20, 1846, Paducah, Ky.	Oct. 29, 1846, "	
660	John F. Maney	"	22	blue	light	fair	5 8½	Virginia	laborer	Oct. 20, 1846, "	Oct. 29, 1846, "	
661	James Curry	Recruit	21	gray	brown	fair	5 4½	Hampshire Isle of W't	sailor	Nov. 17, 1846, Albany, N. Y.	Nov. 19, 1846, Albany, N. Y.	
662	Michael Lawberrow	Rec't 1st art.	30	gray	brown	dark	5 5	Kilkenny, Ireland	labourer	Nov. 4, 1846, Cumberland, Md.	Nov. 15, 1846, Ellicott's Mills	En route to Fort McHenry.
663	Manlof Fowler	6th reg. in. B	25	hazel	dark	fair	5 7	Carrol Co., Ohio	labourer	Nov. 7, 1846, Circleville, Ohio	Nov. 9, 1846, Circleville, Ohio	Discherged by writ of habeas corpus
664	John Bentley	4th art. B	23	blue	brown	fair	5 5½	New York	farmer	June 5, 1846, Newport, Ky.	Sept. 24, 1846, Near San Antonio	
665	Humphrey H. Floyd	"	21	dark	black	dark	5 10½	Columbus, Ohio	rope maker	July 4, 1846, "	Sept. 24, 1846, " "	
666	Steward B. Martin	"	27	black	black	fair	5 9½	Frederick, Va.	miller	May 11, 1846, "	Sept. 24, 1846, " "	
667	James H. Miller	"	22	hazel	d brown	dark	5 6½	Jefferson, Ky.	farmer	June 29, 1846, "	Sept. 24, 1846, " "	
668	Andew J. Roach	"	21	blue	light	fair	5 10	Montgomery, Ky	shoemaker	April 14, 1846, Madison	Sept. 24, 1846, " "	
669	James Robb	"	21	gray	fair	fair	5 10	Butler, Pa.	carpenter	April 17, 1846, Madison	Sept. 24, 1846, " "	
670	William Vickers	"	19	dark	dark	sallow	5 6	Limestone Co., Ala.	farmer	July 15, 1846, Memphis	Sept. 29, 1846, Castroville, Texas	
671	Alfred Ellis	Rec't 2d dra.	22	blue	ligh	light	5 8½	Hudson, N. Y.	carpenter	Oct. 24, 1846, New York	Nov. 20, 1846, Fort Columbus	
672	Michael McGraw	"	24	blue	brown	light	5 9	Tyrone, Ireland	carpenter	Sept. 1, 1846, New York	Nov. 20, 1846, "	
673	James Hatton	Recruit	33	brown	fair	fair	5 8	Tyrone, Ireland	tailor	Oct. 39, 1846, New York	Nov. 20, 1846, "	General service.
674	John Hunter	Rec't 7th inf.	22	hazel	brown	ruddy	5 7½	Fifeshire, Scotland	labourer	Nov. 5, 1846, Plattsburg, N. Y.	Nov. 18, 1846, en route to N. Y.	
675	Dennis O'Roak	Rec't 1st inf.	30	blue	sandy	fair	5 11	Ireland	stonecutter	Nov. 13, 1846, Middletown, Ohio	Nov. 14, 1846, en route to H'mlt'n	
676	Patric Nerny	6th inf.	21	blue	brown	fair	5 5½	Lanesboro, Ireland	laborer	Oct. 29, 1845, New Orleans	Nov. 12, 1846, New Orleans	
677	John Cavanaugh	8th inf. E	23	hazel	brown	florid	5 5½	Holton, Maine	soldier	Nov. 26, 1845, "	Oct. 19, 1846, Monterey	
678	Terence Donohoe	"	21	blue	brown	fair	5 6½	Holton, Maine	groom	Dec. 2, 1845, "	Oct. 19, 1846, "	
679	William T. Wilson	3d inf. A	21	blue	sandy	fair	5 4	Franklin Co., Pa.	brick maker	Nov. 10, 1846, Zanesville, Ohio	Nov. 14, 1846, Zanesville, Ohio	
680	Peter Hannan	2d art.	19	blue	black	fair	5 8	Dunnee, Scotland	tailor	Nov. 2, 1846, New York	Nov. 24. 1846, Fort Columbus	
681	John Meyer	Recruit	29	blue	fair	light	5 8	Germany	apothecary	Sept. 19, 1846, Newport, K. Y.	Nov. 17, 1846, Newport bk's, Ky.	Lieut. Cincinnati volunteers.
682	George W. Bonce	"	34	gray	dark	ruddy	5 7½	Lansingburg, N. Y.	baker	Nov. 9, 1846, Albany, N. Y.	Nov. 22, 1846, Fort Columbus	Enlisted for 7th Infantry.
683	Aaron Bouck	"	21	blue	light	florid	5 10	Middleburgh, N. Y.	farmer	Oct. 19, 1846, Utica, N. Y.	Nov. 27, 1846, "	Enlisted for general service.
684	Edward V. Marsh	"	21	hazel	brown	fair	5 6½	Haverhill, Mass.	cordwainer	Oct. 20, 1846, Lowell, Mass.	Nov. 29, 1846, "	Enlisted for 1st Artillery.
685	William Murphy	"	24	gray	brown	dark	5 3½	Deer Island, Me.	laborer	Nov. 26, 1846, Boston	Nov. 27, 1846, Boston	
686	W. H. Sparks	Rec't 4th inf.	27	hazel	black	ruddy	5 6	Black Rock, N. Y	labourer	Nov. 26, 1846, Syracuse	Nov. 29, 1846, Syracuse, N. Y.	
687	John Stark	"	22	hazel	brown	fair	5 6	Doroff, Germany	labourer	Nov. 16, 1846, New York	Nov. 20, 1846, New York	
688	Wm. Rankin	Rec't 1st inf.	29	blue	auburn	fair	6 2	Augusta co., Vo.	farmer	Nov. 14, 1846, Hamilton, Ohio	Nov. 21, 1846, Hamilton, Ohio	
689	Wm. Maher	R. M't R'n A	28	gray	sandy	fair	5 5	Ireland	labourer	Sept. 14, 1846, Newport, Ky.	Nov. 1, 1846, Jefferson barracks	
690	Ignatius Peeper	" D	34	gray	light	florid	5 9½	Newkise, Prussia	baker	Oct. 12, 1846, Louisville, Ky.	Nov. 12, 1846, " "	
691	David Bricker	" G	21	black	black	dark	5 10	Harrison co., Ohio	farmer	July 27, 1846, Brownstown, Ind.	Nov. 5, 1846, " "	
692	Abel Washburn	" K	21	hazel	black	florid	6 3	Rockingham co., N. C.	farmer	Oct. 16, 1846, Evansville, Ind.	Nov. 7, 1846, " "	
693	Robert Ashley	" K	21	gray	brown	florid	5 9½	Orange co., N. Y.	farmer	Oct. 21, 1846, " "	Nov. 7, 1846, " "	
694	Thomas Embree	" K	23	hazel	brown	florid	5 6	Edwards co., Ill.	cab't maker	Sept. 8, 1846, " "	Nov. 3, 1846, " "	
695	Israel Moore	" K	22	blue	light	light	6 1½	Huntington co., Pa.	plasterer	Aug. 31, 1846, Lafayette, Ind.	Nov. 13, 1846, " "	
696	Michael Fresh	" K	21	blue	brown	florid	5 11	Flemingsburgh, Ky.	boat-maker	Oct. 16, 1846, Evansville, Ind.	Nov. 13, 1846, " "	
697	Joseph Deford	" E	23	hazel	light	fair	5 7½	Washington co., Ohio	laborer	July 24, 1846, Logansport, Ind.	Nov. 4, 1846, " "	
698	Robert Deford	" E	29	hazel	brown	fair	5 8½	Clark co., Ohio	laborer	July 19, 1846, " "	Nov. 4, 1846, " "	
699	Wm. Grandstaff	" E	21	gray	red	fair	5 8½	Clark co., Ohio	laborer	Aug. 3, 1846, " "	Nov. 10, 1846, " "	Apprehended Nov. [illegible], 1846.
700	Wm Chapman	" E	29	black	dark	dark	5 9	Putnam co., Va.	miller	July 31, 1846, " "	Nov. 10, 1846, " "	" "
701	Joseph Haines	" E	23	black	black	fair	5 7½	Putnam co. Ia.	farmer	Aug. 27, 1846, " "	Nov. 10, 1846, " "	" "
702	George Garnel	" H	25	blue	brown	ruddy	5 7	Courtlrnd, N. Y.	blacksmith	Aug. 4, 1846, Michigan City	Nov. 14, 1846, " "	
703	Wm. Woods	" H	23	black	brown	dark	6 1	Chichester, England	labourer	Oct. 17, 1846, Memphis, Tenn.	Nov. 14, 1846, " "	
704	Charles O'Brien	Recruit	23	gray	dark	ruddy	5 8½	Fermanagh co, Ireland	labourer	Nov. 14, 1846, Pittsburg, Pa.	Nov. 23, 1846, Pittsburgh, Pa.	Freckled face, and mark of a scar over left temple.
705	Wm. Thorp	Rec't 8th inf.	26	hazel	black	dark	5 6	Kent co., England	carpenter	Nov. 18, 1846, Whitehall, N. Y.	Nov. 30, 1846, Whitehall, N. Y.	
706	George Hutchison	"	34	hazel	brown	fair	5 7½	St. Lawrence co. N. Y.	laborer	Nov. 25, 1846, Whitehall, N. Y.	Dec. 2, 1846, Whitehall, N. Y.	Very stoutly built, slightly bald; had been a sailor—left in soldier's clothes.
707	Martin Powell	3d inf. A	33	gray	brown	dark	5 11	Strasburg, France	laborer	Nov. 17, 1846, Zanesville, Ohio	Nov. 22, 1846, Zanesville, Ohio	
708	Michael Donahoe	4th infantry	24	blue	brown	dark	5 4½	Co. Clare, Ireland	laborer	Nov. 17, 1846, Syracuse, N. Y.	Dec. 3, 1846, Syracuse, N. Y.	Deserted while under orders for principal depot.
709	H. F. Schermerhorn	2d art. E	24	blue	brown	florid	5 9	Athens, N. Y.	painter	Oct. 3, 1846, New York	Nov. 26, 1846, Fort Columbus	
710	James Young	2d art. E	26	blue	brown	florid	5 10	Pennsylvania	soldier	May 1, 1834, New London	Dec. 2, 1846, Fort Columbus	Third Desertion.
711	Andrew Davis	4th infantry	22	blue	brown	fair	5 5	Dublin, Ireland	blacksmith	Nov. 23, 1846, Boston, Mass.	Dec. 4, 1846, Boston, Mass.	
712	Thomas Wilson	"	28	blue	light	fair	5 9½	Plymouth, Eng.	boot-maker	Dec. 1, 1846, Boston, Mass.	Dec. 4, 1846, Boston, Mass.	
713	Washington Larkins	6th inf. B	19	gray	auburn	fair	5 11	Carrol co., Ohio	carpenter	Nov. 8, 1846, Chillicothe, Ohio	Nov. 23, 1846, Chilicothe, Ohio	
714	James O'Brien	" C	25	hazel	sandy	florid	5 9	Montgomery, Alabama	soldier	Dec. 26, 1845, New Orleans	Nov. 1, 1846, Baton Rouge, La.	Has given himself up to Col. Hunt, and joined his Co.
715	Albert Finch	7th inf. G							soldier		Nov. 1, 1846, " "	Deserted from Baton Rouge, La., Jan. 15, 1845—joined from desertion at Baton Rouge b'ks, La., Sept. 20, '46.
716	John Waggoner	3d inf. G	24	blue	brown	florid	5 9	Perry co., Ohio	laborer	Sept. 2, 1846, Sandusky, Ohio	Sept. 21, 1846, Mt. Vernon, Ohio while on the march to Newport barracks, Ky.	
717	James Johnson	Rec't 6th inf.	26	blue	sandy	light	5 11½	Scotland	chair-maker	July 20, 1846, Evanville, Ind.	Nov. 11, 1846, Newport b'ks	Second desertion. Supposed gone to Canada.
718	William Young	Rec't 6th inf.	26	blue	brown	ruddy	5 7	Glasgow, Scotland	shoe-maker	Oct. 2, 1846, Millwaukie	Dec. 1, 1846, Newport b'ks	
719	Alex. McDonald	Recruit	19	blue	brown	fair	5 4	Ireland	laborer	Sept. 21, 1846, Whitehall	Dec. 1, 1846, Fort Columbus	Enlisted for reg't infantry.
720	Henry B. Bliss	"	24	blue	brown	fair	6 1	New York	farmer	Nov. 9, 1846, New York	Dec. 1, 1846, "	Enlisted for gen'l service.
721	James Farrell	"	28	blue	brown	fair	5 4	Ireland	laborer	Oct. 20, 1846, Philadelphia	Dec. 1, 1846, "	Enlisted for 5th infantry.
722	John Dynan	"	29	blue	brown	fair	5 4½	New Jersey	tailor	Aug. 25, 1846, Newark	Dec. 2, 1846, "	Enlisted for 2d dragoons.
723	James A. Murphy	"	25	blue	brown	ruddy	5 7	Pennsylvania	silversmith	Nov. 9, 1846, Philadelphia	Dec. 2, 1846, "	Enlisted for 1st "
724	Andrew David	"	24	gray	dark	sallow	5 7	Germany	cabinetmaker	Nov. 4, 1846, New York	Dec. 2, 1846, "	Enlisted for 1st "
725	Patrick McFarren	"	34	blue	dark	fair	5 10	Ireland	laborer	Nov. 9, 1846, Philadelphio	Dec. 4, 1846, "	Enlisted for 5th infantry.
726	Samuel A. Hamer	"	24	blue	light	fair	5 7	Norway	shoemaker	Nov. 11, 1846, New York	Dec. 4, 1846, "	Enlisted for 4th infantry.
727	John Barr	"	21	gray	brown	fair	5 7½	Ireland	laborer	Nov. 4, 1846, New York	Dec. 4, 1846, "	Enlisted for 4th infantry.
728	Eli Smith	"	29	gray	black	ruddy	5 4½	England	blacksmith	Nov. 15, 1846, Albany	Dec. 5, 1846, "	Enlisted for 7th infantry.
729	Michael Wilson	"	26	blue	brown	fair	5 9	New Jersey	labourer	Nov. 12, 1846, Albany	Dec. 5, 1846, "	Enlisted for 7th infantry.
730	Charles Bristow	"	21	blue	light	light	5 11	Ireland	boat-maker	Sept. 26, 1846, New York	Dec. 6, 1846, "	Enlisted for 2d dragoons.
731	Joseph Stark	rec't 6th inf.	24	gray	light	dark	5 4½	Bremen, Germany	farmer	Dec. 4, 1846, Brooklyn	Dec. 6, 1846, Brooklyn	
732	Michael White	r'g't m't R. H	28	blue	black	light	5 8	New Market, Ireland	labourer	Oct. 17, 1846, Memphis, Tenn.	Nov. 18, 1846, Jefferson b'ks, Mo.	
733	Michael McCabe	"	28	hazel	brown	dark	5 6½	" "	currier	Oct. 27, 1846, " "	Nov. 18, 1846, " "	
734	Edward Archer	" A	28	blue	dark	dark	5 8	Kilkenny, Ireland	carpenter	Oct. 15, 1846, " "	Oct. 27, 1846, Memphis, Tenn.	
735	William Donovan	"	24	blue	black	dark	5 7	Halifax, Nova Scotia	carpenter	Oct. 15, 1846, " "	Oct. 27, 1846, " "	
736	John McGunnigil	"	26	hazel	brown	light	5 8½	New York	teamster	Oct. 9, 1846, " "	Oct. 21, 1846, " "	
737	Nathaniel R. Maxwell	Recruit	21	blue	lt brown	fair	5 6	Wells, Maine	mason	Dec. 1, 1846, Boston	Dec. 9, 1846, Boston	Boarded at No. 50 Brighton-st., Boston—of slim and prepossessing appearance.
738	Simeon Buddock	"	32	gray	d brown	florid	5 4½	New York	labourer	Dec. 1, 1846, Providence	Dec. 3, 1846, Providence	
739	Wm. Cargil	Arks. vol. A	21							June 10, 1846, Clarksville, Ark.	Oct. 24, 1846, Ft. Gibson, C. N.	Enrolled by Capt. Gray.
740	Wm. Grace	"	21							June 10, 1846, " "	Oct. 24, 1846, Ft. Gibson, C. N.	" "
741	Robert Oadam	"	23							June 10, 1846, " "	Oct. 24, 1846, " "	" "
742	James Reilly	"	22							June 10, 1846, " "	Oct. 24, 1846, " "	" "
743	Willis Holt	"	19							June 10, 1846, " "	Oct. 24, 1846, " "	" "
744	Ismiel Rates	"	18							June 30, 1846, Mulberry, Ark.	Oct. 24, 1846, " "	" "
745	John Williams	"	21							June 10, 1846, Clarksville, Ark.	Oct. 24, 1846, " "	" "
746	I. G. Dillard	" B	22							June 15, 1846, Dover, Pope co. Ark	Oct. 24, 1846, " "	" Capt West.
747	Wm. M. H. Telford	"	19							June 15, 1846, " " "	Oct. 24, 1846, " "	" "
748	Jesse Taylor	"	17							June 15, 1846, " " "	Oct. 21, 1846, " "	" "
749	C. J. Kizer	"	18							June 15, 1846, " " "	Oct. 24, 1846, " "	" "
750	T. J. Linum	"	32							June 15, 1846, " " "	Nov. 5, 1846, " "	" "
751	Ryan Ellis	"	28							June 15, 1846, " " "	Nov. 8, 1846, " "	" "
752	John Laswell	Recruit	19	hazel	dark	fair	5 7	Indiana	labourer	Nov. 11, 1846, Pittsburgh	Nov. 30, 1846, Pittsburgh	Supposed gone to Cincinnati.
753	Wm. H. Quackenbush	"	14	hazel	brown	fair	4 11	Bergen, New Jersey	musician	Dec. 26, 1845, New York	Dec. 10, 1846, Principal Depot, Ft. Columbus	2d des—enl'td to learn music.
754	Adolph Lea	"	21	gray	brown	fair	5 4½	Davis, France	pncl-case-mkr	Oct. 21, 1846, "	Dec. 13, 1846, " "	Enlisted for 1st dragoons.
755	Rufus Case	"	21	blue	brown	ruddy	5 9½	Monroe, N. Y.	farmer	Nov. 13, 1846, "	Dec. 13, 1846, " "	" "
756	James Mulligan	"	21	gray	dark	light	5 6½	Wilkesbarre, Pa.	machinist	Oct. 1, 1846, "	Dec. 13, 1846, " "	Enlisted for 2d dragoons.
757	Edward Batcheler	"	21	hazel	dark	light	5 6	Liverpool, England	printer	Nov. 12, 1846, "	Dec. 13, 1846, " "	" "
758	James Mills	"	23	blue	dark	light	5 4	Gawlay, Ireland	hatter	Dec. 2, 1846, "	Dec. 13, 1846, " "	" "
759	Wm. Omacht	"	24	gray	brown	fair	5 8	Berks Co., Pa.	labourer	Nov. 2, 1846, "	Dec. 13, 1846, " "	" 5th infantry.
760	George Mathis	m'd riflemen	26	hazel	brown	fair	5 10¾	Carroll Co. Ky.	musician	Oct. 12, 1846, Louisville, Ky.	Oct. 31, 1846, Louisville, Ky.	
761	Ignatz Peeper	"	34	gray	light	florid	5 9½	Prussia	baker	Oct. 12, 1846, " "	Nov. 12, 1846, Jefferson barracks	Supposed to be concealed about Louisville.
763	Wm. H. Adams	5th infantry	27	blue	sandy	dark	5 5	Nobleburgh, Me.	machinist	Nov. 24, 1846, Baton Rouge	Nov. 30, 1846, Baton ouge	Not yet attached to a comp'y
764	James Quin	Ord. dep't	23	blue	brown	fair	5 9		labourer	Dec. 1, 1846, Frankford ars., Pa.	Dec. 6, 1846, Frankford ars., Pa.	Enlisted as an ordinance laborer.
765	Sandy Keenen	7th infantry	21	blue	d brown	ruddy	5 4	Kings, Ireland	musician	Dec. 11, 1846, Albany, N. Y.	Dec. 12, 1846, Albany, N. Y.	
766	Albert A. Cook	Recruit	24	blue	brown	fair	5 7	Green co., N. Y	farmer	Dec. 5, 1846, New York City	Dec. 10, 1846, New York City	
767	Thomas Gainer	Recruit	21	blue	black	fair	5 3	Louth co., Ireland	shoemaker	Dec. 8, 1846, New York City	Dec. 10, 1846, New York City	
768	Wm H. Bangs	Rec't 1st art.	22	gray	brown	light	5 4	Baltimore, Md.	baker	Oct. 3, 1846, Baltimore, Md.	Nov. 14, 1846, Ft. McHenry, Md.	
769	Michael Dillon	Ord. dep't	28	hazel	dark	fair	5 9	Limerick, Ireland	laborer	Oct. 5, 1846, Watervliet arsinal	Dec. 13, 1846, Watervliet arsenal	
770	John Dunn	"	22	gray	dark	dark	5 7	Kings, Ireland	laborer	Sept. 9, 1846, " "	Dec. 13, 1846, " "	
771	Denis F. G. Lyons	"	24	gray	black	fair	5 8	Limerick, Ireland	laborer	Nov. 11, 1846, " "	Dec. 13, 1846, " "	
772	James Connell	"	22	dark	dark	dark	5 9	Ireland	laborer	Sept. 1, 1846, " "	Dec. 13, 1846, " "	
773	Joseph Milner,	Serg't 7th in.	20	black	dark	dark	5 5	St. Louis, Mo.	laborer	Jan. 18, 1846, New Orleans, La.	Dec. 10, 1846, Springfield, Mass.	He is an Englishman, born in England, *not St. Louis, Mo.*
774	Simon McCarty	Recruit	33	gray	black	dark	5 6½	Allegheny co., Pa.	tobacconist	Dec 5, 1846, Pittsburgh	Dec. 11, 1846, Pittsburgh	
775	Charles Robedee	Recruit	23	blue	brown	fair	5 7	New York City	farmer	Dec. 14, 1846, New York	Dec. 16, 1846, New York	Of a sullen aspect, and occasional downcast look.
776	Patrick Gairn	Recruit	21	blue	lt brown	fair	5 9¾	Clare, Ireland	laborer	Dec. 11, 1846, Boston	Dec. 17, 1846, Boston	
777	Andrew Davis	Recruit	22	blue	brown	fair	5 5	Dublin, Ireland	blacksmith	Nov. 23, 1846, Boston	Dec. 17, 1846, Framingham	En route to New York—2d desertion.
778	Thomas Wilson	Recruit	28	blue	light	fair	5 9½	Plymouth, England	bootmaker	Dec. 1, 1846, Boston	Dec. 17, 1846, "	Supposed to be 3d desertion.

$30 REWARD.

☞ A reward of THIRTY DOLLARS will be paid to any person who shall apprehend and deliver a deserter to an officer of the army at any Military Post or Recruiting Station.

THE PIRATE OF THE PARKS.

HOW A NEW YORK BELLE TURNED THIEF FOR A WORTHLESS HUSBAND'S SAKE, AS TOLD BY THE "BROADWAY ROUNDER," ON PAGE 4

from William T. Porter in 1856; on this weekly, the first all-around sporting journal, Horace Greeley had once been a typesetter.

In 1876 Richard K. Fox took over the *National Police Gazette* and made a complete change in its appearance and purposes. Under his proprietorship this weekly became a powerful sports and theatrical organ; the forerunner of the present-day tabloid as a picture paper and the dispenser of sensational news; and the means of bringing its head wealth, prominence, and a degree of power. Of the pink decades of the *Police Gazette,* with which many of us are more or less familiar, these will be dealt with further along in this history.

"It sank so low," stated a Fox editorial in reviewing the past history of the publication just taken over, "that it appealed for support to the very class that provided it with subjects for its pages and had regular columns devoted to the lawless classes and printed in their slang, the argot of the New York gutters. Even this did not stem the tide of disaster. The circulation kept dropping until Mr. Matsell, who had come into sole ownership in 1873, disposed of his unremunerative property to two engravers, father and son, who had been providing the pictures for the paper. But it failed to restore itself to its old popularity and so passed into the hands of Richard Kyle Fox."

Now it is patent from a present-day digest of doings in the criminal world, that the primal scheme of the *National Police Gazette,* and as set forth in its prospectus, has not worked out in accordance with its ambitious plan. For the years have proven that crime and the criminal are still with us in spite of the efforts of the original *National Police Gazette.* And the failure cannot be charged to any reluctance on the part of the publishers to acquaint the public with the deplorable propensities and peccadillos of certain of the citizenry. But no matter how primitive an example of journalism the original *National Police Gazette* may be now accepted, its criminal chronicles and rude illustrations struck the public fancy for quite a period, even though it was printed on rather coarse paper and mainly in agate type.

There was one other feature that was special to the *National Police Gazette* pages previous to the Fifties—a rhymed annual address, which poetic effusion gave a partial review of matters that had commanded the attention of the publication during the year, and a sample of which has already been presented. In chapters to come this history will be devoted to some of the outstanding cases. Some reference to these will be found in the address, of which a few of its numerous stanzas are appended:

Then let us not scoff,
Too severe at poor Gough,
Though constrained to exclaim—"What a sad falling off!"

SINS OF NEW YORK

From "tinct. of Tolou" and pure syrup and soda,
To riot and rum in a house of bad odour!
From orthodox slumbers and dreams apostolic,
To the rank ups and downs of an amorous frolic.
"What a sad falling off! What a sad falling off!"
Then mercy, we pray, for the fall of poor Gough!

The next strangest case that the old year has seen,
Is the vexed prosecution of Polly Bodine:
Tried twice—once convicted—the inhuman fury
Gave the scaffold the slip through the loops of a jury.
Oh, Polly Bodine! Oh, Polly Bodine!
Such a case on our records has never been seen!
Such a chapter of horror in which scarce a doubt
Mocks the efforts of justice in tracing it out;
But tho' vengeance is baffled, not hushed is the scream
Of unappeased ghosts upon Polly Bodine!

Bob Sutton, Bob Sutton, bold burglar, come out,
And unravel the train-work which bringeth about
The grasp of the law in its own proper time—
The doom of the felon—the stamp of his crime—
You may wander at large, but naught will disperse
The dark shades of your deeds—their brand and their curse,
Then shrink back, old burglar, shrink back to your den!
And pray for old Time's everlasting "amen!"

     But why further relate
     With name and by date,
The long list of felons disgracing the State,
From Honeyman down to old Parkinson, all—
Some infamous thieves have been pinned to the wall,
And murderers blackened in crime have been tried
And condemned by the laws of the land they defied;
For Justice, though slow, brings at last the poor wretch
Who poisons or stabs, to the string of Jack Ketch.

THE PUBLICAN, THE PEWTERER, AND THE PUGILIST

An Astounding Case of Mistaken Identity

IN ITS initial feature the original *National Police Gazette,* in No. 1 of its series, under the title of "Lives of the Felons," carried the reader back eighteen years. In a serial that ran through several installments, this gave anew and elaborately the details of a criminal episode so extraordinary and unusual as to have all the city of New York lost in wonder for many weeks of the years 1827 and 1828.

Conceive, if you can, a respected and prosperous hotel proprietor who had for his double a member of a daring band of forgers and thieves. Of a resemblance so strong that the tellers of two of the city's prominent banks, which had been victimized, were positive in their identification of the innocent Publican as being the one who had passed on them false checks for the amounts of more than $10,000. Add to the picture how the brand of guilt was further fastened on this innocent man when an unmitigated crook backed up the identification of the bank tellers by false implication in turning state's evidence. And then the clearing of the blameless and broken unfortunate through the persistence and skill of a sagacious officer of the law, whose efforts might have gone for naught but for a trivial accident at the eleventh hour. This is not the imaginings of a novelist or a playwright, but a matter of printed word in the daily papers and of the police records of more than a century ago.

As did the *Gazette,* to make for chronological conception of this amazing case, we shall first deal with the Pugilist, Bob Sutton. He first saw light some ten years after the birth of the United States, and in his early manhood a muscular frame together with, it must be conceded, unflinching physical courage, brought him considerable prize ring renown. As a member of the "fancy," Bob the Wheeler (so nicknamed from his first trade) has his fistic deeds duly recorded in no less an authority on pugilism than *Boxiana.*

Somewhere around his thirtieth birthday, he had fallen so deeply into criminal ways that London became too hot to hold him and he sailed to this country in 1820 and a short time after opened an English beershop at 24 Rosevelt (rose

[N.Y., Jan. 3, 1880.

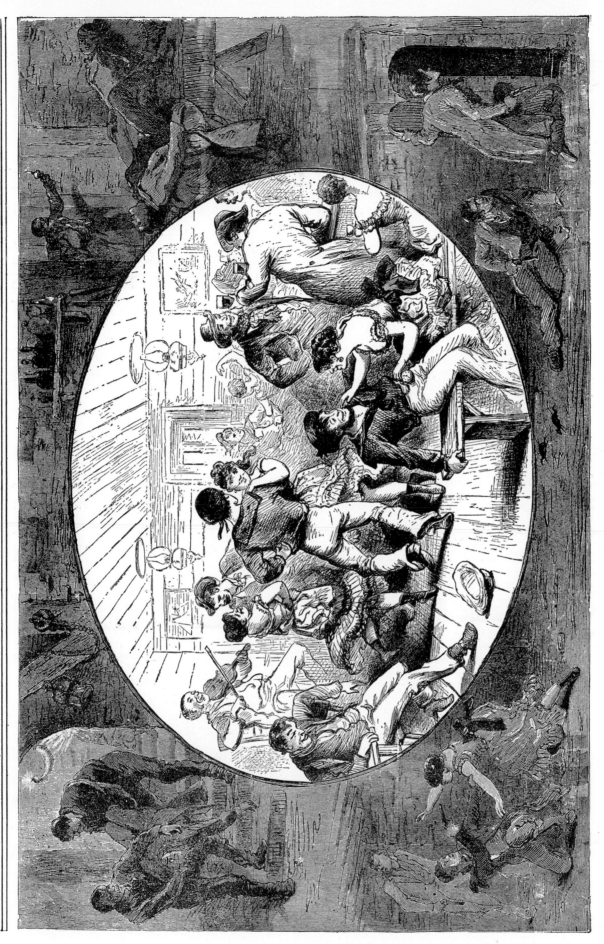

NEW YORK'S GAS-LIT LIFE.—MIDNIGHT PICTURES OF METROPOLITAN SIGHTS, SCENES AND CHARACTERS—LIFE IN WATER STREET—INTERIOR OF A DANCE HOUSE—HAVING A GOOD TIME—THE REAR ROOM—THE DRUGGED WINE—LAID AWAY, WELL SALTED, UNTIL NIGHT IN THE SUB-CELLAR—THE BLIND PASSAGE OPENING INTO THE CITY SEWERS—THE UNKNOWN DEAD—"AH! LIZE, I HAVE GOT YOU"—TRAPPED AT LAST—MEN AND WOMEN WHO MAKE MURDER AND ROBBERY A TRADE.—[SKETCHED FROM LIFE BY GAZETTE ARTISTS.—SEE PAGE 14.

field) Street. Trees still extended along the way down to the waterfront where some years before had been the homes of the early burghers, and which had now given way to the lowest of sailors' dives. The building, a small two-story frame structure painted in blue, became in quick order the resort of English thieves and burglars and of bellicose youth, drawn by their admiration of the proprietor's reputation for fistic prowess. Though business was profitable from the first, Sutton could not refrain from a penchant for pocket picking and other roguery which brought him in occasional contact with the police.

The Pewterer, James Holdgate, came to this country a few years after Sutton, and was also a Briton. It was many months after his arrival in New York before he was able to take up his regular line of employment, which was the making of fancy leaden toys. Before this he was engaged with the Gas Company, being one of the first servants of this new illuminating utility after the president of the company had equipped his own home at 7 Cherry Street, in 1825, with pipes and burners and had demonstrated for a gaping throng that the danger of fire or explosion was merely imaginary. Holdgate's occupation was the repairing of fixtures and meters in the various places of business. While thus engaged he was corrupted by Sutton to the notion of how fine an opportunity his calling presented for getting the impressions of locks so as to enable access to stores and warehouses worth marking for robbery. Several such jobs were put over successfully. Nor was Holdgate weaned from the Sutton influence even after a citizen named Jackson, deceived in the character of the man, furnished backing and established him in a shop at 3 Murray Street for the manufacture of pewter objects, and which venture proved a successful one.

As a matter of fact, the shady connection of Sutton and Holdgate took on a blacker hue with the appearance on the scene of James Stevens, also a Briton. This new member, "a man of fine talents, elegant appearance, liberal education and accomplished manners," was even said to be an illegitimate son of King George III, though on what authority does not seem to be known. This gentlemanly crook, after being forced to decamp from the West Indies, came to know John Reed, a very clever forger, who had already served several prison sentences. When a bold scheme of forgery had been concocted between Sutton, Holdgate and Stevens, one that required the services of an artist in his line, Stevens hunted up Reed and brought him to the Darby & Joan.

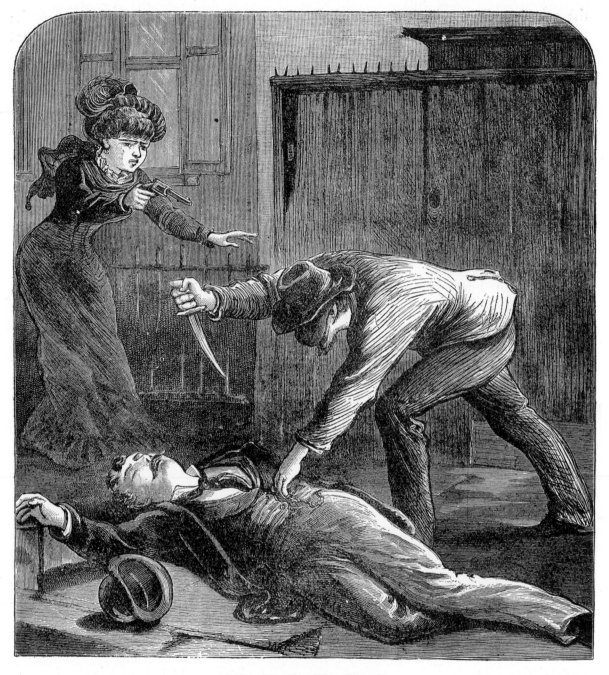

SAVED BY HIS SWEETHEART

THE BIRTHDAY PRESENT WHICH PROTECTED A LONG ISLAND LOVER'S PURSE AND DISCOMFITED A DESPERATE FOOTPAD

As the first move of this daring plan, which was inspired by a number of successful check manipulations for small amounts, an entrance was effected in the prominent banking house of Howland & Aspinwall, in Front Street. Keys for the main door had been fashioned by the Pewterer after impressions procured by himself. As a result of this forced entry the invaders were able to rummage through the premises from midnight until daybreak, and the most prized portion of the spoils was a number of canceled checks. Several of these checks had been merely canceled by writing in ink instead of being mangled by cutting. Of these particular checks, one was on the Union Bank for $7,760, and another was on the Merchants Bank for the sum of $3,500. These checks were renovated by the skillful Reed, who with acids removed the date and cancellation marks and then through his clever penmanship substituted the date of October 15 (on which day it was decided to make presentation of same on the banks) in perfect imitation of the handwriting on the checks.

On the morning of October 15, Holdgate, while sweating over the fires in his Pewterer's shop, and surrounded by his apprentices, suddenly announced that he was going out for a few moments to get a drop of ale. It was proven afterwards, on investigation, that Holdgate was absent from his place of business only a very short time. Yet, inside of much less than an hour, he had gone to the Darby & Joan and replaced his apron and working coat and trousers with his best apparel. After which he visited both the Union and the Merchants Banks, and of such respectability was his appearance and deportment and so perfect the work on the checks, that the tellers surrendered the cash amount called for on the face of each check with practically no questioning. Then Holdgate returned to the Darby & Joan, doffed his fine raiment, and was soon back at work in his shop industriously engaged.

This audacious fraud was discovered on the very next day, and soon the city press was alive with news and conjecture concerning the imposition on the banks, and the entire town was talking of little else, while the search and inquiry was going on in all directions to get trace of the man in the dark olive-colored coat who had cashed the false checks and then disappeared so mysteriously. Among those who shared the prevailing wonderment over the matter was Timothy B. Redmond, keeper of the U. S. Hotel, a large and flourishing establishment on Pearl Street.

Hardly a week later Timothy B. Redmond put on his olive-green dress coat and started out on some business that carried him into Wall Street. As he passed the Union Bank, Daniel Ebbetts, the paying teller who had cashed the check for Holdgate, chanced to be coming down the steps of the institution. The instant his eyes fell on Redmond he was convinced that good fortune had revealed to him the mysterious swindler. He followed Redmond until the latter returned to the U. S.

Hotel, where Ebbetts after a little investigation was surprised to learn that the man that he had been tracking was none other than the proprietor of this prosperous hotel and saloon. Still convinced that he could not be mistaken in his identification he got in touch as quickly as he could with Edward A. Nicoll, paying teller of the Merchants Bank. The two visited the U. S. Hotel and then went into the barroom of the place, where they were waited on by Redmond. The instant Nicoll saw Redmond, he, like Ebbetts, was struck with the conviction that the guilty man had been found. The following day Redmond was placed under arrest.

Almost at the same time a trunk containing much valuable property was stolen from the steamboat *North America* during her passage from Albany to New York. David Ware was the one guilty of the robbery, and as he appeared in sudden affluence and he had a police record he was arrested, but it was on the suspicion that he might have had something to do with the swindling of the banks, the act for which Redmond had been apprehended. The unprincipled Ware, after turning things over in his mind, conceived the plan of confessing to guilt in the matter for which he had been merely arrested on suspicion. His calculation being, that his admission would turn attention away from the misdeeds of which he was actually guilty. He thereupon sent for John Phoenix, the District Attorney of the city of New York, and offered to turn state's evidence and to denounce as his accomplice, Timothy B. Redmond. And when Redmond was brought before him, the unabashed Ware lost no time in identifying the overwhelmed hotel owner, though he had never seen him before. After a hurried examination Redmond was returned to his cell and with little likelihood that he would ever again enjoy freedom. Thus comments the *Gazette:*

> On the day after this gigantic wrong, the journals of the city were loud in their satisfaction at the result of the examination. They recognized the hand of Providence in the wonderful development of the prisoner's guilt and offered their heartfelt thanks to that overruling power which confounds the machinations of the wicked, and which untiringly tracks the offender until it visits upon his head the inevitable punishment of sin. Preachers pointed a moral, or garnished a discourse with the tortures of his guilty bosom; parents dealt out his fate piecemeal to their children as a terrible example, and the clerks who had sworn Redmond to be the presenter of the checks, together with the officers of the Police Department, congratulated each other on the combined efforts of their exertions.

MAGEE DEL.

BRITT Sc.

JACOB HAYS, HIGH CONSTABLE OF NEW YORK.

It is with the most unfeigned pleasure that we present our readers with the above portrait
of our venerable and renowned High Constable. We particularly commend the
character of the original to the attention of all the police officers of the
United States, as a distinguished and honorable example of the
benefits which can be conferred upon society by an
energetic and inflexibly honest man.

Poor Redmond! The hurricane had fairly swept him down. The fabric of his prosperous condition had vanished as a breath; his house was abandoned and deserted, and in addition to the destruction of his character, he saw himself on the road to helpless beggary, maybe lifelong imprisonment. Abandoned by all, other than the idle visitors, who gaped at him through his cage in insulting curiosity, or those unpitying familiars who tortured his innocence for a confession, nothing was left in the prospective but infamy and a felon's doom.

Enter the Policeman, Jacob Hays, who really deserves a place in the title of this account. "Old Hays," as he was better known, was High Constable of New York, the master sleuth of his day, and from all accounts a foe to be feared by the lawbreakers and a friend to be respected by the honest citizen. He was actually the first American detective of note though in his time he was known as a "shadow"; detectives as a distinct corps were not created in New York until 1857. Old Hays was really an able man in his field; it was this same Old Hays who originated an ingeniously effective method for breaking up unruly gatherings. In that period almost every citizen, no matter his station, wore a "topper," or high silk hat. Old Hays would go to work in the midst of the boisterous element and by a deft movement of his wrist with an extremely short "billy," he would knock off "toppers" right and left. Then, when those relieved of their headgear would bend over to recover same, he would administer swift kicks in the pants with a dexterity that might have been the envy of our own Charlie Chaplin.

Old Hays believed he could distinguish the criminal physiognomy from that of the honest man, no matter how much appearances might be against the latter. From the first he felt that Redmond was not a man of criminal tendencies, either by inclination or accident and he strove energetically to prove his intuitions. The bloodhound in this shadow was keen to see the one actually guilty brought to justice. Though further examinations and developments brought to light apparent discrepancies in the Ware confession, public opinion remained strongly against Redmond, and when Old Hays requested of the District Attorney a delay that would permit of additional time for unraveling the mystery, the High Constable came in for some sharp criticism from the press and other sources.

Two things counted in giving Old Hays something in the way of clues; one was due to his own acuteness and the other in a way accidental. Taking up the last we will quote from the *Gazette* by way of explanation:

AN OLD-TIME RACE.

THE GREAT MATCH FOR $20,000 WON BY PEYTONA OVER FASHION ON THE UNION COURSE, LONG ISLAND, MAY 13TH, 1845.

[*From an Original Print.*]

[38]

On the second day of the Redmond trial, moved by the tremendous excitement of the proceedings, Holdgate himself entered the courtroom to see the sport. It was at the opening of the court and Redmond had not as yet arrived. All eyes were at once turned upon the Pewterer, and deceived by the remarkable resemblance, the spectators wondered why the complainant took his seat outside the bar among the spectators. Redmond's appearance a few minutes afterwards dispelled the illusion, though it did not allay the amazement, and the bewildered beholders paid but little attention to the proceedings until the Pewterer, abashed by the general gaze, got up and left the place.

The observing eye of Old Hays also took note of the startling resemblance of the Pewterer and the prisoner, with the result that he made some investigations which merely baffled and led nowhere. It was such an ordinary thing for Holdgate to drop out of his place during the day for his glass or two of ale, and his absence from his shop on October 15 had not seemingly been prolonged beyond the customary stay of the boss, so there did not seem anything suspicious here for the High Constable to work on.

Hays, on account of the expert work in the alterations on the checks, had his suspicions fastened on Reed from the first. Ware, though a stranger to Reed, knew of the latter's reputation as a forger through his underworld connections, and in turning state's evidence the conniving Ware had even dared to implicate Reed. When the latter was placed under arrest on a requisition from the Governor of Massachusetts early in 1828, and he was brought face to face with Ware, the latter failed to identify the man he had accused of being his accomplice. Through his investigations of Reed, Hays got wind of the fact that Reed had been in association with Stevens. So the pursuit for Stevens was on, though for no other good reason than that Hays desired to subject him to some questioning. Hays was led quite a chase, finally losing the scent after he had driven Stevens back to New York, where the prey was searched for in vain. And now it was the 8th of March, the day set for the trial that marked what was apparently the last ray of hope for poor Redmond. And then came one little incident that helped to undo all the perfect planning and the luck of the villains, and that counted even more than the relentless keenness of the High Constable.

On the morning of March 8 some boys were playing in a lumber-yard in Wooster Street, next to the corner of Grand, and they chanced to find a small tin box tied up in a handkerchief. A policeman saw the mysterious box in possession of the boys and brought it down to the station. It was found to contain several blank bills of exchange, some bank notes that had been tampered with, and among them a number of canceled checks that had been gathered on the night of the forced entry into the counting-house of Howland & Aspinwall. Naturally, these interested Old Hays; so much so that he promised the District Attorney in exchange for an additional delay of twenty-four hours that he would produce positive evidence of Redmond's innocence.

Old Hays then proceeded to the vicinity where the boys had found the tin box, and after some careful inquiry he learned that a party calling himself by the name of Atkinson had just moved into a house near by. From descriptions that were had of Atkinson there was little doubt in the mind of the sleuth that he had succeeded in running down the much-wanted Stevens. The persevering officer had the house watched all night and at daybreak the following morning he knocked on the door of the Atkinson apartment, and with the cautious opening of the door, Hays pushed his way into the room. Before Stevens could spring to the table on which reposed a pair of revolvers he was seized and manacled. A search of the rooms revealed all the evidence that was needed. Stevens was soon convinced that he had been caught with the goods and that he was in for a long prison term, and when the crushed and suffering Redmond was pointed out to him the appeal to his manhood brought a confession that completely exonerated the Publican. Relates the *Gazette:*

> In no time the District Attorney, after Stevens had been put upon the stand, arose and touching the abandonment of the defense, stated his firm conviction of Redmond's perfect innocence. It is difficult to describe the sensation which this singular declaration produced in the crowded court-room. The proceedings, which had been strikingly dramatic in all their stages, had wound up with a miracle. The spectators, the Court, nay the prosecuting officers, were not only amazed but thunderstruck, and the majority almost mistrusted that they were the victims of enchantment.
>
> The most powerful effect was visible upon Redmond. His careworn, fixed and haggard features were agitated for a moment with a convulsive tremor, the tears gushed in fountains from his eyes, and sinking his head between his clasped hands, he uttered a fervent ejaculation of "Thank God! Thank God!"
>
> When the confusion and excitement had in some degree subsided, and the repeated admonitions of the crier of the Court had restored a

THE QUEER HOMAGE EXACTED BY AN IMPERIOUS SOCIETY BELLE FROM HER ADMIRERS AS THE CONDITIONS UPON WHICH THEY BE PERMITTED TO ENJOY HER SOCIETY—PERSIAN CUSTOMS INTRODUCED INTO THE CODE OF UPPER-TENDOM'S ETIQUETTE—THE WHIMSICAL FREAKS AND FANCIES INDULGED IN BY THE GIDDY GIRLS OF GOTHAM.—SEE PAGE 2.

partial order, the Recorder, with a moistened eye and a voice quavering with emotion, rose to address the jury. In the brief charge which the consuming anxiety of the whole Court rendered necessary, he observed that Redmond stood before them a ruined man, blighted in character and deserted by his friends. That by the arrest of Stevens, new light had been thrown on the affair, which tended to the irrefragable declaration of his innocence, and that it would hardly expose one to the imputation of superstition to say, "The finger of Almighty God is in this matter!"

The jury then retired, but immediately returned, and upon being questioned by the clerk in usual form, replied by the voice of the foreman: "We find David Ware guilty of wilful perjury."

On rendition of this verdict the excitement broke out afresh. The whole audience betrayed their conviction in accordance with the various materials of which it was composed. There were streaming eyes, murmurs of applause, and mutterings of execration against the malignant wretch who had been so miraculously up-tripped in his deep designs. Redmond was caught up in the arms of his counsel and his previously hesitating friends, and the frantic joy of some of the most mercurial in the dense assemblage expressed itself in violent expressions of delight.

Justice proceeded to make amends and Ware was consigned to the State Prison for five years. Very soon after, Stevens in a further confession told of the full part that Holdgate and Sutton had played in the affair of the false checks, and in a few hours the Pewterer and the Pugilist were in the toils and now it was their turn to be consigned to the same prison which had incarcerated Redmond. Obstinate defense was made for Holdgate by the father of his affianced bride, but when sentence was finally passed it was for life at hard labor. Holdgate, before his confinement, made a full confession.

In 1836, the laws of the state were revised and the penalties of several offenses were altered. Forgery, from a life imprisonment penalty, was reduced to a maximum of five years. The Pugilist regained his freedom, to return to a mode of life that often brought him in contact with the police and that left him free to lead his attack on the *Gazette* sanctum. For the Pewterer:

There was a welcome in store for him which can only be found in the priceless treasure of a woman's love. The true heart which had bestowed the blossoms of its first affections upon the misguided artizan, had never ceased to throb toward his gloomy prison, and though he came back to her a degraded outcast, despised and branded with a felon's shame, it bestowed on him at once the faithfully treasured harvest of its unalterable love. They were married.

As for the Publican: On his return home, Redmond found his house illuminated to receive him, and distrustful friends who had shrunk from him through his ordeal, now gathered shamefacedly in an effort to make amends. The city, wild with a desire to make redress for his wrongs, saw the leading citizens arrange a public dinner in his honor, also a benefit was tendered him by the manager of the Bowery Theatre. The profit from this affair was turned over by Redmond to alleviate the condition of the poor prisoners awaiting trial. His suit against the bank employees was settled for a few thousand dollars, which hardly covered his actual losses. Sad to relate, the strain of his troubles affected Redmond's health, and with his physical decline his hotel never regained its former prosperity. He died a bankrupt in 1843.

VIRGINIA OF VIRGINIA

A Red-Hot Mamma of the Forties

"THIS horrible affair"—citing the *National Police Gazette* of October 31, 1846, in its editorial comment upon the matter which carried through various issues under the heading of "The Richmond Tragedy"—"though more than a month old, has outlived the limit of ordinary horrors [the *Gazette* went strong in its usage of the word horrible]. . . . Apart from the social position of the parties involved, the offense which gave rise to the bloody dénouement is an extraordinary case of adultery in which the bold, flagrant and licentious woman made the weak, vain man convertible to her desires."

Study of this particular illicit love affair, which was quite the topic of its times, would make it seem that the righteous *Gazette* was rather inclement with the man in the case. At least, as it will be seen, he died like a gentleman with a lie on his lips in defense of his lady love, and he was apparently deeply enamored of his charmer. And the frail fair one was not only easy to look at, but her epistolary wooing was so high-powered in romantic expression—well, it is no wonder at all that this poor bachelor was taken by this seductive dame of Richmond, even, as the common phrase has it, this Virginia City was later taken by General Grant. Her letters to the man whose death she brought about were such burning outpourings of a love-hungry heart that it is too bad, indeed, that—but wait.

Strictly speaking, the Richmond Tragedy had little to do with New York and its sinful ways, though the Astor House, in Broadway, then the most splendid hotel in all the country and even all the world, figured slightly in the case, and New York was agog in a ribald and scandalized interest. The circulation of the *Gazette* took a tremendous jump with its issue of October 24, 1846, for in this number the first of the above-mentioned love letters were reproduced in print. They came to light during the taking of the testimony in the Mayor's Court, Richmond, Virginia, in the examination of William R. Myers (husband of Virginia) as principal, and Samuel S. Myers (brother of William) and William S. Burr, as aiders and abettors in the murder of Dudley Marvin Hoyt for supposed illicit intercourse

THE FEMALE RIGHTS' MUSKETEERS.

WHAT MAY BE EXPECTED IF THE SCHEMES OF CERTAIN STRONG-MINDED WOMEN IN AMERICA ARE REALIZED.

[45]

with the wife of the principal. Excerpts from a few of these fervid pennings tell the progress of the tragedy.

Wednesday, Dec. 3, 1845

I trust you will pardon the liberty I take in writing you, and the still greater liberty of begging you the favor of calling here tomorrow at 1 o'clock. . . . I know you will have some scruples as to my request, but I appeal to the kindness of your heart. If you will be so kind as to call at 1 o'clock tomorrow you will find me alone. . . . May I beg of you the kindness to forgive me this note. Yet, when you know the cause you will pardon me. What I have written is strictly confidential, and knowing your high, noble sense of honor, I need say no more. Although I have not the honor of your acquaintance, yet, believe me, I am one of your warmest, most sincere friends. . . .

Virginia M.

"It will be seen," points out the *Gazette,* "that her bold and amorous character is revealed at the outset; that Mrs. Myers, while yet unacquainted with Hoyt, deliberately and of herself contrived the first meeting." She was not so slow for a small city gal, and in a day well before the ladies are supposed to have been taking stock of their various rights. Nor do the facts at hand enable us to enlighten as to what it was about Mr. Hoyt that made for his sex appeal, though his sideburns are described as "very elegant." Anyway, whatever it was that Virginia had need of discussing so urgently with a gentleman whose acquaintance she had not yet enjoyed, a second interview was requested in a letter which contained "warm expressions of satisfaction at the results produced by their first meeting." Her amatory thoughts were expressed to the boy friend thus:

My Dearest and Best Friend:—This morning I received a note from a lady I am to go visiting, that she would prefer my going Monday instead of Tuesday. Now won't you come Tuesday? If you cannot come that day I will excuse myself to her, for on no account on earth would I miss the pleasure of seeing you. You will come, won't you? I had anticipated so much delight in seeing you Monday. . . . The postponement of one day seems very long to me. . . . All Monday, I shall be thinking of the pleasure of seeing you; and I hope the time may pass quickly until our meeting. . . . Don't laugh at this note—for I have written it fresh from my heart. . . . Come, dearest, at 12 o'clock, instead of 1 o'clock. . . . I will go to the theatre tomorrow night if only to rest my eyes on your dear face and tell you with a glance how wholly I love. . . .

THE FEMALE DRUMMER'S ARTS.

A NOVEL AND SUCCESSFUL METHOD ADOPTED AS AN EXPERIMENT BY TWO OF THE MERCHANT PRINCES OF NEW YORK CITY.

No getting away from it, Virginia was a fast worker. So it is no surprise that her next letter, which was written on the Friday following, confessed to being Hoyt's wife, save in the empty ceremony. And by now she was vowing that no other man should touch the lips which he had kissed, nor would her form be

[47]

clasped by another. Which, the *Gazette* seems to intimate, was not at all nice for a married lady.

"This love of you," she wrote, "is raging like a storm in my heart—burning, my sweet, like an electric shock through my soul. I love you better than Heaven, and I call to it to witness this vow, that my whole person is sacredly yours."

In less than the year this correspondence was continued Mrs. Myers must have written more than fifty letters, of which close to one-half were read in the courtroom and every one breathed with love's transports of devotion and its throes of dejection. Such Elinor Glynish self-expression was deemed that of a depraved female. Virginia even feigned illness so she would not have to leave town with her husband and might remain in Richmond with her lover. Finally, during the summer of 1846, she was forced to accompany her husband to New York and from the Astor House her distracted letter sets forth:

> I was unable to close my eyes in sleep all last night, and the distress of being away from you is killing me. You may hear of my taking my life any hour. The only thing that has stayed my hand from taking laudanum is the thought you still love me.

Letters were also read from Hoyt that were almost as long and as love laden, though not so numerous, as those penned by Virginia. In one just before the tragic ending of the infatuation, in endeavoring to reassure as to how sincere was his feeling, he penned these lines that were fraught with a significance that he did not then realize:

> You must know, Virginia, dearest Virginia, how anxious I am to make you a happy woman, that I would willingly give my life to accomplish it, would that but do.

Soon after the return to Richmond an anonymous letter apprised Mrs. Myers' brother-in-law of her intimacy with Hoyt. She soon saw she was under suspicion, which caused her to send a warning that advised the return of her letters. The request was complied with and the letters, unfortunately, were intercepted. The husband, who was out of town, was informed of the state of affairs, and——

> Thunderstruck at the infidelity of her whom he had ever loved, honored and cherished, and stung to madness with the thought of his honor

wounded in the tenderest point, Mr. Myers hurried to Richmond to glut his vengeance where he had been so foully wronged.

In the agitation of her extremity Virginia wrote as follows:

O God! Was ever misery like mine? Wretched days and sleepless nights. What hope is there for me? Tomorrow decides my fate. I am separated from my husband and compelled to return to a house where I well know how I shall be received. My father is a stern-hearted man. What stays my hand when all can be ended in a moment? Oh! that I could see you for one moment—just one instant! I have sat for hours by my window hoping that I might see you. For one hour with thee, I would give up life itself. Dearest, never forget—never forget; swear to me you never will—your promise that my last moments shall be spent with you. You will be sent for, that I promise; and oh, tell me, that you will not refuse to come; then I will be happy, knowing that my last breath will be in your arms. . . . Think of me tomorrow, when my fate is to be decided, and oh! pray God to have mercy on me. . . . All my friends believing me ill, and not having heard the cause of my distress, have called to see me. But I am in too much agony and can see no one . . . only you, I want to see.

And on that same afternoon she wrote one more letter, which was also intercepted, and in which she promised to be waiting by her window at midnight, when she would lower him a farewell note on a string, and that he should attach his reply which she asked to strengthen her through her coming ordeal. "Tell me," she wrote, "you are mine forever and then they may condemn me."

On the next day came the tragedy.

The following was reprinted in the *Gazette* from the Richmond *Inquirer* as apparently pertinent to the case:

The case of the Commonwealth vs. W. R. Myers, S. S. Myers and Wm. S. Burr, was continued, not, however, in the legal sense of the term, before the Hustings Court on yesterday. The whole day very nearly was occupied in the reading of the intercepted letters of Mrs. Myers, introduced in behalf of the Commonwealth. It is understood they are brought forward to rebut the evidence given in the defense, to falsify the dying declaration of Hoyt.

ACQUITTAL OF THE PARTIES—On Monday the argument in the case of the Richmond Tragedy was continued and concluded. The case was then submitted, and the Court stood FIVE TO TWO for acquittal, and the parties were discharged. The courtroom was crowded almost to suffocation with spectators, who lingered through the long argument, full

RUM ON TAP.

THE WOMEN OF KYANA, IND., GO TO THE RAILROAD DEPOT AND DEMOLISH A CARGO OF LIQUOR.

of anxiety for the result. When that was ascertained, such a burst of applause took place as we never heard in a court of justice.

In this wise the *Gazette* correspondent dramatically gives the particulars of the tragedy:

> William Myers, his brother Samuel, and Burr, forced their way into Hoyt's room at about 7 o'clock in the morning, while the latter was still in bed. Burr thrust a letter before Hoyt which he demanded must be signed. It was a pledge that Hoyt would leave Richmond and never return to the city under penalty of death.
>
> Hoyt stoutly refused.
>
> Col. Samuel Myers then brandished a stick over Hoyt and said that he must sign or take the consequence. Hoyt answered coolly:
>
> "Gentlemen, I shall decline signing this paper."
>
> Whereupon William Myers drew a revolver and fired twice as Hoyt started to rise from the bed. The weapon was only a foot away from his person as the trigger was pressed and the bullet was discharged full in his face and pierced the brain above the right eye. He was instantly blinded with the blood of his wound, yet still attempted to defend himself, when he received a second ball, which passed through the fleshy part of one thigh and buried itself in the other.

And in this brave fashion the honor of a Virginia gentleman was avenged. And the villain in the case? Why, as he fell to the floor blinded with the gush of his life-blood and believing the words would be the last (which they were) he would ever utter, cried:

"She is innocent!"

This chapter should be rounded out with an account of how Virginia committed suicide over the resting-place of her lover, or at least pined away in sadness to an early grave. Only that was not what really happened. Hardly a month later she was trying to exonerate herself at the expense of her dead lover in a letter to a friend, which she took pains to have given out to the public, and which wound up as follows:

> May God enable me to bear my trial meekly, assured that high heaven will not always shroud the pure innocence of
>
> Your afflicted friend,
Virginia Myers

At which point the *Gazette* waxed very indignant editorially and lost interest in Virginia of Virginia. Which, by now, is possibly the case with the reader.

GOUGH AND THE *GAZETTE*
The Trials of the Tippling Temperance Talker

WHEN the *Gazette* removed John B. Gough, one of the foremost of the temperance lecturers of the Forties, from a bawdy house on Walker Street, and in a very intoxicated condition, New York's crusading weekly started something that not a few out-of-town papers were not pleased to copy. Notwithstanding, the business got plenty of play in print all over the nation. In fact it got the press quite roused, for some of the newspapers were strong temperance organs, and certain dailies, particularly of Boston, tried to undermine the *Gazette* articles and came back with all manner of charges, and the *Tribune* and the *Journal of Commerce,* both of New York, became very much embroiled. Really, it was a sad business.

On the one hand, as we have said, the *Gazette* claimed to have found Mr. Gough right where they said and under conditions as stated. And, unfortunately, as the paper proceeded to bring strong proof of its charges the temperance disciple was forced more or less to admit as much, but—there was the Gough side of the affair to be taken into consideration. It would appear from Gough's own lips in explanation, that he was the victim, nothing more or less, of very dirty work on the part of dastardly enemies to the cause of temperance. His story, which he stuck to, explained how a most mysterious Jonathan Williams, or it might have been Williamson, invited the temperance talker to partake of a drink of raspberry soda, the Williams, or Williamson, person "looked into my face with a devilish expression of exultation which I never shall forget."

John B. Gough, it would appear, arrived in this city on his way to Albany and put up at the Croton Hotel. After tea he went out and for an entire week was among the missing. Alarmed at his disappearance, his friends issued conspicuous placards with a description of his person and attributing his singular disappearance to accident or foul play at the hands of the rum-dealers. "The entire city was in a fever," so we read, "and the press and the public made up their minds at once for an interesting horror."

Alas, acting on information which was brought to the *Gazette* in a mysterious

BEAUTY AND THE BEER.

AN INCIDENT OF THE BEER-MAKER'S STRIKE IN NEW YORK—HOW THE DASHING DAUGHTER OF A BREWER SUPPLIED THE PLACE
OF ONE OF HER FATHER'S STRIKING EMPLOYEES—A PRETTY GIRL'S PRACTICAL PROTEST AGAINST TEETOTALISM.

way, instead of directly to the police, George Wilkes, one of the owners of the paper, made an investigation of the Walker Street address given, which was located in a labyrinth of rookeries. After mounting two flights of stairs in a rickety rear-building, directions were followed through a passage that led to a bedroom and——

[53]

There we found him, John B. Gough, the mere shadow of a man, pacing the floor with tottering and uncertain steps. He was pale as ashes; [his eyes glared with a preternatural luster], his limbs trembled, and his fitful and wandering stare evinced his mind was as much shattered as his body. The pompous horror had dissolved from its huge proportions, and shrunk into a very vulgar and revolting commonplace. The man was drunk.

That was all that was the matter with him—the man was drunk (and apparently did not carry his liquor well). But if you think the *Gazette* picture was a bit

GOING FOR HIS SCALP.

TWO INEBRIATED DUDES, ON BEING EXPELLED FROM A THIRD AVENUE TOBACCO STORE, VENT THEIR RAGE ON THE HARMLESS INDIAN SIGN.

lurid, you should bear in mind that it was the end of a hard week for the temperance advocate and naturally he did not look so good. After calling in an officer from the police station this representative of law and order was sent to accompany Gough back to his distressed friends, who were probably more distressed when they saw what had been brought back to them. No immediate reference was made to the business by the *Gazette* "out of respect to a worthy cause," so it was said, though neither Wilkes nor Fox, judging by the examples of their artists, had much respect for the temperance advocates. One cannot help having suspicions that the spot was awaited until the desirable moment had come for its "revolting revelations." Silence was maintained until Gough issued his "confession" from Boston in explanation of his disappearance. Then the *Gazette* was indeed heard from and from then on things got rapidly no better.

It was rather unfortunate that Gough had to be so vague in his facts concerning the identity of Williams or Williamson; the exact location of the place where he had imbibed the efficacious draught of raspberry soda; even the name of the shop where he had been betrayed, to say nothing of other essential details. And he questioned that the building in which he had been found was a house of ill-fame and had much else to say, all of which was endorsed by the Mount Vernon Congregational Church and other religious bodies, by various temperance societies, and by quite a few newspapers as "a free and artless confession of the truth." Against this there was plenty of public, press, and even pulpit derision of the confession, and the temperance advocates, themselves, came to odds over the business.

An article that got the *Gazette* going well was published in the Boston *Star* under the signature of "Corporal"—"to distinguish his rank among the literary understrappers of his city," opines the *Gazette*. "Corporal" even went so far as to insinuate that blackmail was back of the exposure of Gough and that the *Gazette* was an inveterate enemy of not only temperance, but all religion as well.

To which the *Gazette* came back with the news that it was quite true there had been some money handled. That friends of Gough, when the latter had been delivered in their hands gave up one hundred dollars to the officer under the impression that he had been the main agent in the backslider's restoration. Evidently, the policeman did not feel that Gough's return was worth all that money; though that may not have been the reason he brought the amount back to the office of the *Gazette*. "And," reports the said *Gazette,* "we refused the money, but divided it in two parts, giving half to the officer and a like amount to the person who had furnished us with the information that led to the discovery of Gough in the Walker Street brothel—we kept the balance."

And then the *Gazette* started to fire its hottest shrapnel in the way of printer's ink and proceeded to impart the news that the Walker Street visit which had been exposed was not Mr. Gough's first escapade; that he was neither a stranger to the use of liquor, nor to the slums of the thoroughfare in question, and that he picked up a female on the Broadway stage-coach. Which brought into the case "the woman

ALMOST TRAPPED.

AN EPISCOPAL MINISTER IN NEW YORK JUST MISSES BECOMING THE VICTIM OF A HORRIBLE AND SCANDALOUS
BLACKMAILING RACKET

in black" (who was apparently the one who had supplied the *Gazette* with the information as to Gough's whereabouts when he was where he most certainly should not have been). Let us lift from the pages of the righteous *Gazette:*

> We will now claim the privilege which the unjust imputations of the "Corporal's" article confers upon us, of stepping beyond the immediate transaction of the memorable week referred to, and examine some other

MACHINATIONS OF A FEMALE TEMPTRESS.

PERILS WHICH BESET THE PATH OF YOUNG MEN WHO RIDE IN BROADWAY STAGES; NEW YORK.

features that pertain to the same story. In these we will preserve the same candor which has distinguished every portion of our statement.

One day, about six or seven weeks previous to the 6th of September, the period of Gough's last arrival in New York, he accosted a certain tall, good-looking woman dressed in black and with dark hair and eyes while in the Broadway stage. This was between the hours of nine and ten o'clock in the evening. In the conversation which ensued, he said he had been out riding on horseback, that he was very much fatigued, and that he wanted to accompany her home.

To this she replied that she could not take him to her home, but would take him somewhere else. The arrangements being thus concluded, she conveyed him to the same house in Walker Street which he afterward rendered so memorable. We are further informed, that for certain reasons nothing further of a criminal nature took place, and that the parties after an interview of considerable length, withdrew to different rooms, Gough giving his interesting new acquaintance a five-dollar gold-piece before retiring, and leaving the house at an early hour in the morning. Nothing more is heard of him in this quarter until the afternoon of Friday, September 6, when he arrived in the New Haven steamboat at Peck Slip, with the intention of proceeding to Albany. Immediately, on landing from the boat, he was seen by a gentleman of high standing and unimpeachable character, walking up the pier in company with a woman who must have met him by agreement. That we may no longer grope in mystery, we will mention the name of the gentleman, Dr. Joel G. Candee, Dentist, No. 20 Park Place, of this city, and our informants on this point are Mr. Flanagan, a Deputy United States Marshall, and Mr. Stockwell, keeper of the Temperance Croton Lunch, on the corner of the Bowery and Division Street.

That this circumstance is positively true we therefore cannot doubt. It is certain that the lady was not Mr. Gough's wife, for that lady was in Albany. It is certain that Mr. Gough's friends, upon his recovery, made him acquainted with the charge. Well, Mr. Gough gets to the Croton Hotel that evening, goes out after tea and with the "woman in black" goes to the Walker Street house, and by which time he is already intoxicated. He remained there until the following evening, when he slipped out, went privately to his hotel and returned again immediately to his cyprian retreat. On the following Monday the "woman in black" came back to the house to pay a visit to a friend there. Her female acuteness at once detected that there was more than ordinary mystery in relation to an inmate of an upper room, and setting in operation that ingenuity with which woman is so ready, she induced the girl in charge to go to the corner for a pint of cherry brandy. During which absence she slipped into the mysterious closet, and at once recognized the occupant of the room, and he immediately recognized her. It was Gough, and with the exclamation that she was the person he wanted to see, besought her to remain.

But the owner of the apartment coming, the conversation was broken off, and poor Gough lost his inamorata altogether. His subsequent delivery from the house is already known.

Then the *Gazette* proceeded to show Gough up even further. For attention was called to "two other drunken sprees of the drunken apostle," and evidence was then produced of his fall from grace some months later, "both these cases of fatigue taking place in Massachusetts." Before closing with the regret that they should be accused "of writing in a bitter and unfeeling spirit" the Gough career was reviewed in this wise:

Take one look back through his whole history, and the mind reels back sickened and disgusted with the spectacle. We first find him a mere brute wallowing in the mire and degradation of continual drunkenness; next a temperance apostle and member of a church, who, notwithstanding his solemn vows and pledges before the altar of his God, and his sacred pledges before man, returns back to his vomit, and seeks solace for his forced abstemiousness in the secret orgies and caresses of drunken prostitutes. A beast in the commencement, next a mountebank and a hypocrite; and a wretch and villain in the last. And he must remain so branded until he can translate a brothel to an honest dwelling and make a holy sanctuary of a harlot's bosom. . . . We do not consider the letter of Mr. Bates as any testimony at all, for though it represents the writer as traveling with his wife (whom he had married the day before) and in company with Gough from the 4th to the 7th of August, inclusive [dates when the *Gazette* accused Gough of being elsewhere] it says he was not out of the company of Bates for a single hour in the whole four days. This was a very extraordinary way of passing the honeymoon, to say the least.

AN OYSTER AND WINE CLERICAL CONFERENCE.

Mr. Candee was prevailed upon to come to the defense of Gough, but did so rather weakly by saying that he had no knowledge that the lady seen walking the Peck Slip pier with Gough was no lady, but might have been the latter's wife. This refutation did not help the Gough cause to any extent, as it was known that Mrs. Gough was elsewhere at the time. Other papers than the *Gazette* asked pointedly why Gough did not act on the request of the Mayor of New York, to furnish such information as was needed to further an investigation that would permit of getting to the bottom of his alleged drugging.

Gough advocates rallied vigorously to his support and tried their utmost to pull down the *Gazette* charges, only to be confounded completely when such a high personage in temperance work as B. F. Goodhue came through with the report of his personal investigation of the sad business. "I love the temperance cause—but will not lie to bolster up hypocrisy," he said in a letter that teemed with the straightforwardness of a sincere man. Goodhue had been instrumental in bringing about Gough's entry into the field of temperance. His letter was about 3,500 words in length and took up more than three columns of the *Gazette*. It is sufficient to reproduce the headlines and it can be judged quite well, whether or no, this was another *Gazette* victory.

THE LIAR'S DOOM!

STATEMENT OF
Mr. B. F. GOODHUE,
THE CELEBRATED TEMPERANCE MISSIONARY,
Of the DRUNKENNESS, DEBAUCHERIES,
and BLASPHEMIES of
JOHN B. GOUGH,
WITH AN EXPOSURE OF THE FORGERIES AND
OTHER VILE AND VILLANOUS PRACTISES WHICH
HAVE BEEN RESORTED TO BY HIS UNPRINCI-
PLED ASSOCIATES, TO SUSTAIN HIM IN HIS IN-
FAMY.

And in the end, when Gough failed to make good a threat to sue the *Gazette,* then the *Gazette* started suit against Gough. This led to a backdown on the part of the tippling temperance talker and the suit was not pressed. The *Gazette* being satisfied to make Gough take water, especially as Gough would not seem to have liked so doing, having a preference for raspberry soda.

THE MERRY YULETIDE MURDER

Thrice Tried, Once Convicted, Polly Bodine Escapes Gallows

WHAT a paper so strident of expression as the violently moral *Gazette* could do with a really grisly murder story can be imagined. The *P. G.* of its early days saw that its pages were never without a horrific murder and if the country at large did not come up to expectations in this respect then Messrs. Wilkes and Camp would turn to the journals of England, France or Germany to provide such entertainment for their readers. The murder of Adeline M. Spencer over in Jersey City by her husband, and the murder of Maria Ann Bickford up in Boston by some other lady's husband, each provided ghastly perusal features in the late Forties. However, we will take for our subject a murder from earlier in the decade to which you are being carried, and which, though it occurred almost two years before the *Gazette* came into existence, still got plenty of attention from that paper as the accused, Polly Bodine, was being tried for the third time as said *Gazette* started to flourish. It was known as the "Staten Island Murder" and was harrowing and mystifying in the extreme, the mystery being—how Polly Bodine came to escape the gallows.

This particular case had to do with the murder of Mrs. Emeline Houseman and her infant child under conditions that brought many a shudder. The alleged murderess was first tried on the 24th of June, 1844, in Richmond County, Staten Island, where the crime was committed. Conviction failed when one of the jurors stood out against the other eleven "because of his personal opposition to capital punishment, though he subsequently confessed to being convinced of her guilt." The second trial, held in New York, April, 1845, brought in a verdict of "guilty," but this conviction was rendered void by adverse decision of the Supreme Court, which disputed the presiding judge, John W. Edmonds, on a number of vital points. "When it was found impossible to panel a full jury, since twelve men out of a community of 400,000 persons could not be found who had not already arrived in their own mind as to the guilt of the prisoner, the venue was changed and the accused stood trial for the third time in Poughkeepsie, in April, 1846." The facts in the case, as near as they were ever arrived at and as set forth by the *Gazette,* were as follows:

On Christmas Eve, 1843, while the tiny Staten Island settlement known as Granite Village was busy in its own modest and rural way of spreading the spirit of "peace on earth, good will to man, the bodies of Emeline Houseman and her babe were being butchered by an atrocious hand in the little home on Staten Island." At half-past nine the following evening (Christmas night) the home of the Housemans was found to be on fire. The merriment in the neighboring homes soon gave

THE BOSTON TRAGEDY.

TIRRELL MURDERING MARIA A. BICKFORD,

WHILE IN A STATE OF SOMNAMBULISM.

way to universal commotion as the villagers hurriedly gathered to save the dwelling and its occupants. The house was completely closed and ingress was had only with some difficulty, and this was the sight, as pictured in the *Gazette,* that met the eye:

Having extinguished the flames, they lifted the mass of ruins formed by the smouldering bed, and there to their astonishment discovered the charred remains of Mrs. Houseman and her infant. Every soul present recoiled with a shudder of unmingled horror, and cause for the non-appearance of the unfortunate woman during the day stood horribly revealed. She had been murdered! There was a red mark around her neck; around her wrists were the fragments of a handkerchief, which from the position of her hands and knees, showed plainly that she had been bound to her sacrifice. A part of her head had been burned away, and nearly all the cranium of the child was consumed to its base; a fragment of the infant's skull, with the scalp and hair attached, was found among the ruins, with the blood on the inner side fresh, proving that the fire had been but the sequel of the

"Graceless action of some heavy hand."

THE STATEN ISLAND TRAGEDY.

Murder of Mrs. Houseman and Child, by Polly Bodine.

The victims of the tragedy were the wife and child of George W. Houseman, a prosperous trader in oysters. His business had called him to Virginia and it was early in December when he bade good-by to the loved ones he was not to see in life again. For he did not return to Granite Village until the day following the discovery of the murder. The finger of suspicion, for various good reasons, never pointed to the husband. On the way to his house of death, as he took passage from Pier 1, on the half-past one boat for Staten Island, there came an accidental meeting that was fraught with significance in the viewpoint of the *Gazette*.

On this very boat, as accident would have it, the wifeless and childless husband, met the woman (his sister, Polly Bodine) who was shortly to be branded as the murderess. On seeing him she burst into a flood of tears and touchingly bemoaned his sad misfortune; but Houseman, as if nature instinctively refused the hollow offering, avoided her presence and sought a refuge in solitude in the forward cabin.

Two days later, Thursday, the 28th, the Coroner's Jury brought in a verdict of willful murder and a committee of investigation was appointed from among the inhabitants of the place. It was at first supposed that a gang of murderers had descended upon the island, their cupidity incited by the rumor that the sum of $1,000 was in the possession of Emeline Houseman. This amount, which had been realized by Houseman just before the trip referred to, came through the sale of a schooner, and, it later turned out, had been secretly placed in the safekeeping of his mother, who lived nearby. So the only spoils that had come through this

POLLY BODINE, ON HER RECENT TRIAL AT NEWBURG.

horrible deed was some jewelry and personal effects of small value. This money, which had apparently cost the bereaved husband the life of his wife and child, was offered by him as a reward for the detection of the murderer, or murderers, and was accompanied with a minute description of the stolen property.

It would seem only then that suspicion was first directed toward Polly Bodine. She expressed herself in strange ways as being in opposition to the offer of the reward, and she further attempted to pervert it by giving wrong descriptions of the articles stolen until corrected by other members of the family. How suspicion was still further fastened on Polly Bodine and how these suspicions culminated in her arrest will be left to the *Gazette* to relate. But first, for clearer understanding, a brief history of the alleged murderess is in order.

Polly Bodine, at the time of the murder of her sister-in-law, was in the middle thirties. At the age of fifteen she married one Andrew Bodine, by whom she had two children, Eliza Ann, age fifteen, and Albert, slightly older. The couple separated after about five years due to misconduct on the part of the wife, and Bodine "became blunted in every moral sense and fell in with a woman much of the same stamp as himself, named Simpson, whom he married, despite the existing bonds with Polly." For this unlawful marriage Bodine, one year before the House-man murder, was sentenced to the State Prison for two years. In the meanwhile, Polly, after some traveling about, fell in with a man named Waite, an apothecary with a store at 252 Canal Street, New York, and during this liaison, placed her son, Albert, as a clerk in the Waite store.

On Friday, the reward was decided on, and the advertisement was sent up to the city in time for the evening papers. From this moment Polly Bodine seems to have lost the greatest portion of her self-command and in the extremity of her uneasiness is known to have sent the following dispatch to Waite, which was taken to the city by her son Albert.

Mr. Waite, you can't imagine my troubles, as I slept with Emeline last. I want you to get a soot of clothes and come to see me with Albert. Close the store—you will be examined on my coming to New York on Monday. You and Albert must say that Albert came to the ferry for me and I remained with you all day, with the exception of going to Spring Street for about 10 or 15 minutes to get a basket mended, went out the next morning about the same length of time, was going to stay some days, but her brother-in-law came to let her know about accident. I and my son returned to the island immediately, you will be treated well. We are all worn out with examinations. Your store and all is going to be searched and other places. Hide the things I left and put them where they cannot be found. If [writing obliterated for half a line] should ask [another obliteration] your house, say no.

Going back to Sunday, December 24, we find that Miss Matilda O'Rourke visited the deceased at her house, left on 5 o'clock of that after-noon, when Polly Bodine came in for the evening, and for the purpose of sleeping with her sister-in-law, Houseman having arranged with his mother that his wife should be left alone in the house at night as little as possible, Emeline being of timid disposition. Miss O'Rourke testified that when she left the house Mrs. Houseman put away the silver spoons, the sugar tongs, her gold watch, and also observed around the child's neck, the coral beads and clasp, which were afterwards pawned, with other things

QUEENS OF THE LOBBY—FASCINATING SIRENS WHO CAPTIVATE SUSCEPTIBLE STATESMEN BY FEMININE BLANDISHMENTS, AND MANIPULATE LEGISLATIVE JOBS SUCCESSFULLY FOR WEALTHY CORPORATIONS, WHERE "BAR'LS" OF GREENBACKS PROVE UNAVAILING—CURIOUS WIRE-PULLING BEHIND THE SCENES AT ALBANY THAT EXPLAIN THE SECRETS OF MANY LITTLE OPERATIONS THAT PUZZLE THE TAX-PAYING PUBLIC OF THE EMPIRE STATE.— SEE PAGE 2.

(and by one recognized as Polly Bodine), on the very day the murder was discovered.

After having gone over to Mrs. Houseman's house as above described, Polly Bodine did not return home until six o'clock of the following morning Monday, when she was let in by her mother. Early that morning, Christmas, she journeyed to New York and went to Waite's store, where young Albert Bodine was gotten rid of on some pretense for fifteen or twenty minutes. Polly Bodine, after leaving the store on Canal Street two or three times, departed with the announcement that she was going to sleep for the night at the house of a Mrs. Strang.

We must now go back for an hour or two for the purpose of inquiring what took place during the periods of Polly's absences from the Waite store; and the while the bodies of Emeline Houseman and her child lay butchered in that silent, noiseless house on Staten Island. During the period of this absence a woman dressed in a cloak, hood and veil, went to the pawnbroker's shop of A. Adolphus, at 332 William Street, and offering a gold watch, wished to obtain a loan of $70. upon it. Adolphus offered $35. and the woman agreed, received the money, and gave the name of Henderson, of Bergen, N. J. It was the watch that had been given to Emeline Houseman by her husband. We next find this same woman at the pawnbroker's shop of John J. Levy, No. 32 East Broadway, where she pawned the gold chain belonging to the same watch. She obtained a loan of $25. and gave the name of Ellen Henderson, of Bergen, N. J. We find her also at the pawnbroker's shop of Davis, in Chatham Street, where she pawned the silver spoons which Miss O'Rourke had seen in the possession of the deceased; also to Hart's, 27 Chatham Street, where more of the spoons were pawned and the same name and address given. [Later, in three cases out of five, Polly Bodine and Ellen Henderson were identified as one and the same person.] And finally a woman visited the store of Thompson & Fisher, jewelers, No. 331 Broadway, and changed the earrings of the deceased, and the clasp of her infant and a breast-pin, for a hair bracelet, and received 50 cents change.

Polly left Waite's on the eventful Christmas afternoon, to go as was stated before to Mrs. Strang's, to sleep that night; but Mrs. Strang, who lived at the time in Eighth Street testified that the accused did not sleep there that night, and had not slept there in three or four years. Polly's whereabouts, from the time of departure from Waite's house, on Christmas afternoon, until the following morning, stands to this hour unaccounted for. At half-past nine on that night the dwelling of George Houseman was discovered to be on fire.

The fire was entirely confined to the corner in which the bed stood. All of the witnesses who saw the fire swear that the fire appeared to be under the bed. The post mortem examination by Drs. Harrison, Clarke and Eadie proved conclusively that violence had been used previous to the fire. The radius of the left arm was broken and the end of the fractured bone charred, showing that the fire had been communicated subsequently through the fracture. Near the fracture was a flesh wound an inch, or an inch and a half in length, with extravasated blood, denoting that it must have been inflicted previous to death. The right wrist had a black silk handkerchief bound tight around it, and was consumed to the knot. Other marks, with the position of the body, indicate a violent death. The front kitchen door was found unfastened by the lock, bolt and bar which usually fastened it. As John Thompson, a neighbor's boy, tried the door in the morning, and found it fastened, it appears most certain, the person who fired the building entered that way, and must have had the key.

When was this horrid deed performed?

Who did the deed?

This question, from the circumstances which have been elicited, connects itself with a further query—where was Polly Bodine when it was done? The last we have seen of her was on Christmas day afternoon about 4 o'clock. We next hear of her on Tuesday morning between six and seven o'clock after the fire at Staten Island, going on board of the boat to New York (though she knew it did not start until eight). She then had something to eat and took a seat in an obscure part of the cabin and never moved until the boat reached New York. On the same boat was Mr. S. B. Freeman, on his way to New York to find Polly Bodine and acquaint her with the murder. Neither met the other during the trip and Freeman left his information at Waite's store. A few minutes later Polly came in. She returned to Staten Island with her son, Albert, on the half-past one o'clock boat. During the passage she met her brother, George, under the circumstances already related.

And it was during this passage that she turned over to Albert a newly purchased hair bracelet with directions to give it to his sister, Eliza Ann. But on arriving at Port Richmond Polly resumed possession of the hair bracelet, and all trace of this damning piece of evidence was lost trace of from then on.

On the following Friday, the day on which the reward had been offered for the discovery of the guilty, as she waited impatiently the coming of Waite, Polly suddenly got up and departed from the house of her mother. After she had been absent a short time, search was made for her high and low. The house was ransacked, and even the well was looked into, on the presumption that she had committed suicide, but the search was fruitless, and the dreadful suspicion by her own family of her guilt stood half confirmed.

How and where she spent that dreadful night, no one but herself can tell. She had on neither shawl nor hat when she left the room and her dress was a thin one, and the night was freezing cold. But on the following morning (Saturday, 30th), she again presented herself at the steamboat and went by the first trip to the city.

In the meanwhile Waite came out on the first boat that same morning in company with the boy. After remaining on the island for a few hours and evincing marked uneasiness at Polly's sudden disappearance, Waite set out to return to his place of business, but was placed under arrest on board of the boat and taken into custody. On searching him, the letter from Polly Bodine was found. This letter changed every doubt of her guilt, and the cry was up for Polly Bodine. The officers went first to Waite's house, arriving there between six and seven o'clock that evening and found the bird flown, though the bed was still warm.

The following noon she was accosted on Spring Street near Hudson by a Mr. Coddington, who recognized her, and called her attention to the fact that he had read a notice in the *Herald* that her arrest was desired. She told Coddington she had not eaten or had sleep for many hours, had walked over the city from Harlem back. Coddington took her to the house of Alderman Vandervoort, and after a short stay she was driven to the Tombs in a carriage. The same day she was taken to Staten Island and consigned to Richmond County Prison.

In face of all this evidence, how did Polly Bodine escape the gallows? Was this one more miscarriage of justice?

The facts against her were certainly most damning in contrast to those which saved her.

Judge Barculo, who charged the jury in the final trial—the one in which she gained her freedom—stressed this point: If the murder was committed on Christmas, when Polly Bodine stayed in the Houseman dwelling, then the presumption must be almost irresistible, that she was the one who had committed the deed.

Against this fact, three witnesses, who could observe the house of murder from their own windows, testified that they saw some woman whom they presumed to be Emeline Houseman at work on her porch during the afternoon of Christmas Day.

No stress seemed to be placed on the fact that the stolen jewelry and silverware, which was being pawned that day in New York, would have been a sufficient excuse for Emeline Houseman to raise an alarm if she was still alive at the time, since she would almost surely have discovered the disappearance of her valuables.

The identification of Polly Bodine by the pawnbrokers as the one who disposed of the stolen jewelry was deservedly a weak point against her. The mode of identification adopted by the prosecution was irregular, particularly in view of the fact that a reward of $1,000. was practically on the head of the accused. The three witnesses who identified Polly Bodine as one and the same person were taken to the prison room in which she was confined alone, instead of having her picked out from among a number of persons.

No significance, in this trial where Polly Bodine fared best, was seemingly attached to the disappearance of the hair bracelet which she retook from her son on the boat trip from New York to Staten Island.

SUBSTITUTE FOR THE DEATH PENALTY.

As to the mystery of the whereabouts of the accused on Christmas night, when fire was set to the Houseman residence, here is what Judge Barculo's charge had to say on that point:

> The prisoner does not attempt to prove where she was on that night. She told her son, Albert, that she was going to stay with an acquaintance in the city, but it is proved she did not do so. Why she told this falsehood does not appear, except that her counsel attempts to explain it by saying she slept at Waite's that night and did not wish Albert to know it. It is submitted to you, however, to say whether this explanation is satisfactory, when Albert expressly swears he slept with Waite in the same bed that night.

Needless to say, the escape of Polly Bodine brought its meed of vitriolic comment from the astounded *Gazette*. A two-column editorial paid its respects to the "blockheads of a sheriff's panel and the drivelers of the bench." It was inclined to take the case as another evidence of increasing opposition to capital punishment and added with a note of hopelessness:

> We must have a reform and that right speedily, or the community must resign themselves to a state of things which will outhorror the darkest ages of crime. . . . The verdict of NOT GUILTY in this case, it is needless to say, has been received with mingled sensations of horror and indignation but little short of those excited on the first discovery of the crime. Every man and woman feels it, and the cheeks which blanched at the original recital of the barbarous deed, now kindle with indignation that the ghosts of the butchered innocents must forever wander unavenged.

WHEN MEN WERE—MANHANDLERS

About John Morrissey and Murder, and Bill Poole and Politics

PHYSICAL combat, professionally, (and for its present-day standing the Fox *Gazette* carries no little responsibility) has long since been reduced to a business of boxing contests in which two well-conditioned athletes belabor each other with padded mitts before tremendous gatherings which, in the case of very important matches, include many of the most representative men and women of the country. A few hours later, the combatants, usually little the worse for their conflict, are paid a fortune for their efforts; in one instance one combatant, Gene Tunney, was paid very close to one million dollars for his thirty minutes within the roped arena. The outcome may be followed by some bitter discussion, but that is all.

Three-quarters of a century ago, when John Morrissey fought it out with Bill Poole to determine which was entitled to recognition as the champion rough-and-tumble fighter, this was decidedly a brutal life-and-death business and a mere boxing contest was then in utter defiance of law and order. Though no reams of advance publicity appeared in the newspapers concerning the impending conflict, the battle between the two had been brewing for long and the entire city of New York and most of the country looked forward with anxious dread to the meeting of the two. And the fight and what followed became a very important news item through the press of the country after it had come about. For it was a matter that held political import.

Although the *National Police Gazette,* through the efforts of its subsequent owner, Richard K. Fox, laid the foundations for the tremendous prominence that has since been given to the sport of pugilism, a quarter of a century was to go by before what was probably the clearest story of the Morrissey-Poole fray and its relative details was set down in print. In 1880 Fox prevailed on Theodore Allen to assist in its writing. "The" Allen, as he was generally known, was then the proprietor of the "Bal Mabille," one of the leading resorts of the fast and the fancy. He then had back of him a record of thirty years as a political bully, keeper of gambling houses and worse; had been concerned in many rough-and-tumble fights and

[72]

shooting frays and had figured in numerous other transactions that made him amenable to the law, though until then he had always managed to escape conviction. Allen had been more than a mere eyewitness to the Morrissey-Poole epic; he had played an important part through the entire momentous violence.

Tammany's political despotism was more than challenged by the Native American, or Know Nothing organization and factional antipathy then did not even halt at murder. Each political party had its representation of tough henchmen. Under the banner of the Native Americans were Tom Hyer, who had licked Yankee Sullivan in

BILL POOLE, THE FAMOUS SPORTING MAN, POLITICIAN, AND FIGHTER—SEE PAGE 14 FOR DESCRIPTION OF HIS GREAT BATTLE WITH MORRISSEY.

JOHN MORRISSEY, CONGRESSMAN, STATE SENATOR, GAMBLER AND PUGILIST—FOR REMINISCENCES OF HIS EVENTFUL LIFE SEE PAGE 14.

17 minutes and 18 seconds in a fight for the American heavyweight pugilistic title, and his friend Bill Poole, rated the peer of rough-and-tumble fighters. Morrissey had aligned himself with the Tammany force, which boasted such fearless sluggers and merciless roughs as Yankee Sullivan; Pat "Paugene" McLaughlin, a cruel little manhandler, who had parted with his nose by the teeth of Murray the Mick; and among others, Lew Baker, who attempted to assassinate Hyer, and who finally did Poole to death. Morrissey not only challenged the ring supremacy of Hyer, but declared himself a better man than Poole in an "everything-goes" battle. He styled

himself the American Champion on the strength of a decision over Sullivan after Hyer had announced his retirement, the bout in question terminating in a general fight after 53 minutes of milling and Sullivan being ruled the loser for having left the ring. This bout was in October, 1853.

It was soon after the New Year in 1855 that a row started in a saloon in the basement of Wallack's Theatre on Broadway, the Morrissey challenge to Hyer being the basis of the quarrel. Before the argument had progressed very far Baker's confederate, Jim Turner, drew a gun and shot at Hyer, the ball grazing the champion's neck. Hyer, a quiet man for all his fighting record, but a dangerous person when roused, turned on Turner and drawing his own gun contemptuously discharged his shot into the wall. The smoke was still curling from his pistol when he saw the reflection of Turner in a mirror in the act of again cocking his pistol. Wheeling quickly he grasped Turner by the neck and threw him violently to the floor. At the same time Baker attacked Hyer from the rear, using the butt of his gun on Hyer's head. The latter then gave his attention to Baker and was proceeding to treat him the same as he had Turner, when a policeman entered and Hyer turned Baker over to the officer for arrest. The representative of the law declined to interfere in what was termed a private dispute, even though Baker had drawn a knife. So Hyer proceeded to finish with Baker and deposited him in the gutter in an insensible condition, though he had his hand severely cut before this task was accomplished to his own satisfaction.

And so the war was on in earnest between the rival political brawlers. Baker got another licking a few days later from Poole, who would probably have had both of Baker's eyes out if the police had not happened along in time. Whereupon, Morrissey told the world that he was going out to get Bill the Butcher.

Poole, by now, had given up his butcher business and started a drinking-place on the corner of Broadway and Howard Street and which was known as the Bank Exchange. His admirers, in celebration of the venture, arranged a grand ball in his behalf in the Chinese Assembly Room, so-called on account of its oriental decorations, and where the first masquerade ball on skates was held. Deputations of sports and fast women and men from New Orleans, Charleston and Savannah and other large cities attended and there has seldom been such a free and easy company gathered as was present for this occasion. Morrissey and many of his followers also attended, but nothing of a troublesome nature happened until

A MASQUERADE ON SKATES.

THE LATEST PHASE OF THE ALL-CONQUERING CRAZE OF ROLLER-RINKING AS ILLUSTRATED IN THE CITY OF NEW YORK.

shortly after the ball was over and the two met in the bar of the City Hotel, which was opposite Poole's place of business.

From this point we will let Allen tell the story. "The" was privileged to take a very intimate part through the entire business. He had been a helper in Poole's market and had resigned to become a political protégé of Bill the Butcher, who had been taken with the way young Allen had handled himself against several desperate ruffians.

Morrissey was standing at the bar as Poole entered and advanced toward him. The place was full of people and all talk died down until there was not even a whisper. The two eyed each other coldly and alert. Morrissey was the first to speak. He spit his cigar from his mouth and then said defiantly:

"There stands the black-muzzled American fighter."

"Yes," responded Poole, sneeringly, with his favorite expression, "and I'm a dandy."

"I can lick all the dandy out of you tomorrow morning," responded Morrissey. "What is more, I'll bet you five hundred dollars you don't dare meet me, and you can name the place." And he put fifty dollars as a forfeit in the hands of George Deagle, chief clerk of the hotel.

"How about the foot of Christopher Street?" asked Poole. He had named a location within two or three blocks of his own home.

Big Tom Burns, one of Morrissey's bosom friends, protested and broke out excitedly:

"Don't go there, John; that's Poole's headquarters. His gang will never let you get away alive."

After a moment's hesitation Morrissey tossed over fifty dollars to Poole and dared him to name another place.

"How will the Amos Street dock suit you?" asked Poole.

"That's satisfactory," was the bold answer.

"I'll be there bright and early," promised Poole.

Five o'clock in the morning Poole came up to the Amos Street dock in a coach accompanied by "Smut" Ackerman, Tommy Culkin and myself [Allen]. Amos Street wharf was the next one above the Christopher Street dock. It was the only pier the opposition Albany boats landed at uptown. It was also used as a wood wharf, cordwood being heaped there in great piles. Numerous admirers of Poole had already put in appearance and they had cleared a place for the fight and were now camped on the piles and in the street, or rested themselves on sails that they had unbent from the spars of the sloops and schooners that were at anchor in the slip.

It was more than an hour and a half from the time set at which Morrissey was expected to put in appearance and as there was a nipping coolness in the air of this February morning Poole decided to warm up by enjoying a bit of exercise. Poole and a couple of his boon companions and myself rowed across the river to Barker's Gardens, a resort over in Hoboken, near the ferry. There we had a few drinks, Poole calling for his favorite, milk punch. He took his turn at the oars on the way back so as to limber up. We pulled into the Hammond Street dock and then

SCRAPPING FOR LOVE.

THE EXCITABLE YOUNG LADIES OF APPLETON, WIS., INDULGE IN A FIGHT AT A BALL.

left Bill to rest in the Village House, while I went down the street to see if Morrissey had yet put in appearance.

Morrissey had not yet got uptown. A number of his friends, however, had started up Hudson Street in coaches. Poole's friends were laying in wait for them and every carriage that appeared was stopped and either upset or emptied of its inmates. A fight invariably ensued, which ended in "Old Smoke's" supporters making their departure for home or a hospital.

[77]

It was nearing 7 A.M. before news, which traveled ahead of him, apprised that Morrissey was driving up with a friend in a light wagon. I had time to get Poole to the wharf before Morrissey arrived. He came with Johnny Lyng, proprietor of the "Sportsman's Headquarters," at Canal Street and Broadway, and they walked toward us arm in arm. The crowd which swarmed on the dock made a lane for them to pass through and everything was very orderly thus far. Even the hundreds who crowded the roofs and windows of the adjacent buildings were quiet. But among the people on the pier was John Poole, Bill's brother. He had undergone a frightful mauling in Lyng's Place and burned for revenge. As Lyng passed John Poole, Bill's brother struck his enemy a smashing blow on the jaw. In a second there was a general fight. No one attempted to molest Morrissey, who stood quietly looking on. But his followers fared badly. They were given a thorough thrashing after which their revolvers were taken from them and tossed into the river. After this slight delay the principals were permitted to get down to business.

There was no ring, but by general consent the throng had kept a space open for the combat. Poole, in his undershirt, as he had rowed across the river, was ready. It did not take Morrissey long to peel.

Throwing off his coat and white shirt, he stood in his red flannel undershirt, as brawny a young bruiser as the most enthusiastic admirer of muscle could desire to see. Poole had a powerful physique and carried himself the more gracefully of the two. Each stood over six feet and weighed close to two hundred pounds.

The fight began with some light sparring, Poole holding himself principally on the defensive as his opponent circled about for a chance to close. For about five minutes this child's play of the giants lasted. Then Morrissey made a rush. But Poole was too quick for him. As "Old Smoke" made his lunge "Bill the Butcher" ducked with remarkable agility and seized him by the ankles. In a flash Poole threw his opponent clean over his head and as "Old Smoke" went sprawling he had only time to roll over to his back when Bill pounced on him like a tiger. Then followed terrible minutes of fighting.

Clutching each other in grips of steel they butted and pounded their heads and bodies together, tearing at each other's face with their teeth and gouging for the eyes with talon-like fingers. It was sickening to watch, for in no time they were frightfully punished. There was a long gash in Poole's cheeks where the flesh had been torn by his opponent's teeth. The blood was streaming from Morrissey's both eyes. They never changed positions while the struggle went on, for the minute they were down the crowd closed in on them and the surging bodies of the combatants pressed against the feet and legs of the surrounding onlookers. The wonder is that the two on the ground were saved from being trampled to death. Not a hand was raised to interfere with or favor either contestant during the two or three minutes this inhuman struggle lasted. But Morrissey was underneath and was doomed to defeat. And soon his voice was heard, hoarse, breathless and suffocating with blood.

"I'm satisfied," he gasped. "I'm done."

A cheer went from the crowd and the shout rang out and repeated till it swelled into a roar that carried through the streets half a mile away:

"Poole's won! Poole's won!"

That was the end of the great fight between John Morrissey and Bill Poole, but not of the day's excitement, nor of many more days of turbulence. A number of outsiders had drifted by to see the battle. They had reason to wish they had stayed away before the pugnaciously inclined Poole minions were through celebrating. An attack was started on Morrissey as he started to depart from the scene of his defeat and but for a few brave friends and the aid of some fair-minded ones among the enemy he would have been carried off bodily to Lord knows what fate. He finally got safely away to the Bella Union saloon on Leonard Street, of which he was part owner.

Within less than an hour after the crowds had cleared from the Amos Street dock "Smut" Ackerman, in trying to illustrate how his friend Poole had thrown Morrissey, slipped and suffered a fatal fracture of his skull in the fall. As the dying man was being taken in a cart to the New York Hospital, then at the corner of Broadway and Anthony Street, they drove by the Bella Union saloon. The street was jammed with friends of Morrissey all hot with rage against any one who had concern with the man who had worsted their champion, and soon the cart and dying man were hemmed in by this threatening crowd. Directly opposite the Morrissey saloon was the Fifth Precinct station-house. As the infuriated Morrissey men closed in on their prey the door of the station-house opened and the knights of the club made a sally. Beating back the mob they escorted the cart to the hospital. That same afternoon Ackerman died in the arms that had beaten Morrissey into submission.

Ackerman was not even in his grave before the two factions were fighting again. The Bowery Boys and the Short Boys, who supported Morrissey, had it in for Allen for the part he had played in Poole's victory. "Paugene" McLaughlin soon after ran into Allen and challenged him to a fight on the New York Hospital grounds. At that time, though the gates to the hospital park were padlocked, there were many who had keys that fitted the lock and it was a common practice to fight out differences there. "Paugene," however, was so "spoiling for a fight" that he smashed Allen in the jaw on the way and there was scrimmaging all over the street. "Paugene" had enough for the time being, but Harry O'Donnell, who had fired a pistol at Allen during the scrimmage, was challenged to battle on the Harrison Street wharf on the following night. The gangs rowed down to the wharf, for this was in the era before street-cars roamed this district. O'Donnell, though he boasted some reputation as a professional pugilist, was well handled by Allen and wound up by being thrown into the water. The evening was topped off with a general fight in which knives, slung-shots and brass knuckles were brought into play. This succession of defeats had the Morrissey men thoroughly aroused and greedy for revenge.

A few nights later Allen and two friends were trapped in Brady's Hall, at Bayard Street and the Bowery, which was close to the headquarters of the Bowery Boys, which was at No. 40. In the desperate fight for life of the Poole trio two policemen, Rogers and Sullivan, were so terribly beaten that the latter died soon after. Allen was taken away insensible to the Star Hotel, Frankfort and Williams Streets; his eyes had been gouged from their sockets and hung out on his cheeks. A skillful operation restored them to place; he lay in bed several weeks stone blind. The first day he was permitted out by his physician, he hunted up Bob Linn, who had been the ringleader of the attack against him. Linn was found at supper in Spring Street and almost brained with a vinegar cruet.

And the following morning Allen lent a hand with the sandboys—all Poole followers—in an attempt at revenge against a crusty mail-agent named Peck. The sandboys were in the habit of loading their carts from the hills of sand left by the sloops and schooners before daybreak each morning. There was so little room between the dock and the railroad-track that the carts would be backed up against the sand piles and the forelegs of the horses would be on the tracks. Peck was in the habit of speeding down in the mail-car without warning and smashing over carts and horses. The mail-car was stoned this morning and in response to pistol-shots from the car window by Peck, Allen procured an ancient blunderbuss loaded with nails, which was possessed by one of the sand-schooner captains, and blazed away at the mail-car.

For this, three days later, Allen was arrested and taken before Judge Davidson in the Jefferson Market Court. Poole accompanied him to go on his bond.

Morris Underhill, a court officer and friend of Morrissey's, got into words with Poole and soon the two were fighting wildly right there in the courtroom and Underhill lost the use of one of his eyes. Poole, however, was never to have to answer for this disrespect to the court. He was to suffer his death wound a few days later. But first he was to have the pleasure of one more good rough-and-tumble-fight.

A night or so after the court fracas Charley Lozier, who was in the butcher business in Barrow Street, held his annual "Slaughter House Ball." Lozier had his slaughter house cleaned out specially for the event and here the followers of the

THE NATIONAL POLICE GAZETTE'S SPORTING GALLERY

"THE" ALLEN. THE FAMOUS POLITICIAN, GAMBLER, AND PROPRIETOR OF THE NOTED "BAL MABILLE;"
FOR HISTORY OF HIS ADVENTUROUS LIFE SEE PAGE 7

Poole aggregation and their good ladies, danced and drank and a grand time was had by all. During the festivities Poole and Bill Travers got into an argument as to their respective manhandling abilities, and though they were of the same political faction, nothing remained but that this matter must be settled once and for all and in the usual way.

So at 5 A.M., when the ball broke up, all adjourned to the blue-stone yard a step away and the two Bills went to it. In no time the two were struggling on the ground, which was strewn with chips of stone that cut through their clothing

THE CHICAGO CRAZE.

EVERY GARDEN CITY BELLE WANTS TO HAVE HER HAIR CUT LIKE A LITTLE MAN'S.

[82]

and gashed into their skin. The friends of the combatants perched on the mounds of stone and made a living wall about the two and cheered impartially as they battled away in the gray of the dawning day. When Travers finally agreed he had enough he was in need of one new eye, and Poole, who was well damaged himself, assured his opponent that never before had he enjoyed such a fine struggle for his honors. Which was well, for in less than forty-eight hours the Tammany thugs got him.

We will let "The" Allen tell how.

Bill Poole met death on the night of February 24, 1855. A little after 10 o'clock that evening Charley Lozier, Cy Shay, Jimmy Acker and myself [Allen] dropped into Stanwix Hall, which had been newly opened opposite the Metropolitan Hotel, then regarded as the finest of the two hemispheres, and where on that particular day William Makepeace Thackeray was quartered after delivering his delightful lecture on the Four Georges. The Stanwix, with its glistening mahogany and cut glass, was one of the handsomest liquor stores and bars in the city. There was a yard in the rear giving access to Mercer Street, and which in warm weather was to be used by Charley Dean, the proprietor, as a summer garden. There were several parties in the barroom, including Mark Maguire, who was known as "king of the newsboys." He was said to be in control of five hundred newsies, and boasted that among his customers were or had been, Andrew Jackson, Henry Clay and Daniel Webster.

Poole did not like him, for some reason or other, and invited everybody to have a drink with the exception of Maguire. Mark resented this and said if he was as big as Poole he would show him what he thought of him. Poole took a bread-knife from behind the counter and tossed it to Maguire with the remark that the two were now equal, as he was unarmed, and he exposed his pockets in proof of this claim. Chris Hogan, of the detective force, came between the two to smooth out the trouble. At this juncture the door opened and in came Morrissey with several of his friends.

Morrissey immediately walked over to Poole and began pouring out a torrent of abuse, to which Bill responded by stripping off his coat. Morrissey tore off his collar and ejaculated a remark, that while pointless, was equivalent on his part to saying that he was primed to do bodily injury. "I'm John Brown, the Button Man," he said. There was an attempt by Hogan and some of the onlookers to prevent the fight, which only enraged Morrissey more than ever, and drawing his revolver he snapped it three times at his enemy's head, but the gun missed fire. Some accounts have it that Poole then drew a pistol and would have fired at "Old Smoke" only that Maguire asked him reproachfully if he would kill a helpless man in cold blood. The truth is, Poole was unarmed and the coolness of the unarmed man only made Morrissey wilder than ever and he hurled his own pistol to the floor and begged some one to loan him another.

Then the police, led by Captain Charles Turnbull, arrived and Morrissey was placed under arrest, while Poole and I escaped by the back way into Mercer Street. Chris Hogan tried to stop Bill, but I yanked the detective aside by his tie and Poole got away. He went right to the Eighth Precinct station-house, where Morrissey had been taken, and gave himself up. There were no charges, so the foemen were not held. Before releasing them, however, Captain Turnbull exacted a promise from Morrissey that he would not come above Canal Street again that night. Morrissey is understood to have gone down to Lyng's sporting headquarters at Canal Street and Broadway, where he remained until he went home to his newly married wife. Poole and the rest of us went back to Stanwix Hall, as Bill insisted on making his apologies to Charley Dean. We stayed there drinking and talking until some time after midnight. The saloon was supposed to be closed and the curtains were all down. Poole had just announced that it was time for him to go home when the front door opened.

In walked Lew Baker, "Paugene" McLaughlin, Dad Cunningham and several others of the Morrissey bunch. Among the party was Jim Turner, who had just come back from California, having been run out of San Francisco by the Vigilantes. "Paugene" was the last to enter, and as he came in he turned the key in the lock and made the door fast. Every soul present knew there was to be bloodshed. Poole leaned coolly against the bar and watched "Paugene" drop the door key into his pocket. "Paugene" returned the glare and asked:

"What are you looking at, you black-muzzled bastard?"

"At you," was the reply.

"Well, you're looking at a better man than yourself when you take a look into the glass. So you're the American fighter? Why, Morrissey can lick you on sight."

As he said this "Paugene" leaped at Poole, seized him by the lapel of his coat and spat in Bill's face. At the same time there was a general drawing of revolvers among McLaughlin's followers. Poole calmly shook his insulter off and offered to bet $500. that he could lick any of the party fairly, and he drew five golden eagles and slapped them on the bar. Turner, who had been fidgeting about nervously, yelled:

"Oh, hell! Let's sail in." And with that he pulled aside his heavy cloak and drawing a long-barreled "taranta" pistol of the type then in use by the Mexicans and the miners, leveled it over his arm at Poole. As he pulled the trigger some one jostled him and the ball ploughed through his own arm.

[84]

That was the signal for a general fusillade, and also for a general scamper. Unable to get out, those who had no stomach for the deadly sport took refuge behind counters and stools. One chap, George Deagle, actually walked into a pier mirror, supposing it in his terror to be an open door.

One of the shots had taken effect in Poole's leg. He clinched "Paugene" and as they struggled toward the door another bullet hit Bill in the shoulder and he dropped across the door, which some one had forced open by now. Lew Baker made a rush for the prostrate man, bounded upon him, and with his knee pressing into Bill's chest and before his friends could get to him, he placed the pistol against Poole's body and fired twice. One bullet lodged in the heart and the other in the abdomen. There was scarcely a second's interval between the two reports.

The sharp barking of the revolvers, the jangle of broken glass, the oaths, blows and cries suddenly ceased. Then, as Poole's friends sprang for the assassin, Baker jumped to his feet and dashed through the open door. He would never have escaped then had it not been for Turner. Directly after that personage had injured himself he dropped down and, hugging the floor during the shooting, he had dragged himself toward the door. He was close to the exit when Baker fired his last shot and leaped away over him. Lozier, Shay and several others of us tripped over Turner and were still mixed up on the floor when the police came surging in.

Poole was alive, but insensible. The ambulance was sent for as he lay there breathing in short gasps. In the wrecked saloon, filled with smoke that hung over it like a gray pall, he was cared for by his anxious friends till the ambulance arrived. The dawn was brightening in the east as his body was borne away through the city streets on his last ride in life.

The entire police force was set to work to capture Baker. He concealed himself in Lyng's saloon until the following night, from where he was smuggled through the scuttle and over the roofs to the Apollo Hall Assembly Rooms and then out of the cellar into a coach that had been provided for the purpose and was driven to Jack Wildey's place on Broome Street. It was from here he shipped aboard the brig *Isabella Jewett* as a common sailor. This vessel was already cleared for the Canary Islands and the next day, March 10, sailed. Five days later the secret of Baker's flight was divulged. George Law thereupon placed his speedy clipper yacht *Grapeshot* at the disposal of the authorities and she was dispatched with a strong crew and a number of officers aboard. The *Grapeshot* made Teneriffe two hours before the *Isabella Jewett* made that port. There were no extradition laws in those days and the Portuguese minister in Washington had already refused to give up Baker, should he come ashore in Teneriffe. So the *Isabella Jewett* was boarded on the high seas and Baker was placed under arrest and removed from the brig, to the indignation of her captain. Baker was brought back to New York and was indicted along with Turner, McLaughlin, Morrissey and others. After three trials, each of which resulted in a jury disagreement, the authorities abandoned the prosecution and no punishment was meted out by the law.

In the meanwhile Poole lingered for two weeks before the end came. He had been removed to his home and examination showed that, while the heart had not been reached by the bullet, the pericardium had been pierced and there was no possibility of saving the victim's life, as it was impossible to reach the bullet. Poole recovered consciousness and made a statement that his death was due to an organized plot of Morrissey. Further, he swore that he had been unarmed on the night he had been shot.

His recuperation was only temporary and on the fourteenth day the physician in attendance announced the last hour was at hand. Poole heard the announcement with a placid face, looked up at Hyer, who had been constantly at his bedside, then drew his last breath and managed to gasp:

"I die a true American!"

In the meanwhile New York existed in a condition of excitement no words can adequately describe. The entire affair was fraught with a significance that was political as well as personal. It would have been worth the life of any person even suspected of being remotely connected with the Morrissey faction to come anywhere close to the district of the home on Christopher Street near West where Poole lay dying. The vicinity had taken on the appearance of a camp. A steady line of vehicles poured through the street depositing their freight of anxious inquirers at the Poole door. Not alone the comfortable equipage of the sport, but the wagons and carts of the venders and butchers halted long enough for the latest bulletin. Many strangers from out of town traveled to Christopher Street before seeking their hotel. The *Herald, Tribune, Times* and every other New York paper of consequence had their reporters on hand day and night. But there was no serious outbreak until the day of the Poole funeral. That was a day in New York to be remembered. It was a pageant, this funeral, the like of which the city has probably never witnessed. The funeral was set for Sunday and it seemed as though all New York was out on that eventful day. Again we let "The" Allen resume the story:

The sidewalks all along the route of the funeral procession were jammed, and every housetop and window was clustered. The very trees, awnings and projecting signs were seized on as points of vantage and the air was alive with the great roar of the multitude. Opposite the dead man's residence was a carpenter-shop owned by a man named Onderdonk. It was a sturdy two-story frame building with a stairway on the outside giving access to the upper floor. The spectators packed this stairway as one solid mass and every inch of roof space was also taken up. The structure began to creak ominously, then the roof and stairway gave way, and the people and the timbers fell together in one common wreck. Four people were killed and thirty injured. To add to the excitement, the firebells were set ringing and several companies were called to the scene of the casualty.

It was amid this turmoil that the funeral cortège got under way. It was headed by a detail of several hundred of the old police force. The van of the procession was led by the Poole Association, 2,000 strong. Then came deputations from the Order of the United Americans from various cities forming a body twice as great. The famous Shiffler Hose of Philadelphia followed with about 1,000 members, and then came various local and visiting fire companies headed by the Red Rovers, Engine No. 34, of which Poole had been a member. Deputations of the volunteer fire companies had traveled hundreds of miles to do the occasion honor, the Mash Markey Hose coming from Baltimore, and Boston also being represented. Then came thousands of citizens in advance of the hearse in which the casket rested under the stars and stripes and which was guarded by two companies named in the dead man's honor as the Poole Guards, and the Poole Light Guards, captained respectively by Captain Jim Bannon and myself.

The course lay through Christopher and Bleecker Streets on to Broadway and every foot of the way had to be cleared as the cortège slowly made its way downtown. At Grand Street, a body of five hundred men in the familiar attire of working butchers knelt with their heads uncovered as the procession passed. They fell in behind and accompanied the march to the ferry. The funeral and its immediate escort crossed to Brooklyn and continued on to Greenwood Cemetery. There, after most impressive ceremonies, Bill Poole was committed to that last long rest which comes to busy and troubled lives such as the like of his as well as to those of less troubled men.

After the ceremony the procession broke up into parties and returned to New York by various routes. The Poole and the Light Guards marched together and reached Broadway and Canal Street late in the afternoon, where the New York and New Haven Railroad depot then occupied one corner. Opposite the depot a house was being torn down and work had been stopped in consequence of the parade. Behind the brick and timber

THEY COULD TAKE CARE OF THEMSELVES.

A PARTY OF GAY GIRLS OF NEW YORK BOHEMIAN CIRCLES DECLARE THEIR INDEPENDENCE BY DISPENSING WITH MALE ESCORTS DURING
THE MASQUERADE BALL SEASON, AND ENJOY A PERIOD OF PLEASURE UNADULTERATED BY MASCULINE RESTRAINT.

barricades made by the wreck and that lined the gutter a strong party of
Morrissey followers had ambuscaded themselves. They consisted of members of the 36th Engine, known as the Original Hounds, reinforced by a
gang of Buttenders and Short Boys, led by Larry Aiken and Dan Linn.

As the Poole volunteers came within range a volley of stones and
bricks darkened the air. Another and another followed. The attack was

so sudden and unforeseen that the spectators who were gathered in the street watching the parade had no time to get out of the way and a woman on the other side of the street was killed, while a number of men and women were badly wounded. Five of the Poole Guard were included in the list of the injured. They were not long in recovering their order and Canal Street soon became the scene of a pitched battle. The howls of the ruffians and the cheers and shouts of the volunteers made a ringing chorus, through which was heard the sharp crack of pistols, the crash of stones smashing windows and doors, and the shrill screams of the wounded.

The fight continued for an hour, when the Morrissey men, having used up pretty much all of their barricades for missiles, were left without cover and the Poole Guards proceeded to charge them with their bayonets. The Morrisseyites had no stomach for cold steel and they scattered just as the Seventh Regiment, which had its armory in National Hall over the depot, and which had been called out to suppress the riot, appeared upon the scene. The assailing party had a number of its members disabled and two lay dead. The Poole Guards marched off to the Village, bearing their wounded with them.

That night the Hounds were gathered around the stove in their engine-house discussing the events of the day, when a menacing murmur fell upon their ears. In a moment more there came a crash which shook the building and split the doors. Another and another followed until the doors fell open. Then, dropping the beam that had been used as a battering-ram, the besiegers poured in upon their demoralized foes. The assailants were the Poole Guards which had come down bent on vengeance.

Separated into a number of detachments to prevent the suspicion which would have been roused by the passage of such a large party as their combined one through the streets, they had come together undiscovered at the portals of the enemies' stronghold, which they lost no time in storming. When they got through there was nothing left of the engine-house but four blackened and smoking walls. The Hounds narrowly escaped with their lives. After which the Poole legion returned to the village and celebrated long into the night. Bill Poole's burial had certainly been a grand and exciting occasion.

"The" Allen's story was not exaggerated in the least, as reference to the old newspaper files readily verifies.

His was a true picture of New York and of politics in the Fervid and Frantic Fifties.

A little more than two and one-half years after the Poole murder Morrissey returned to the prize-ring and defeated John C. Heenan. Soon after he was being acclaimed as the great American prize-ring champion, even by the Poole adherents, and he became the owner of many prosperous and luxurious gambling houses in New York and branching out to Saratoga; in time he was a Tammany Hall leader and climbed to the Legislature and to Congress.

Some historians have endeavored to make Morrissey out a heroic figure of the prize-ring and an admirable one in other ways. But the *Gazette* estimate finds him "a bold man, a strong and courageous man, also a shrewd one in a bluff and rugged fashion. Luck played him well in his career until his downfall started with the overthrow of the Tweed ring. Luck played an important part in his ring eminence. He was by far the worst punished of the two when his fight with Yankee Sullivan broke up and he was ruled the victor. Tom Hyer would almost surely have bested him in a square fight; they were matched once and Morrissey forfeited his appearance money, and after another meeting was agreed upon the Hyer's following was so greatly outnumbered by the armed Morrissey gang that the match fell through. When he did fight Heenan, the latter had the misfortune to injure his hand against a ring post. Morrissey declined a subsequent challenge and retired from the ring thus forfeiting the title to Heenan."

So Morrissey lived and prospered long after his enemy, Bill Poole, was cold in his grave.

THE MANSION BUILT ON BABY SKULLS

Why Madame Restell Added Her Own Life to the Many She Had Taken

ON the corner of Fifth Avenue and Fifty-second Street, during the Seventies, there stood a dignified residence that commanded unusual attention. "Upon 'most any day that was inviting to the outdoors, a grim-visaged, but elegantly dressed woman might be seen making her way down the high front stoop with a stride that was firm, for all her advancing years and a bearing that flaunted a callous defiance. At the walk waited a glittering equipage and a prancing pair of horses ready to join fashionable Gotham on wheels. A liveried coachman held open the door of the carriage to bow his mistress into the interior. No sooner had he resumed his seat and the reins and started the afternoon drive, with the first roll of the wheels, around the corner there came scurrying a band of unkempt street urchins, who only turned on their heels sufficiently long to chorus in derision:

"'Yah! Your house is built on babies' skulls!'"

For a way these ill-mannered boys would chase after the carriage the while they kept up their offensive yelling. There was no change of expression in that grim-visaged countenance, even while the carriage occupant was within hearing of her tormentors. There was something about the woman that suggested she was utterly adamant to public regard as her shocking vocation would make her seem— and she was an abortionist of most unenviable reputation. So, when finally she came to the end of her hardened existence, and with an estate officially inventoried at over $1,000,000, it came as amazing news that "she merely added one more life, that of her own, to the many she had taken, by committing suicide in the bathtub in her palatial home."

Madame Restell, or Mrs. Ann Lohman, with whose life and death this chapter deals, carried to her grave secrets that would have wrecked the peace of many a respected household, and that would have affected the names of many of the powerful and widely known of New York and even throughout the entire country. Madame Killer, the Abortionist, as she was long known, was one of the most noted birth control practitioners, so to put it, in all the land for many years.

[91]

GOTHAM ON WHEELS.

THE CARRIAGE PEOPLE OF THE METROPOLIS, AND HOW THEY DRIVE FOR BUSINESS AND PLEASURE, AS TOLD BY "THE BROADWAY ROUNDER", ON PAGE 6.

While she saved many fine reputations from disgrace through her handiwork, she made her own name one of the most hated. Anthony Comstock is generally credited with having driven Madame Restell to do away with herself in 1878. The *National Police Gazette,* however, which was harrying her with vigor almost as soon as Comstock was permitted his first glimpse of this immoral sphere, puts quite a different motive back of this sensational suicide case. One year after Anthony Comstock opened eyes on a world that he was to find such an offending one, the *Gazette* of February 21, 1846, printed the following torrid editorial:

RESTELL, THE FEMALE ABORTIONIST—The exposures which we have recently made of this base woman's practices, have excited the profound attention of the community; and moved by the deep necessity of providing a punishment adequate to her horrid and unnatural crimes, an association is already in the process of formation, whose intention it is to petition the legislature to make abortion a State Prison offense; and also to take such measures as may lead to the punishment of its practices, and the prevention of any future murders at hand.

It is well known that Madame Restell keeps a large number of apartments in her golgotha in Greenwich Street for the accommodation of females in *accouchement,* and the number that avail themselves of such facilities in a city where licentiousness stalks abroad at midday may be guessed at, but not counted. It is well known that females frequently die in *ordinary* childbirth. How many, then, who enter her halls of death may be supposed to expire under her execrable butchery? Females are daily, nay, hourly, missing from our midst who never return. Where do they go? What becomes of them? Does funeral bell ever peal a note for their passage? Does funeral train ever leave her door? Do friends ever gather round the melancholy grave? No! An obscure hole in the earth; a consignment to the savage skill of the dissecting knife, or a splash in the cold wave, with the scream of the night blast for a requiem, is the only death service bestowed upon her victims. Witness this, ye shores of Hudson! Witness this, Hoboken beach!

We do not wish to speak in parables. There is a mystery yet to be cleared up which sent a thrill of horror and a sensation of profound excitement through the length and breadth of the land! We speak of the unfortunate Mary Rogers. Experience and futile effort have proved that we have heretofore followed a wrong trail. The wretched girl was last seen in the direction of Madame Restell's house. The dreadfully lacerated body at Weehawken Bluff bore the marks of no ordinary violation. The hat found near the spot, the day after the location of the body, was dry though it had rained the night before! These are strange but strong facts, and when taken in consideration with the other fact that the recently convicted Madame Costello kept an abortion house in Hoboken at that very time, and was acting as an agent of Restell, it challenges our minds for the most horrible suspicions. Such are these abortionists! Such their deeds, and such their dens of crime!

We now ask again, if a community professing to be civilized will any longer tolerate this wholesale murder under their very eyes? Will a city possessing courts and a police, wink at such an atrocious violation of the laws, and if it will, and the demon murderess Restell be too rich to be within the power of the law, will the community, in the last resort, suffer her to go on unrebuked by some sudden application of popular vengeance?

We are not now demanding justice upon the perpetratress of a single

THE FEMALE ABORTIONIST.

crime, but upon one who might be drowned in the blood of her victims, did each but yield a drop, whose epitaph should be a curse, and whose tomb a pyramid of skulls.

This was inflammatory stuff to be printed in a paper of the already considerable circulation owned by the *Gazette*. But before setting forth what followed the publication of this editorial, which sounds as though it might have been phrased by a William Jennings Bryan, it would be well first to give some attention to the inference that the Restell woman may have been in some way connected with the death of Mary Rogers, "the beautiful cigar girl," a case that goes down in the history of crime as one of the greatest of the unsolved death mysteries.

Less than four years previous to the appearance of the above editorial the city of New York knew no other topic of conversation than the assassination of Mary Rogers, whose beauty back of the cigar counter of John Anderson, well-known snuff manufacturer, played havoc with many masculine hearts and made her the bright attraction of the store at 319 Broadway. She lived with her mother, who kept a boarding-house at 126 Nassau Street. Sunday morning, July 25, 1842, she knocked at the door of one of the young lodgers, Daniel Payn, to whom she was engaged to be married. She told Payn she was going to the house of her aunt and requested that he call for her that evening if she had not returned home by supper-time. She never crossed the threshold in life again. The following Wednesday her murdered body was found on the shore of Weehawken Heights.

"The annals of crime are gorged with mysteries. The red band of murder has set its mark on many of its pages, but left no other sign of its identity. Of all the episodes enshrouded in this somber vagueness, there is none more tantalizing than the case of Mary Cecilia Rogers." Thus wrote the *Gazette* in review of the mystery when it was again brought to attention through the death of John Anderson, Mary's employer. This was in 1881.

The corpse that was buried over in New Jersey after a primitive inquest was not immediately known, according to most versions, to be that of the beautiful cigar girl. But, shortly after, a New York newspaper demanded that the remains be dug up, and the disinterred body was laid out in the dead-house in City Hall Park, New York, and though decomposition had already set in, portions of the attire were positively identified and all doubt was removed that the corpse was that of Mary Rogers. The search for the murderer was next in order. Newspapers started an untiring pursuit of the mystery and the unsatisfactory results worked the public mind to fever-heat. Meetings were held and public and private subscriptions made as rewards for the unveiling of the death secret. Various suspected persons were arrested, yet, as the *Gazette,* long years after, commented: "In this case murder will not out. The murderer of Mary Rogers never was and never will be definitely known. His crime is buried forever in the grave in which its victim long ago mouldered to dust, so thoroughly forgotten that to-day no one knows where she is buried."

Mary Rogers did not go to the home of the relative toward which she was supposed to have been headed the Sunday she left her abode. She was last seen

FIFTH AVENUE BELLES ACTING AS STREET-SWEEPERS.

TWO WEALTHY GIRLS, TO SHOW THEIR SYMPATHY FOR THE TAXPAYERS, SWEEP THE STREET IN FRONT OF THEIR RESIDENCE—ONE OF THE RESULTS OF THE STREET-CLEANING AGITATION IN NEW YORK.

in New York in the company of an unknown young man in the vicinity of Barclay Street not far from the Restell dwelling on Greenwich Street, but she was presumably walking toward the Hoboken ferry. Her companion was supposed to have been a young naval officer, who was among her legion of admirers. But somehow his identity remained ever somewhat vague, for all his undoubted importance in this puzzling tragedy.

Of the various suspects there was none on whom the crime was ever fastened, and few death mysteries have ever been kept so long alive. No sooner had interest commenced to flag than something happened to give it a fresh start. Some boys roaming close to where the body had been found discovered in a thicket a white petticoat, parasol, silk scarf, gloves and a handkerchief on which, for all the discoloration and rot of mildew, the initials of Mary Rogers worked in silk thread were still legible.

Some months later, and to further add to the mystery, young Payn, who had been her betrothed, contributed no small share. After the death of Mary he had taken to dissipation and seemed obsessed by a settled melancholy. He drank hard and deep and one day he staggered out of a saloon and was seen no more until his dead body was found in the thicket where the relics of his dead sweetheart had been found. There was an empty laudanum bottle by his side and in his pocket a letter which read:

"Here I am on the very spot. God forgive me for my misspent life."

And then came two other incidents shortly after and almost at the same time that further helped to sustain interest. Edgar Allan Poe, who had written an amazing mystery story, "The Gold Bug," which in the year 1843 had won the $100. prize offered by The Dollar Newspaper of Philadelphia, wrote a short story which purported to be the solution of the murder, and which was entitled, "The Mystery of Marie Roget." In this Poe paraphrased the events of the Mary Rogers tragedy, only giving the actors different names and locating the crime in Paris instead of New York. His theory was that there had been an indiscreet intimacy with her mysterious sailor lover which had resulted in her pregnancy, and finally her murder.

It is in order to insert here, there is a standing *Gazette* tradition that Poe, some time between 1846 and 1849, the year of his death, had been temporarily on the staff of this journal. How much actual foundation there is to this tradition remains a question. The same year that the *National Police Gazette* came into existence, the firm of Wiley & Putnam, 161 Broadway, brought out the first edition of a book, "Tales by Edgar A. Poe." It included "The Gold Bug," yet the book did not enjoy much in the way of success, though its author was, too late for his satisfaction, to be accepted as a genius. More attention was attracted to the author by his poem, "The Raven," which saw print in 1845, the year the *Gazette* came into existence. That year Poe was for a time the assistant editor of the *Broadway Journal,* a weekly paper published in New York, but he did not prosper in the connection. In fact, the closing years of Poe's life were such a discouraging struggle for existence that it is easily possible that he may have been pressed to do some hackwork for such a successful weekly as was then the young and robust *Gazette.* If such was the case, Poe never attached his name to any scrivening that he may have been driven to do for Messrs. Wilkes & Camp.

Coming back to the other happening that livened interest in the Rogers case, the very month in which the Poe story of the crime was published, over in Weehawken a woman was fatally wounded through the accidental discharge of a gun. The woman was Mrs. Loss, who kept an inn, which was close to the scene where the body of the beautiful cigar girl had been found. Mrs. Loss was the mother of the children who had made the discovery of the Rogers girl's handkerchief and other belongings. She made a deathbed confession that would lead to the assumption that the objects found in the thicket had been specially planted there by herself. According to the dying words of Mrs. Loss, Mary Rogers had come to breathe her last through the performance of a criminal operation. Why no special credence was placed in this confession is something of an enigma, but such seems to have been the case. Yet, it obviously came nearer to the truth than any of the various surmises that were offered instead. It was probably the basis for the *Gazette* charge that the Rogers girl was a victim of the abortionist, Restell.

Just where Madame Restell was involved in the case, as the *Gazette* hinted, is something beyond answer. The result of the *Gazette* article, however, is a matter of record. From the issue of February 28, 1846, we cull the following:

> RESTELL'S CHARNEL HOUSE—Great excitement existed in the vicinity of the house occupied by this wretch, in Greenwich Street, on Monday last, owing to the circulation of a handbill, calling a public assemblage, to induce her to leave the vicinity and abandon her horrible profession. We take the following from the "Morning News," not being present at the period alluded to:
>
> ALMOST A MOB—The residence of Madame Restell in Greenwich Street, was beset yesterday afternoon by a vast concourse of people of all classes, many of them, doubtless, drawn thither by curiosity, or a vague idea that something extraordinary was about to be enacted in reference to the notorious woman, and not a few who apparently came with the in-

tention of being actors in some scene of violence and popular outbreak. There were very many of our most respectable citizens noticed among the mass—a result unlooked for, and certainly ominous of a deep and abiding feeling of abhorrence and detestation among the better classes, for the practices of this miserable female, which may yet prove of fearful import to her, and to those who countenance and support her in the vile and unholy occupation, the known existence of which, in defiance of all laws, and outraging every sense of decency and morality, has been suffered so long to rest, as a foul plague-spot upon our city.

We learn that in anticipation of some energetic demonstration in the course of the day, Madame Restell early left her house and secretly repaired to the dwelling of some unknown friend, seeking a shelter, in her fears, in a hiding-place far from the scene of her iniquitous practices.

Meanwhile, though the Chief of Police, aided by a strong body of officers, were upon the ground of the disturbance, it seemed as though for some hours the neighborhood was slumbering upon a volcano, which a mere breath would inflame into swift and terrible action. Curses loud and deep upon Restell and her coadjuters were rife amid the crowd, and cries of "Haul her out!" "Where is Mary Applegate's child?" "Where's the thousand children murdered in this house?" "Throw her into the dock!" "Hanging is too good for the monster!" "Who murdered Mary Rogers?" and other inflammatory exclamations of a like nature were continually uprising from the excited multitude. Through the whole vicinity, the windows on both sides of the streets were upraised and filled with anxious faces intensely watching the movements of the mass below; and there were not wanting those among the inmates of the neighboring houses, and those inmates too, females of respectability and refinement, who joined in the universal cry for vengeance and retribution. It did indeed seem as though the strong feeling of popular indignation was about to be manifested in an outbreak of serious character, and that the unhappy object of their dislike was about to realize that there is in this land a power above all law, whose mandates would—when the arm of justice became paralyzed and insufficient, and was daringly sneered at by those who depend upon their ill-earned wealth and *certain peculiar influences* for immunity from the just reward of crime—be suddenly executed in violence and confusion. Owing, however, to the prompt exertions of the energetic Chief of Police, under whose directions one or two arrests were made of the most active spirits among the assembled mass, the threatened disturbance was finally put down, and at this time (late in the evening) order and quiet are restored to the neighborhood.

We do not envy the feelings of the wretched woman during the existence of the threatened outbreak, for, although at some distance from the scene, yet, she very well knew what was going forward, being made acquainted at short intervals with the position of affairs. We trust from the expression of yesterday, Madame Restell is now convinced of the necessity of immediately closing her unlawful business; otherwise there seems to be a most fearful certainty that *the end is not yet.*

It was the affair of Mary Applegate that brought about this storm of public indignation and which culminated in the Applegate woman being brought before Mayor William F. Havemeyer, in whose presence she made a sworn statement of the following facts:

That she was a seamstress residing in Philadelphia, in which city she had been seduced by Augustus Edwards, who had a connection with the offices of the Reading Railroad. That she had been placed in the home of Madame Restell by Edwards, and after a stay there she had been delivered of a living child. That Mrs. Restell took her child from her (Mary Applegate) on the pretense that it was to be sent out to a nurse, and that she (Mary Applegate) had never had sight of her child again. Mrs. Restell had subsequently denied any knowledge of the deponent and insisted that no female had been delivered of a child for several months past in her house. Later Mrs. Restell claimed that she was unable to locate the nurse to whom she had delivered the Applegate infant.

In a subsequent affidavit Mary Applegate described some of the things that had come to her attention while an inmate of the Restell house on Greenwich Street. She stated that there were so many women present during her stay that several were placed in the same room and even occupied the same bed "when they were sick." She met there a widow from Albany who was being supported by a married man from the same city, who was president of one of the banks. Another from Philadelphia was having her expenses defrayed by "one of our Congressmen." Another was the daughter of a New York family "in the first circles" who had been brought to the care of Mrs. Restell by her own mother, who had been heard to say she "would rather submit to anything else, than the disgrace."

In spite of the furor that was thus aroused, and that the *Gazette* finally accused Mary Applegate of having accepted a substitute infant in the one that was subsequently restored to her, Madame Restell somehow escaped the meshes of the law for all the exposure and indignation that was aimed her way, and she continued in her peculiar business for more than a quarter of a century longer. There can be no doubt that she had strong influences in high places. When the *Gazette* was finally forced to admit that Madame Killer was plainly beyond the pale of the law, Messrs.

GROOM VERSUS BRIDEGROOM.

THE DOMESTIC AMUSEMENTS OF THE YOUNG WIFE OF AN OLD MILLIONAIRE, WHICH GAVE AN ADONIS OF THE STABLE THE RUN OF
THE PARLOR AND PLAYED HOB WITH THE CONFIDENCE AND THE WINE CELLAR OF THE ABSENT LORD; NEW YORK CITY.

Wilkes & Camp printed her picture and gave expression to their feelings in no uncertain terms.

The public knows the character of Madame Restell, but none know it so well as the corrupt minions in official place who have for years tampered with her crimes and secretly received her gold in exchange for an immunity in wholesale bloodshed. For years she has triumphed over the law, defied public indignation, and laughed at the denunciations of the press. Others of her mystery—understrappers and retailers in the work of death—have felt the pinch of power, but she has gone scot-free of any check, and proclaims to the world her readiness to stifle human life at so much per deed. The law has swept every rival from her path, and she remains mistress paramount in a scheme of practical destruction. In the heart of this metropolis she holds her bloody empire. In this city, so vain of its good name, she sits in a spacious den, tricked out in gorgeous finery for the superficial eye, but crowded in its extensive labyrinths with misguided frailty, and teeming with the groans and misery of death.

What becomes of the children thus delivered we can readily imagine from the numerous infants, alive and dead, which are sprinkled about our city on stoops and in areas in the course of every week; but there arises at this point a more fearful inquiry: What becomes of the groaning mother if she perchance expire under this execrable butchery? Alas, we have no longer even the consolation of a doubt. The question has been answered in the developments of a public trial . . . the carcase is thrust uncleansed into a sack, lugged to some secret death-house, and there tumbled out for a medical orgy and the mutilations of the dissecting-knife. Thus perishes all trace of the murders of the abortionist. The refuse bones that are scattered on a dung-heap, or the skull that grins from the top of a doctor's cabinet, afford no trace of the blooming cheeks and rounded form of the once beautiful victim of these chartered murderers.

We are not led to these remarks with the view of spurring the authorities to bring this woman to justice. That hope is past. Our intention is not to arouse public indignation to her course—for already her name is never mentioned without a curse; but we would warn the misguided females who invoke her aid in the hope to hide their shame, that they had rather consign themselves to the mercy of a fiend and desperately seek their death.

For all of which Madame Restell continued in business and waxed prosperous until finally she committed suicide. What prompted her to put an end to her life? The *Gazette* asks and answers the query. The answer purports to be secret revelations secured by Richard K. Fox from a detective who had been in the Restell employ while she was doing battle with Anthony Comstock, and who kept her apprised of the doings of her enemy, all of which was published in the *Gazette* shortly after the Restell suicide.

According to this account, she professed, with apparent good reason, that she had very little to fear as to the result of her trial on the Comstock charges. It was fear, we are led to believe, of a "more serious" charge which impelled her suicide. What was this "more serious" accusation? The implication is, that the answer lay in the fear that certain facts surrounding the death of her second husband, "Dr." Charles R. Lohman, seemed about to be brought to light.

Originally, it is explained, Mrs. Restell during her first years in this country following her arrival from England, was actively engaged in dressmaking. She is believed to have already taken up the pursuit that brought her so much money when she contracted the marriage with Lohman. Lohman was in the business of manufacturing quack medicines. Their marriage did not turn out a happy one and they were separated at various times. The two had one fault in common, which was the source of continual disputes—namely, an inordinate greed for money. Though each had acquired money fast, they clung to it as though its possession was all that life was worth living for, and their quarrels over their money affairs, to-gether with a radical incompatibility of temper, had them generally on bad terms except during occasional spells of reconciliation.

Lohman, when real estate was very low uptown, had purchased the lots front-ing on the east side of Fifth Avenue, between Fifty-second and Fifty-third Streets, and just one block away from where the spires of St. Patrick's Cathedral were to raise their architectural beauty. With the rise in real estate Lohman sold the upper portion of the property, but kept the 125 feet front where the Restell residence and the Osborne flats were subsequently erected. When he built the Restell house he had to raise the sum of $27,000. and executed a mortgage for that amount to the Mutual Life Insurance Company. Mrs. Restell, while on bad terms with her hus-band, succeeded in buying up the mortgage without his knowledge. For the erec-tion of the Osborne flats she advanced $147,000. in cash to her husband. The two mortgages aggregating a total of $174,000. on properties then valued at $600,000.

During one of their periodical reconciliations, when Mrs. Restell's harsh temper toward her husband was softened, he executed a will in her favor, which also in-cluded title to a valuable store which he owned in Chambers Street. Soon after, on January 5, 1876, Lohman died. The *Gazette* tells a curious story concerning that death-bed scene.

> The "doctor" did not seem particularly ill when he took to his bed. While he had not been feeling right for some time, no grave apprehension was felt concerning his condition. Lohman raised himself in bed and said

to a young man who had been visiting him every day: "Hand me the medicine-bottle from the bureau, will you?" The visitor looked around and seeing no bottle, replied: "What bottle? There is none here." "Why, it was there a few minutes ago," the invalid exclaimed. "Who could have taken it?" In a fit of angry impatience he rang the service bell. His wife appeared in answer to the summons, holding a medicine-bottle in her hand, and looking, so the eye-witness stated, strangely excited. "What the devil did you take my medicine for?" Lohman asked impetuously. "Well, I thought the bottle was getting empty," she replied, "and I had better replenish it." He was by no means reconciled with the explanation: "It was more than half full when I had it before and didn't need renewing." "Well, I thought it did," was the reply, and with that she deposited the bottle, which was now nearly full, on the bureau. That very night Lohman died.

No clergyman was called in before the removal of the body, which omission could, of course, be attributed to the general isolation of the Restell household from all religious associations. At a very early hour, when the neighborhood was still and but few people were astir in Fifth Avenue and the neighboring street, the coffin was quickly carried through the rear entrance and taken to Tarrytown, where the remains were interred.

At the time of her committal Madame Restell seemed strangely distressed, though strong legal advice gave it as the opinion that she would have little difficulty beating the Comstock charges, since the confession he was supposed to have obtained from Restell was had by trickery. But there was also a strong hint of an investigation to ascertain the possibility of there having been foul play in the death of Charles R. Lohman. Grounds for the belief came to light that Lohman had blood relations in Prussia who would have some claim on his estate. There was talk of exhuming his body.

Madame Restell thought much less of the sacrifice of life than she did of money.

THE MOST BEAUTIFUL ILLICIT LOVE TRAGEDY

Murder in the Tribune Office, Death Drama in the Astor House,
and Travesty in the Court of Justice

"Why talk you of the posey or the value?
You swore to me
That you would wear it till your hour of death,
And that it should lie with you in your grave."

Nerissa declaimed the somber beauty of Shakespeare's prose with a voice that had more tenderness in its thrush-like softness than ever before. This night Portia's waiting-maid was not making response to the supplications of her doubleted suitor on the stage. Her heart was in her mouth and her tongue had only message for the lover she knew was watching her eagerly from among the sea of faces that made up the dark background beyond the proscenium arch. Soon the play would be over and the footlights dimmed, and he would be waiting by the narrow alley leading to the stage door of the Winter Garden Theatre.

Could she be one and the same with the Abby Sage whose girlhood had been spent in the little Massachusetts mill town of Lowell, and who had been the teacher of a tiny rural school in Manchester, New Hampshire, only ten years ago? Was it no more than a dream that this same Abby Sage now found herself a successful actress filling an engagement at the munificent salary of twenty-five dollars a week and playing in support of no less a stage luminary than the eminent Edwin Booth in "The Merchant of Venice"? And she had written little pieces about children and nature that had not only been published, but paid for; and a book of poems under her signature had already appeared in print. And it would be only a matter of months now before the error of her early marriage would be legally erased and she would be the wife of one who had already taken a place of some importance as a successful man of letters.

Maybe it was well that Abby Sage should have her dreams for a little while. She was not far away from stark tragedy—days when her name was to be vilified through the pitiless publicity of a notorious court case of many weeks' duration, that followed in the April, five months after the country had been startled by the sensational murder that happened on Thanksgiving evening, 1869, in the offices of the New York *Tribune.* But we are meeting Abby Sage two and one-half years before her discarded husband fired the death bullet into the body of the man who had taken his place in her affections. On the night of March 13, 1867, of which we are writing, and which was to mark Abby's last appearance on the stage for several years, her lines were fraught with no foreboding significance when the thrush-like softness of her voice murmured of the posies of love, and

"That you would wear it till your hour of death,
And that it should lie with you in your grave."

When Abby Sage, or Mrs. Daniel McFarland, as she then was, kept her tryst with Albert D. Richardson, neither knew that her husband was skulking in the shadows close to the stage door. Three weeks previous she had found the intemperance and cruelty of this man unbearable and had fled with her two children to the home of Samuel Sinclair, publisher of the *Tribune,* and whose wife had done much to befriend Abby. There, in the presence of the Sinclairs; of her father, who had been summoned to the conference; and also before several other witnesses, Mrs. McFarland told her husband she was through with him forever, and he agreed to abide by her determination. That same evening Richardson, whose friendship with Abby and the Sinclairs shall be gone into later, called at the house. As he was about to leave, Abby followed him to the door, and as they stood alone in the hallway, she murmured with an emotion she could not hide:

"You have been very kind to me. I cannot repay you."

"How do you feel about facing the world with two babies?" he asked.

"It looks hard for a woman, but I am sure I can get on better without that man than with him," was her answer. All the while her hand was still in his. His voice was so low his words were almost a whisper as he said:

"I wish you to remember, that any responsibility you choose to give me in any possible future, I shall be glad to take." And he hurried away without even bidding her good-night. Two days later he called on her again and told her he wanted to give his motherless children to her care, and that he wanted to marry her so soon as she was free. She had but one answer to give.

"It was absolutely impossible for me not to love him," was later the simple admission in her affidavit.

After this proposal, to pick up the *Gazette* story in our own words, Richardson departed for Hartford, where he went to complete work on a book he was then writing. He returned to New York on the night of March 13 and waited to escort Abby home from the Winter Garden Theatre. As these two under the spell of love moved eagerly toward each other, McFarland came up from behind and fired three shots at Richardson, only one of which took effect and resulted in a slight wound of the hip. (The second attempt on Richardson's life resulted in the fatality.)

WOULD-BE VOTERS.

A BEVY OF STRONG-MINDED AMAZONS MAKE A SENSATION AT A NEW YORK UPTOWN POLLING PLACE.

But, notes the *Gazette,* "this triangle came prominently to the public attention with the first attempt at murder, and when it finally had culmination in death it became exceptional not only for its tragic romance and the fact that it involved so many important personages, such as Horace Greeley, Whitelaw Reid, Rev. Henry Ward Beecher, Edwin Booth and Daniel Frohman (then a mere youth), but it involved abnormal religious, political and editorial controversy." Moreover, "women were getting too strong-minded." Already there was much talk of the "Sorosis," the first women's club to be incorporated in New York, and which came into existence the following year.

Incidentally, it is interesting to examine into the somewhat different point of view that the same paper, the *National Police Gazette,* takes of this same case at different periods. At the time of the happening this publication seemed to be aligned with those who regarded McFarland as justified in taking the life, through emotional insanity, of the man who had shattered his domestic peace. Fifteen years later, which was in the Fox régime, whether due to a more clarified viewpoint or a change in the trend of thought, the review of the case is more than favorable to the murdered man, and to the woman who had been the indirect cause of his death. The writer even refers to this as "the most beautiful of illicit love trage-dies." Let us look at its outstanding figures through the eyes of the *Gazette.*

Albert Deane Richardson, who so manfully gave his life for love, as we shall see, was in the middle thirties at the time of his meeting with Abby, who was seven years his junior. Franklin, Massachusetts, was his birthplace, and he was a teacher in Boston for a while. He formed an early taste for journalism and after various experiences through the Midwest, where he gained some prominence as corre-spondent for various New York newspapers, he joined the staff of the *Tribune.* By that paper he was sent into the South as a secret correspondent during the Civil War. He was finally captured by the Confederates and consigned to Libby Prison in Richmond. After a five months' detention there he was removed to Salisbury Prison in North Carolina, from where he succeeded in making his escape in 1864 and traveled four hundred miles on foot until he reached the Union Lines in Knox-ville. His story in the *Tribune* telling how he came "Out of the jaws of death and out of the mouth of hell," was a thrilling one and had prominence, in its time, as one of the outstanding newspaper stories.

On his return to New York Richardson made his adventures into a book and this, and one or two other literary ventures, had sales which netted him what was a considerable fortune in those days. With the means thus accumulated he pur-chased six shares of *Tribune* stock. He became one of the featured writers on that paper and his accounts of his overland trip for the inauguration of the Pacific Railroad also kept his name in the foreground. So he was a man of no little standing at the time of his first meeting with Abby Sage, which happened in 1866.

And from the first, though a twelvemonth and more went by ere she admitted this to him, he was her ideal of an interesting and romantic personage. What is more, he was a fine figure of a man, tall and straight of carriage and weighing well over two hundred pounds. His ample whiskers of a ginger color and his steady hazel eyes gave him what was then regarded as a distinguished appearance.

While incarcerated in Libby Prison, the young lady whom he had married during his sojourn in Cincinnati passed away. Upon his return to his fireside he found his three children motherless. At the time of his death their ages were respectively, thirteen, ten and six. These were the charges he left to the care of Abby Sage.

Daniel McFarland, who brought to an end the earthly existence of Richardson, was the senior of his wife by a score of years. As a youth he showed an early promise that his mature years failed to realize. He was close to forty years of age when he took Abby Sage as his bride, and he must have already found himself face to face with the bitter knowledge that he was destined to make a failure out of the ambitions that had stirred him to something in the way of early achievement. Though Abby had no gleaning of this when she plighted her troth, intemperance had already made him something of a weakling, though he still carried himself with egotistic optimism.

As a youth he had broken away from an apprenticeship to a harness-maker, scraped together enough money before the attaining of his majority to take a course at Dartmouth College, where he gained his degree of Bachelor of Arts and was an assistant to one of the professors of chemistry. By this professor he was sent abroad, but on his return he took up the study of law in Boston and gained admission to the Bay State Bar, but never practiced. This last fact probably revealed the weak link in his character. He had ambition without the determination to fulfill a purpose. For a short time he was Professor of Logic, Belles Letters and Elocution in Brandywine College, but when Abby became Mrs. McFarland he had been in turn a lecturer and speculator. Through the ten years of their married life his undertakings met with one failure after another.

At the outset Abby was undoubtedly deeply enamored of her mate. To her he was a man of the world. His pale, sallow features were not uncomely. He dressed and talked well; he probably lied beautifully of himself and his prospects. Anyway, the fortune of between $20,000. or $30,000. that he claimed before becoming a benedict quickly evaporated into nothingness with the depreciation of some mysterious land interests, which probably never existed. They knew wretched poverty from the start. Within a few months after making their first home in Madison, Wisconsin, Abby was forced to return to her father's roof and to his charity.

All the unfair testimony that was turned loose against Mrs. McFarland when her character was so bitterly assailed in the trial following the death of Richardson, did not disturb the truth, that she had been a loving, true and encouraging help-mate through those early years of disillusionment. They were forced to set up makeshift homes in New York, Brooklyn, Newark and Croton, establishing a second residence in Madison on the very day Fort Sumter was fired on. Three children came to them during those early years of marriage, the first-born dying within a few months. Time and again her father was forced to save her from starvation. When her second child, Percy, was born the physician's bill was paid through her earnings out of the proceeds of a public reading that she had given in 1860, when she had already shown some early talent as an elocutionist. But very little of this, or other facts that might have shown the husband in his true light, was permitted to come out in the McFarland trial, or if it was, then it was always distorted in his favor. In particular, little or nothing was given out of the facts that he owed his desk in the Provost Marshal's office, and later in the office of the City Assessor, to the help of Mrs. Calhoun, of the *Tribune,* and Mrs. Sinclair, whose friendships had been so valuable to Abby. Later McFarland publicly charged through his lawyers that these women were "the procuresses through whom his wife's affections had been alienated to the keeping of her lover."

But let us now turn our attention to the woman in the case. We find some differences in the descriptions of her appearance that make up the pen pictures that have been handed down by various writers. At least they all agree that she had grace and beauty and charm of person, which is something that can be readily accepted, since she was given her engagement by Booth even on her limited stage experience, which had been had through her several public readings, though she prepared for this work under the schooling of Mr. and Mrs. George Vanderhoof. This schooling was at the instigation of McFarland, though in his trial he had it made out that he had always been able to support his wife and had therefore discouraged her dramatic ventures from the first.

As to her appearance, I like best the *Gazette* estimate, which pictures her as molded into a slender elegance. With hair of a dark brown hue through which glinted fleeting glimpses of strands that had grayed soon after life had brought its severest ordeal—the dying whisper of the man she had learned to love, who had murmured to her when he knew the end was near: "Sweetheart. Yours was a love worth living for. Even more, it is a love worth dying for." And he must have loved her eyes, for the velvet brown of their luster was set off by dark lashes that gave a regal arch to her brow. Though the inflexibility of her Puritan stock was strongly in evidence, yet there was somehow a hint of the fires of a personality. To her lover she must have been even more of a breathing, throbbing loveliness than she appeared back of the footlights, where her work seemed to be marked more by preciseness and comeliness than inspiration.

Her literary efforts were a fair example of the innocuous stuff that then went into the reading that was prepared for small children. Her first book, which was brought out by the Houghtons was no doubt inspired and written out of love of her second child and was a collection of poems under the title of "Percy's Year of Rhymes." It is said to have returned her several hundred dollars. Her most ambitious effort was published by the American Publishing Company, of Hartford, and was entitled "Pebbles and Sunshine." Richardson had some hand in its acceptance. A number of selections from this work appeared in the *Gazette* shortly after McFarland's crime. Though it may react against your sympathies for Abby Sage, all the evidence will not be in unless we inflict just one example of her muse. You will note that she rhymes "drest" with "priest." Notwithstanding, Richardson thought well of the effusion, which was not the worst of those reproduced by the *Gazette,* and he encouraged her ambitions to write. Possibly, you will not doubt after reading this, that the man was very much in love.

LITTLE DAN

Little Dan has eyes of radiant blue,
And hair of a wonderful golden hue—
The roundest, merriest, baby face,
And movements of the airiest grace.

He's full of the oddest pranks—
Of merry jests, and quips and cranks—

THE NEW SONG OF THE SHIRT.

HOW AN ACTRESS WHIM BROUGHT COMFORT INTO A MISERABLE HOME AND AIDED A VICTIM OF THE SLOP SHOPS TO STAVE OFF
STARVATION ON AN IMPROVED PLAN; NEW YORK CITY.

Now, he's a baby, and now a grown man,
And acts his parts as a mimic can.

Sometimes, he puts on a princely air—
Tosses back his flowing golden hair—
Assumes a look of regal pride,
And orders his carriage to take a ride.

Anon, he's a jolly beggar boy—
Kicks little bare feet with shouts of joy—
Scoffs at sorrow and turns up his nose,
If you tell him "Earth is a vale of woes."

Again, he will play a tragic part—
Will tell a tale to break one's heart—
And before the tears are fairly dried,
The wag will forget he has ever cried.

At night, in his flowing night-gown drest,
He turns to a little white-robed priest,
As he says with a wondrous, solemn air,
In his lisping way, an infant prayer.

Oh, a wonderful mimic is little Dan,
And he plays as only an actor can.
And you'll scarcely believe it when you're told,
Our darling is just only three years old.

Mrs. L. G. Calhoun, who wrote an interesting column on social and other doings for the *Tribune* and whose kindnesses were so misrepresented during the murder trial, first interested herself in the future of Abby, while the young wife had her home for a short time in Newark. She brought her to the attention of Mrs. John F. Cleveland (a sister of Mr. Greeley) and Mrs. Sinclair, who also became exceedingly fond of Abby. Through their assistance she gave several dramatic readings in Steinway Hall, which never netted less than one hundred dollars, since Mrs. Sinclair disposed of tickets among her numerous friends. She had her husband use his influence with Horace Greeley, through whose intercessions McFarland gained his city appointments. It was Mrs. Calhoun, and not Richardson, as was made out, who secured for Abby her engagement with Booth.

Five years after their marriage, in 1862, McFarland, in one of his drunken rages, which were now more than periodical, turned on Abby suddenly as she tried to soothe him and struck her in the face, sending her reeling backward. "There was a look in her eyes that made him burst into a paroxysm of tears and to beg wildly that she should forgive him."

"But from that moment," she said, "I could never tell him that I loved him or forgave him, because it would not have been the truth."

Four years after this incident came the first meeting with Richardson, who, as can be readily understood, moved in the circle with Mrs. Calhoun and the Sinclairs. In January, 1867, the McFarlands rented rooms from Mrs. Mason at 72 Amity Street. One month later Richardson moved from 61, on the same street, and was not only under the same roof with Abby, but had the rooms adjoining hers. Needless to say, much was made of this point in the trial, though an explanation of how this came about was brought out to the annoyance of McFarland's lawyers. It seems that Richardson was first shown a single room on another floor, but this was objectional to the would-be tenant for the reason that he would use it in part for his office and for his writing and that ladies would call and "it would be indelicate to receive them in a room where there was a bed." Which brought the comment from McFarland's lawyer: "Imagine a butcher ashamed of blood." Anyway Mrs. Mason effected the transfer of tenants that enabled Richardson to have the two rooms beside the McFarlands.

The two, Abby and Richardson, were often seen in each other's rooms. This was naturally brought out very strongly during the trial and while any sort of construction can be placed upon the extent of their intimacy, for all that was brought to light in court, they must at least be credited with having been discreet. William D. Norris, a Negro servant, was examined and the following dialogue took place between the lawyer and the witness:

Lawyer: "You know what liberty is—now. Did you ever see Richardson take liberties with Mrs. McFarland?"
Norris: "Yas, sah, I did. I've seen them shake hands together."

These facts are not inserted with a view of creating the impression that Abby was steadfast to her marriage vows. She may have safeguarded herself within a bulwark of treasured ideals; she may have found the tides of human emotion too treacherous. Yet, who would begrudge her a few drops of pleasure, who had to drink so deeply of sorrow. There were many ready to believe the worst—naturally, the *Gazette* included.

A letter in Richardson's handwriting that had been intercepted was read in court and was thought to give strong evidence of their intimacy. The envelope bore the postmark "Hartford, Conn. March 9, 1867." It was addressed to Mrs. A. S. McFarland, care of Samuel Sinclair, Esq., Tribune Office, New York City, and had been inadvertently turned over to Daniel McFarland. On the back it was sealed with red wax on which were stamped the letters "D.A.R." The letter read:

> What a goosie it is about my coming home. Of course, I shall come, whenever my business compells or will let me. What judgment shall you fear, doing no wrong? The circumstances make it right and unnoticeable, and I will not stay away for 40,000 Mrs. Grundies. I will not neglect work to come; but it is quite possible I may have to come next week. I have not been waiting for you, darling, all these long years to wear haircloth and serve seven years now; I want you always. A hundred times a day my arms seem to stretch out toward you. I never seek my pillow without wanting to fold you to my heart, for a good-night kiss and blessing, and the few months before you can openly be mine will be long enough at best. No grass shall grow under my feet, but I never let public opinion bully me a bit, and never mean to; so, Sunbeam, I shall come whenever I can and stay as long as business will permit. I will decide about the summer just as soon as I can, darling; can probably surmise by Monday or Tuesday.
>
> Darling, I should be afraid if you had fascinated me in a day or a week. The trees which grow in an hour have no deep root. Ours I believe to be no love of a noonday hour, but for all time. Only one love ever grew so slowly into my heart as yours has, and that was so tender and blessed that heaven needed and took it. My darling, you are all I would have you, exactly what I would have you, in mind, body and estate, and my tired heart finds in you infinite rest, and riches, and sweetness. Good-night my love, my own, my wife.
>
> Burn this—will you not?

Less than three weeks before the above letter was written—February 19, was the date—McFarland found his wife in conversation with Richardson before her own door. As soon as he was alone in the room with Abby he made all manner of charges against her. The next day she left McFarland and was taken in by the Sinclairs. After the first attempt on Richardson's life, arrangements were planned for Abby's divorce. On October 31, 1869, she returned from Indianapolis to the home of her parents a free woman. There Richardson spent Thanksgiving Day. He returned to New York and to his death.

At five o'clock on the afternoon of November 25, 1869, Daniel McFarland came into what was known as the counting-room of the *Tribune* from the Park Row entrance and lingered in a corner without attracting attention. On the testimony of Daniel Frohman and others who were employed in the office, McFarland had a wait of fully fifteen minutes before the object of his vengeance appeared. Yet his act was made out as an unpremeditated one. Richardson entered from Spruce Street and walking to a desk at the end of the counter asked for his mail. Several letters were passed over to him and as he started to examine them a figure sprang toward him; not until then was Richardson aware of the presence of McFarland. There was only time for an exchange of glances. The room echoed to the detonation of a pistol. For a moment Richardson clutched at the edge of the counter, then he staggered off and on wavering legs he climbed two flights to the editorial rooms, where he threw himself on a sofa. He lay there in dreadful agony; he had been shot through and through the body and the wound which was two inches below the breast-bone on the left side was a mortal one.

The wounded man was carried across City Hall Park to Room 115 in the Astor House. There, with his life ebbing slowly away he was made as comfortable as medical attention would permit. Before he breathed his last, one week later, two dramatic scenes took place in the death room. Within less than five hours following the shooting McFarland was found in the Westmoreland Hotel by Captain Allaire of the Fourth Precinct and was told he was under arrest for shooting with intent to kill. He was brought to the room where Richardson lay dying. The stricken man raised himself feebly, gave one look at his assassin and said:

"That is the man!"

Three days before the end came, Richardson requested of Horace Greeley that arrangements be made so that he could marry Abby without delay, as he felt the end was near. And that same day the ceremony was performed by Rev. Henry Ward Beecher and Rev. O. B. Frothingham that made Albert D. Richardson and Abby Sage McFarland man and wife. This tender and touching marriage was described in the trial as "a horrible and disgraceful ceremony to get the property of a dying man and that tended to hasten his demise." Mr. Beecher was forced to answer to his flock. When he got through they knew they were answered. And the members of the church board lost no time in asserting that they stood behind their brilliant pastor.

Albert Deane Richardson died on the morning of December 2. His hand was in that of his bride of three days as he passed away.

BOSS TWEED,

AS HE APPEARED WHEN FOREMAN OF BIG SIX, FROM AN OLD PHOTOGRAPH IN THE POS-
SESSION OF THE N. Y. FIRE DEPARTMENT.

[117]

April 4, 1870, Daniel McFarland was brought to trial, if the travesty that was enacted may be described as such. But first let us draw a little picture of the era in which this case happened. "The political ring which was the golden setting for Tweed greed," had had virtual control through six years of incorrigible corruption.

AN ENGINE DRAWING THE WORK-TRAIN ON THE METROPOLITAN ELEVATED RAILROAD JUMPS THE TRACK AND PLUNGES INTO THE STREET BELOW, ITS OCCUPANTS NARROWLY ESCAPING A FEARFUL DEATH.

Greeley, a Republican, and other editors, were fighting the Democratic administration for a cleaner government; and the Republicans were outnumbered three to one in the city of New York and the citizens were taking politics as a serious matter. Editorial comment was often inflaming and subsidized; Tweed and his gang manipulated the policy of his several newspapers and swayed the courts to his

SHE GRABBED THE REINS.

THE SENSATION PRODUCED ON A BROADWAY CAR BY AN IMPATIENT YOUNG LADY PASSENGER.

THE LAST STAGE.

"OUR OLDEST DRIVER" MOURNFULLY SUCCUMBS TO THE NEW DESPOTISM ON BROADWAY.

THEY BUTTONED HIM TO A POST.

HOW HIS FRIENDS DISPOSED OF A FAT BALDHEADED PRINTER WHEN THEY WANTED A DRINK.

own interests to no little extent. The man on trial was a Catholic and the man he had put in his grave was a Protestant, and religious tolerance was less mildly practiced then. During the trial Greeley and his friends were accused of extending financial donations so that the case would go against the accused. And yet there was a District Attorney whose duty it was to bring about the punishment of an offender against the laws, and no one inquired where the $10,000. fee was coming from that was to go to the McFarland defense, though the accused was known to be practically penniless. The Greeleys, Sinclairs, Calhouns and the Woodhulls and Claflins were branded believers in free love and Mormonism and worse; they were "immoral persons who had conspired to steal Abby from her lawful husband."

Roebling had just announced his plans for a bridge over the East River. The Arcade Railroad had submitted diagrams for a proposed subway that would extend beneath Broadway—an absurd proposition that was quickly vetoed. A successful trip had been made by officers of the Elevated Railway from Cortlandt to Thirtieth Street. As yet the road was laid only on one side of the street, but "it is intended to have two roads, so that passengers may go uptown, while others are going down." Some of the onlookers were heard to declare that this was "flying in the face of Providence." One reporter who made the trip informed that he knew precisely what housekeepers were doing their spring cleaning, and that he had seen fair ladies putting up their back hair and thought elevated traveling very interesting. The ride had taken only sixteen minutes. If *Gazette* pictures are to be relied on, this must have been a highly dangerous mode of transit.

The New York Circus had opened for a short season on Fourteenth Street, opposite the Academy of Music, and featured "The Wonderful Cynocephalus," though what this might be, aside from being "the most unique of novelties," could not be learned. "Little Dorrit" was nearly ready in the Plum Pudding Edition of the works of Charles Dickens published by D. Appleton & Co., and the author was to give a reading from his new book at Steinway Hall. Mr. J. W. Wallack was playing "Rosedale" at his own theater. Mr. and Mrs. Blanchard "and the dogs" were doing "The Watchman and His Dogs" at the Bowery Theatre in conjunction with "The Signet Ring, or the Triumph of Greece," also "Sixteen String Jack." Ouida was writing what were then judged to be very sexy novels, though they would read as tame stuff now. Also, in scanning the old *Gazette* files, we learn that "Bret Harte, a young Western writer, has turned out a moving and realistic tale in 'The Luck of Roaring Camp.' "

It took four days to panel a jury of twelve men after six hundred and twenty triers had been examined. McFarland was represented by John Graham, Elbridge T. Gerry and Col. Charles S. Spencer. For the prosecution District Attorney Garvin had the assistance of Noah Davis. The hearing was before Recorder Hackett. Col. Spencer delivered the opening address to the jury for the defense. It took up practically all of the fifth day of the trial and was described as eloquent and thrilling. "He was thrice applauded. Once the large audience, which listened with eager attention to catch every word that dropped from his lips, burst out in a perfect storm of applause." This is what caused the storm: during the address, which was embellished by extracts from no less than five poets, Spencer made reference to the Richardson letter already reproduced here.

"I believe it is my best trait," the gentlemen of the jury were informed, "that I love my wife, and I believe she is as pure as an angel; but if ever I discovered a letter like that to her from any man, I would shoot him whether it made me mad or not."

Spencer imparted the information that insanity was to be the grounds of defense. McFarland had been "an insane man who simulated sanity."

Then John Graham took charge for the accused man and his work was a masterly exhibition of witness-baiting, browbeating of the court and of an absolute distortion of the actual evidence in the case. It was prolonged into the eighth week and almost two days were taken up by Graham in his summation for the jury; and he broke down and wept as he finished. In short, Attorney Graham was privileged to run the affair pretty much as he pleased and whatever he did was right, and what the other side did was wrong if he so decided. Here are just two examples of the manner in which he jockeyed proceedings during examination of witnesses:

Witness: "I call myself an inventor."

Graham: "I should call you the same."

Witness: "I am a dentist."

Graham: "If you don't pull teeth any quicker than I pull your answers from you, then you can't make much of a living at your business."

Now note the difference when the witness is there with the snappy answer.

Graham: "Did McFarland strike you as a drinking man?"

Witness: "I should not take him for a temperance lecturer."

Graham: "That is not very becoming, Mr. Pomeroy. A man is on trial for his life, and your wit is out of place here."

When Attorney Davis, for the People, could stand the high-handed proceedings no longer and endeavored to explain to the Court just how infamous was the course of his opponent, then Graham threatened with his fist and called Davis "a damned coward."

"If you say another word," he blustered, "I'll have the clothes off your back. God damn you, I can lick you. I'll teach you what is due one gentleman to another."

He did not quiet down until McFarland came up to his counsel and said to him: "I hope you won't do anything to hurt my case." Which was a sane thought for an insane man.

It can readily be imagined how, under the circumstances, the murderer was made out a paragon as a husband and father, and a model of temperance and as a provider as well, while "Richardson's grave was his well-earned tomb," and all his associates were vile people. The law was made to take a back seat and Attorney Graham earned his $10,000. fee.

Graham wound up his long harangue with the following telling words for the consideration of the jury:

"Let those who dare dishonor the husband and the father, who wickedly presume to sap the foundations of his happiness, be admonished in good season of the perilousness of the work in which they are engaged. As a result of your deliberations, may they realize and acknowledge the never-failing justice of the Divine edict that [and the concluding words were fired with rhetoric intensity] JEALOUSY IS THE RAGE OF MAN AND THAT HE WILL NOT! CANNOT! AND MUST NOT! SPARE IN THE DAYS OF HIS VENGEANCE!"

Little was made of the facts presented by District Attorney Garvin: That Richardson's record in the days of the war between the North and the South proved him a man of proud and brave spirit; that the prisoner had taken the law in his own hands and sent the dead man to his last account without trial or question; that men seldom marry their mistresses except upon compulsion; that insanity was claimed as the excuse for crime, and the insanity was not proven; that—but why go on. The District Attorney spoke long and well, and while his summation was more able, if less flowery, than that of his opponent and not so prolonged, it could not carry the same weight.

Apparently it was altogether beside the point that McFarland was guilty of a premeditated murder. Also, through all the mass of testimony and the long examinations of the witnesses and evidence, the real legal weakness of the defense was never brought forward. McFarland was permitted to justify his crime on the grounds that Richardson had robbed him of his wife—yet: *Abby Sage had not been morally the wife of McFarland for more than two years and one-half before he shot Richardson, and at the time of the killing Abby had not been even the legal wife of the man on trial.*

At two minutes after three o'clock on Tuesday, May 10, the jury retired. A storm which had been lowering all the day burst forth in a thunderstorm of unusual violence and flash after flash of lightning lighted the gray sky and reflected through the windows of the courtroom. Amid this disturbance of nature the jury returned with its verdict at 4:50 P.M.

Taking all things in consideration, maybe it was cause for wonder that the jury was out as long as it was before the verdict was found:

"Not guilty!"

THE MOST REVOLTING UNSOLVED MURDER MYSTERY

*The Case of Many Clues That Led Nowhere and $50,000. Reward
That Was Never Claimed*

BARELY had the McFarland trial ceased to intrude itself into the daily papers
and the general conversation, when the city of New York found a new and appalling murder, this time an exceedingly mysterious one, to chain its interest. "Love,
illicit or otherwise, but that had the redeeming quality of flowing deep from at
least two hearts," thus points out the *Gazette,* "lent the virtue of romance to the
Richardson tragedy. The murder that happened sometime in the early hours of
the morning of July 29, 1870, in 12 West Twenty-third Street, this was as utterly
an abhorrent business as murder can be. That a citizen so respected and benevolent as Benjamin Nathan, one who should have had not an enemy in all the world,
that he should have had his life-spark extinguished with such shocking brutality
made for a revolting and horrible affair."

Years were to place it in the fore of the most puzzling of the unsolved New
York murder mysteries. Of the great cases of slaying within the confines of Manhattan Island that have ever defied unravelment, none has left trails so apparently
distinct and yet so confusing. In no other instance where justice had finally conceded its utter bewilderment, has even the public mind been so far at sea. Even
the *Gazette,* which has usually arrived, sooner or later, at what might be accepted
as the lost key that could have unlocked these mystery doors of death, is forced in
the end in the Nathan murder to advance conjecture that can at best only be accepted
as fantastic.

The murder of Helen Jewett, one of the first of the big crime mysteries of
the last century, was after all merely just one more instance where justice had
grossly miscarried. For the killing of this beautiful courtesan on the night of April
11, 1836, in the house on Thomas Street of which she was then an inmate, her
quondam lover, Richard P. Robinson, there is almost conclusive evidence, escaped
the gallows through the bribery of one of the jurors. As for the Mary Rogers

THE BUZZARD IN DOVE'S PLUMES.

HOW GRADUATES IN VICE MASQUERADE AS SCHOOL-GIRLS AND SNARE UNWARY MEN WITH ARTS BORROWED FROM INNOCENT CHILDHOOD: NEW YORK CITY.

case the guilt could probably have been pinned on the right person if her obscure sailor lover had been compelled to reveal himself, as shown in the chapter devoted to Madame Restell.

The murder of Dr. Harvey Burdell, famed as the "Bond Street Mystery," which took place in the house numbered 31 on that street in January, 1857, was pretty well fixed in the public mind as the outcome of black collusion between Mrs. Cunningham and John J. Eckell, a boarder, who was alleged to be her lover. While the *Gazette* gave it plenty of space at the time of its happening, on the occasion of a review a quarter of a century later it was conceded that the case had been made more of than it merited. The curiosity of an ingenuous public helped to make this more than the nine-day wonder that it was, and the introduction in the case of the "phantom baby" gave it a bizarre angle. Mrs. Cunningham, who claimed to have been mysteriously married to the murdered man before his killing, was the only one tried for the death of Burdell. The trial lasted no more than three days, and as a result she was pronounced "Not guilty." While in prison she pretended she was about to become the mother of an heir to the considerable property of the murdered man.

Once back in the Bond Street house Mrs. Cunningham continued her deception. She went about it systematically, and in her "make up," showed herself a true artist. Her form became gradually more in accordance with the Hogarth lines of beauty. Unfortunately for Mrs. Cunningham, she had to have a doctor to assist her in her deceit, and the practitioner she made a confidant of was Dr. Uhl, a friend, it so happened, of the District Attorney. Uhl, with the connivance of the authorities, secured a new-born baby from Bellevue Hospital, which was brought in the care of a nurse who turned out to be a police woman. So Mrs. Cunningham was forced to come away from playing at confinement to endure real confinement once more and in the Tombs.

The scheming woman, as mother of a posthumous child of the deceased, would legally have come into control of the bulk of the property left behind by Dr. Burdell. However, no more of this particular murder, other than to add that little Justitia Anderson, the baby used in the attempted hoax, was secured along with her mother as one of the attractions for Mr. Barnum's Museum, and there exhibited at "twenty-five cents a head, half price for children."

It might be added that A. Oakey Hall happened to play a prominent part in both the Burdell and the Nathan mysteries. He was the District Attorney who conducted the Cunningham prosecution and was also the author of a dreary farce with the unseemly title of "The Coroner's Inquest," which had to do with the trial and its curious outgrowths. He was the same A. Oakey Hall later to be referred to by Thomas Nast during the Tweed ring exposure in the famous *Harper's Weekly* cartoons as O.K. Haul and who happened to be mayor of New York at the time of the Nathan tragedy. Of the reward amounting to almost $50,000. that was offered for the detection of the murderers of Benjamin Nathan, $5,000. was from out of the Hall pocket.

As for the crime for which Polly Bodine went on trial, and which made one of the early features of the *National Police Gazette,* there has never been much doubt as to her having been the guilty party. A study of the famous American crime cases makes one wonder why this case in particular has chanced to be so generally overlooked by students of these phenomena. But from out of the Bodine and the Nathan cases, no Edgar Allan Poe, Conan Doyle or S. S. Van Dine ever strove to fictionize a mystery that led up so many blind alleys and yet arrived nowhere, and this despite the strong monetary incentive in the way of reward in the Nathan affair.

Benjamin Nathan, around whose foul and mysterious murder this chapter centers, was one of the first citizens of the community. For three generations the Nathans had a high place in New York business circles; his father, Samuel Nathan, had helped to found the New York Stock Exchange, of which the murdered man was a member. Benjamin Nathan was bound by ties of blood and marriage with several of the distinguished Jewish families. Judge Cardozo and Rabbi Julius J. Lyon, were brothers-in-law. His fifty-seven years had been well lived and bespoke the man who was devout and benevolent in inclination and honorable in his business dealings.

In appearance he was of good medium build and with a kind and even strong and distinguished face framed in white side-whiskers and with a still thick thatch of gray-white hair; metal-rimmed spectacles were necessitated by his imperfect vision. He was in business as broker and private banker on Wall Street, where his repute was of the highest, and he played a pronounced part in laying the cornerstone for the Mount Sinai Hospital, to which he had given generously of his fortune, and of which he had been the president for a number of years. And this was the man who was found horribly dead on a sultry July morning, and why and how he came to his end in this way, no one, it seems, will ever really know. The basic facts, which the various sources examined seem to make out as fairly correct, were summarized in the *Gazette* as follows:

Sometime during May, 1870, the Nathan family had moved for the summer to their country seat at Morristown, N. J. Once or twice a week it was the habit of Mr. Nathan to come to his office and consult with his confidential clerk, and occasionally he would stay overnight in his luxuriously furnished city home at 12 West Twenty-third Street. He came to New York on Thursday, July 28, and made what was to be his last appearance at his Wall Street headquarters. As the following day was to be the anniversary of his mother's death and he desired to commemorate this event at the Nineteenth Street Synagogue he decided to sleep overnight at home. He found the house in the hands of carpenters and temporarily upset. At his request four mattresses were heaped into a makeshift bed in the front parlor on the second floor by Mrs. Anne Kelly, the housekeeper. Four people were known to have been in the house during the hours of the killing.

Among these four, were two of the sons of Nathan, who were in business in New York, Frederick and Washington, ages twenty-five and twenty-three. The other two were Mrs. Kelly and her son, William, who acted as a sort of general helper about the place. It was a few minutes before 6 o'clock of the following morning, a morning that had broken bright and glorious after a night of storms, when the first alarm of the dreadful happening was had. Patrolman John Mangam, of the Twenty-ninth Precinct was walking along Twenty-third Street with his thoughts on his relief and making the last turn of his beat, when his attention was arrested by voices vibrant with terror:

"Officer! Officer! For God's sake, hurry!"

He turned in the direction of the cries, and noted on the stoop of the brownstone house which he had passed only a few seconds before, the figures of two intensely agitated young men, who were still in their nightshirts. They were recognized instantly as Washington and Frederick Nathan. The nightshirt of the latter was stained with blood, and his white socks had trailed unsightly stains to the stoop.

"Father! He's lying upstairs! He's been murdered!" the horror-struck voices of the two young men exclaimed together in broken words. The officer followed the two into the house and up one flight of stairs. The door to the front room was still open. There was the ghastly spectacle.

The fearfully battered body was stretched on its back over the threshold of this temporary bedroom with the feet extending into a small room that broke off to the hallway and that was used as a study and office. On the body, later examination revealed, there were marks of no less than twelve distinct blows. The gruesome details of the murder are essential in connection with an important point in the case. Five wounds were about the head, two of which could have caused immediate death; one had split the left ear as though with a knife, another, the most frightful one, was near the temple and had crushed the skull. Two of the blows had been of such power as to break three fingers on the right hand and to fracture the knuckles. The other marks were on the arms, breast and back. A welter of blood had changed most of the right side of the dead man's nightgown from white to crimson. The implement of death was discovered within a few minutes after Officer Mangam came into the room.

Near to the street door Washington Nathan had noted a heavy bar about eighteen inches long with both ends turned down at right angles. The discovery had been made while Frederick Nathan had gone with Officer Mangam to summon Superintendent John Jourdan and Chief De-

WAR ON THE WIRES

HOW A YOUNG WIDOW WHO KNEW HOW TO TAKE CARE OF HERSELF RESENTED THE APPROPRIATION OF HER HOUSETOP BY A TELEGRAPH COMPANY, NEW YORK CITY

tective James J. Kelso by telegraph. They had only to go a few steps to the Fifth Avenue Hotel, where there was a telegraph station. [Incidentally, the *Gazette* was conducting a campaign at the time condemning the manner in which housetops were being appropriated.]

Careful note was made of the condition of the room. It revealed other evidences of the terrific struggle that must have taken place. The walls and frame of the door, as well as the floor, were blood smeared. Chairs and other objects were overturned. [The finger-printing system had not been brought into usage by the police as yet, otherwise on one of the four persons who had been in the house during the time of the murder, guilt would have been fastened where it belonged, or else they would have been exonerated from a suspicion that was never lived down.] Robbery had been committed, whether as a blind or the work of a thief

PLAYFUL PRANKS OF MARCH BREEZES.

HOW THE WIND TAKES ADVANTAGE OF WOMENS' DRAPERY AND GIVES THE NAUGHTY MEN A CHANCE TO STUDY ANATOMY ON BROADWAY, NEW YORK.

was a subject for vague supposition. The keys had been taken from the dead man's body, the safe in the private office had been unlocked and rifled, but there was nothing of much value to be taken. The safe never contained more than a few hundred dollars. A Jurgenson watch and three diamond studs had been secured by the murderer; the timepiece was valued at $600. In the basin in the bathroom were indications that bloody hands had been washed there.

That no signs of this deed of violence had come to any of the four who occupied the house at the time, would have been grounds for strong suspicion, had this not been explained by the architect who had built the house. The architect testified that the walls and passage to Nathan's room had been specially deadened, and made soundproof at the owner's desire, so that one could very well sleep at one end of the floor and be ignorant of a life or death struggle at the other end.

These were the facts that were brought to the attention of the world at large through the newspapers on the morning of Saturday, July 30, 1870. Of such import was this happening as a matter of news value that it all but crowded the Franco-Prussian War off the front page. The *World,* for example, gave more than four entire columns of its front page to the murder on Twenty-third Street. Only the final of the six columns was devoted to "The War on the Rhine," and to the account of the skirmishing between outposts, the neutrality of England, the arrest of newspaper correspondents, and the claim of a German success at Volklinge. All else in the newspapers was overshadowed by the murder. The reader on this day probably gave but a casual glance to the progress of Horace Greeley's proposed candidacy as a successor to General Grant as the White House occupant. A few lovers of sport may have taken time to read about the triumphant tour of the Red Stockings of Cincinnati, a team that appeared unbeatable at the sport called baseball. The new traction system for Broadway was spoken of and the passing of the stage-coach was foreboded. There wasn't much doing in the theater, anyway, at this time of the year, aside from J. K. Emmet, the sweet-voiced singer, at Wallack's in his character of Fritz Vanderblinkenstoffen in his new play "Fritz, Our German Cousin." Joe Jefferson was not to reopen the Booth Theatre in "Rip Van Winkle" till the middle of the coming month; and Patti was being advertised for a new concert in the Academy of Music. One story did get more than a column and it dealt with how Lydia Thompson, the dashing British blonde, who set off a pair of fleshings so satisfactorily, had been pursued by (so tells the *Gazette*) a Miss Griffin with an "intense, intolerable and peculiar love," which caused the Griffin dame to follow Lydia Thompson wherever she toured and to write her burning letters by the hundreds.

All day Saturday and Sunday and for many days thereafter Twenty-third Street in the vicinity of No. 12, found its walks flooded with an awe-struck and babbling populace. This street was then one of the most notable of the city thoroughfares. Many fine residences stood on each side of its broad roadway and well-kept trees edged the sidewalks. Directly opposite the Nathan home was the quite new Fifth

MASHED BY A MIDGET.

PATTI, THE PRIMA DONNA, FALLS IN LOVE WITH A MIDGET IN BUNNELL'S NEW YORK MUSEUM AND ENTERTAINS HIM AT HER HOTEL

Avenue Hotel, which rose to the then unusual height of six stories, and which, on account of its altitude had been equipped with a new-fangled contrivance known as an "elevator." No. 5 was the home of Professor S. F. B. Morse, inventor of the telegraph. Lily Langtry, the beauteous Jersey Lily, had her home on this street soon after.

Eagerly the newspapers were devoured and their least revelations of new development were discussed at great length. The coroner's inquest, which proceeded

SPRING OPENINGS ON THE TURF.

EPISODES OF THE PREPARATIONS FOR AND OPENING OF THE SPRING RACING SEASON AT JEROME PARK AND
SHEEPSHEAD BAY.

I—Mrs. Langtry Visits Eole. II—Dividing the Winnings. III—The Jockey's Mash. IV—Their First Race. V—George H. Engeman, Manager of the Brighton Beach Track.

the following week, was awaited with positive excitement. The city was buzzing with rumors that conveyed a repellent suspicion. Was this a parricide? Had it been the hand of Washington Nathan that had done his father to such an appalling death? August 2nd was the date when the inquest got under way. That same day one could read of the Nathan burial, which had occurred the day previous. The procession of carriages had proceeded to Cypress Hills Cemetery and passed through an entrance over which was the Hebrew inscription, "Congregation B'nai Jeshurun" and with the words "Gate of Prayer" above. Through this the long lines of vehicles was driven and the casket borne to its grave in a lonely little spot in the hillside. Whose was the guilty hand in this sad taking off? The *Gazette* report of the inquest follows with but few alterations:

One of the first to give testimony was Major-General Francis P. Blair. In addition to being a veteran of the Mexican and Civil Wars he had been the nominee in 1868 for the Vice-Presidency of the United States on the ticket headed by Horatio Seymour, and which had given little opposition to the one headed by General Grant. About twenty minutes before the discovery of the murder the General had looked from the window of his room in the Fifth Avenue Hotel into the room on the third floor of the Nathan home and had seen Frederick Nathan in the act of getting out of bed. Blair's observations before returning to his own couch had made note of another fact. The front door of the Nathan house leading to the street was open to almost the full half distance.

This fact was quite at variance with the statement that came out in the examination of John Mangam, the officer on the beat. Mangam declared he had examined the front door of the Nathan house at 1:30 and 4:30. It can be seen where more credence can be placed on the word of Major-General Blair than of the policeman so far as this contention may be concerned. The point can have held importance since Dr. Joseph E. Janvrin, the physician attached to the Fifth Avenue Hotel, testified that he had examined the body of the deceased some few minutes after 6 A. M. and that Mr. Nathan had then been dead not less than three or four hours, in his opinion. Someone could have been concealed in the house and escaped after the fell deed.

Walton H. Peckham, whose house stood at the southwest corner of Twenty-third Street and Fifth Avenue, and which was the nearest to the east from the Nathan residence, admitted to having heard some noise during the night, but could not determine the significance of same. Considering that so many windows must have been open close to the Nathan house the presumption is that the noises of the death struggle must have attracted some attention unless the murder happened at a time when the night storms had broken loose again. There was heavy rain and rumblings of thunder between 2 and 3 o'clock in the morning.

There was other inconsequential testimony which was made much of for the time being. A nephew of the dead man was among those sworn in, an act that led to an odd incident, though one that had little bearing on the case. One speaking for the witness declared to the Coroner that since said witness was of the Holy House of Israel, the requirements were that to be sworn in "he must have his hat on his head, his face to the east, and his hand on the five books of Pentateuch." The witness, however, was sworn in accordance with the customary court procedure and his testimony was of no import.

Frederick Nathan, when it came his time to describe the happenings of the fatal night and morning, gave a satisfactory account of how he had spent the evening. He was slender-framed, and luxuriant "Burnside" whiskers gave his face dignity. He reached home at about midnight and he exchanged a few words with his father, who desired to know if he wished any of the ice-water that had been placed in his room. Frederick had slept undisturbed during the night, not even taking note of the homecoming of his brother, Washington. He had arisen shortly before 6 A. M. and had begun to dress, when his attention was attracted by the calls of his brother and had rushed to the floor below. He knelt down over the body of his father hoping to find that life still remained. In this way his nightshirt and socks became stained with the blood of his parent.

Washington Nathan was, of course, the one on whom all waited for his testimony. So far as was ever made known, he was the last to see his father in life and the first to look upon his dead body. He was slender, like his brother, but carried himself more gracefully; he had only a slight mustache and looked much the younger of the two. Suspicion, which he was never able during his life to altogether live down, had been directed his way on a very strong current. He had enjoyed a rather interesting evening the night of July 28, and admitted to having been from 9 o'clock until midnight in the well-known and fashionable *maison de joie* kept by Irene Macready, at 104 East Fourteenth Street. He reached home at 12:20, noted that both his father and his brother were sleeping soundly and he retired without disturbing either. A few minutes before 6 o'clock the following morning he arose and, as he was to take part in the ceremony that had kept his father in the city, and as his father, moreover, was a heavy sleeper, he went down to call him. And then his eyes met with the sight that caused him to call for his brother.

[135]

The hearing had extended to August 11, when the Coroner produced something of a sensation by calling the name of Miss Clara Dale. This was the young lady who had entertained Washington from the hours of nine until midnight in the house on Fourteenth Street. We read that "her face was full and fair and her physique and carriage were stately." As to how ladies of her trade in the Seventies dressed, the following may not be a fair criterion, since "she had divested herself of all showy ornaments, causing her to appear as an elegant lady." However, "she wore a green and white striped silk dress, with panier, flesh-colored kids [gloves], and the hair was done up in waterfall and puffs. Her gaiters were the latest style worn by fashionable ladies, with the preposterous high brass heels, and white pearl buttons, and tassels."

Her testimony was brief and to the point and her examination was in no ways embarrassing. The District Attorney, we are informed, "treated her with a manner polite enough to be called Chesterfieldian." It was much nicer treatment than was accorded Mrs. Anne Kelly, who had appeared on the scene a day or so earlier.

Mrs. Kelly was subjected to far more personal questioning than was the fate of Miss Clara Dale, which brought a letter of caustic rebuke from Dr. Mary Walker. Mrs. Kelly was even made to confess to an unhappy event in her early life that had no bearing on the case. She had been the housekeeper in the Nathan house for four years and according to her story her master had reached home around 10 P.M., and after carrying ice-water to his room on the second floor and arranging a bed for him on the floor according to his direction, she had fastened the doors and windows, retired to her room at the other end of the second floor and had heard nothing thereafter until she had been awakened by the cries of Washington in the morning.

Her son, William Kelly, followed Miss Clara Dale on the stand, and his was a severe grilling. His examination could not have been more severe if he had been on trial for the murder. A pale young man of insignificant build who gave his age as twenty-four and whose sunken cheeks and hollow eyes made him rather sickly-looking. He had been discharged from the Union Army in 1865 and was receiving a pension of $8. a month from the Government. He lived on this and odd change he picked up around the Nathan house, where he lodged and had been sleeping on the night of the murder in his room in the attic. He had heard nothing during the night. He had risen shortly after 5 on the following morning and after dressing had gone to work in his room blackening the shoes of the Nathan men, which he had taken to his room the previous evening.

SHE KNOCKED IT OUT.

HOW DR. MARY WALKER, WHILE TRAVELLING ON A CONNECTICUT RAILWAY, RESENTED THE SMELL OF A QUEER CIGAR.

His attention to the tragedy had been first attracted by the calls of Washington Nathan.

There you have the stories of the four persons who were actually known to have been in the house while Benjamin Nathan was being beaten to death. Nothing vital was ever made out of their mass of testimony. Could either of these be the guilty one?

[137]

Frederick Nathan, it should be said at once, was never under suspicion, nor was there any good reason why he should be. In fact, so utterly was he free of suspicion that were this a narrative of fiction instead of fact, right here we would have the guilty party.

Mrs. Kelly had few fingers pointed her way, though there had been some discrepancy in some of her statements. First she said she had heard nothing on the fatal night, then she said she had been awakened by the storm. But on the whole she told a straightforward story and impressed every one as a hard-working and harmless being.

William Kelly, there is little doubt, was the one on whom the police tried to fasten suspicion, at least as an accomplice. It was hinted that he might have opened a door to let in the one who had done the murder; that he might have committed the deed himself. One version, which the *Gazette* held in derision, drew a picture of the boy slinking into the room to rifle Mr. Nathan's pockets. Suddenly the sleeping man wakened and recognized the sneak-thief. Before he could make an outcry Kelly struck Nathan over the head and knocked him unconscious, then proceeded with the brutal killing so that the danger of accusation would be forever removed. Somehow, the *Gazette* seemed to take the view that William Kelly was too supine a character for such desperate work. This was a point of view strongly taken by Edmund Lester Pearson in his book "Studies in Murder," in which is to be found the most able and interesting review of the Twenty-third Street murder.

This leaves only Washington Nathan of the quartet to whom attention has been turned. Suspicion, of course, pointed all the more strongly in his direction when it was discovered that his feminine associations leaned toward ladies of easy morals. And there was only his word for it that he, the last known to have seen his father breathing in life, had reached home at the time he claimed, twenty minutes past midnight. And no living soul but Washington Nathan could know whether he had slept undisturbed through the hours of the murder. He died abroad practically in exile twenty-two years after the burial of his father with the mystery unsolved. His hair was white and his health had been broken for several years. His character never seemed to take on any of the strength of that of his father. In 1879, the same year that marked the passing of his mother, he got mixed up in an unpleasant escapade in the Coleman House in which he was shot in the neck by a woman named Fanny Barrett. In 1884 he married the widowed daughter of Colonel J. H. Mapleson. Bequests of more than $100,000., of which $75,000. came to him from his father, enabled him to round out an idle and misspent existence. But for all the general worthlessness of his character it never betrayed anything in the way of vicious symptoms such as could have turned him into a parricide so fiendish as to inflict the brutal wounds that had caused the death of his father.

More than a week was taken up with the proceedings of the inquest and the list of those examined was an extended one, and never got anywhere. All sorts of leads were followed, and they were many. Chief Jourdan of the Police received almost five hundred letters ere the murder was ten days old, and most of them advised him how to handle the case. Several times there were arrests that gave hope that the murderer had been found, and then the expectations proved to have no genuine basis.

One of the arrests, that of Thomas Dunphy, was an odd business. Mr. Dunphy, a quite prominent lawyer, was spending an evening with some ladies in a house over in Brooklyn in the week after the excitement on Twenty-third Street. Dunphy, like most barristers of the period, had a tendency toward dramatics. He reacted the tragedy with gestures and resonant vocal effects for the ladies in the parlor and took the part of the imaginary murderer. His acting was so realistic that one young lady, who had been listening in at the keyhole, ran out of the house in her agitation and convinced an officer of the law that the murderer had been found. Dunphy was collared by the policeman and carted off to the station-house and it took him an entire evening, most of which was spent in a cell, before he proved his innocence. Strangely enough, he had been co-author of a book on murder trials which had been published in 1867 under the title "Remarkable Trials of All Countries."

Following the inquest there came a number of other suspicions and arrests. Most of them were "confessions" by convicts who wished to get free passage to New York. Then George Ellis, a convict in Sing Sing Prison, was brought into the case. He had been heard to say that he could give the name of the Nathan murderer. He was brought down to New York and he identified the "dog" from out of a score of such implements that had been gathered from various shops. Ellis said that before his commitment to Sing Sing he and a burglar named George Forrester had planned to rob the Nathan house. The plan had been to enter the house while the family was away in the country. Forrester, in the opinion of Ellis, had undertaken the job alone and had been surprised to find Nathan in his room. Forrester was arrested in 1872 after quite a chase and was represented by the celebrated criminal lawyers, Howe and Hummel. The case against Forrester never got very far. It was felt that the testimony against the man would not stand up and he was discharged, only to be sent to Joliet, where he was wanted on another charge.

Ellis, who was not permitted to testify against Forrester, explained his identification of the "dog" as an implement with which the two had often worked. The *Gazette* refers to one of the "leads" noted in the "Recollections of a New York Chief of Police," by George Walling, who was thirty-eight years on the force. According to Walling, while Ellis was under guard in the Sixth Precinct Station during the pursuit of Forrester, Ellis, in conversation with Detective Patrick Dolan, said one day:

"I'm going back to State's Prison and Superintendent Jourdan is going to die. Isn't it too bad?"

"How do you know that?" Dolan inquired.

"Well—his clothes don't fit him," was the answer.

The implication that Walling would seem to convey is that the Police head was burdened with some haunting secret and that Judge Cardozo had used strong influence to force Jourdan into shrouding with mystery certain facts that might have reflected unfavorably on some one in the Nathan family, and yet $30,000. of the amount of reward for detection was put up by the wife of the murdered man. Nor does the Walling deduction coincide with Walling's surmise that William Kelly had been a confederate in the murder. In fact, the one-time Chief of Police of New York is very vague in some portions of his account. Anyway, Walling has it that Jourdan failed from the day of Benjamin Nathan's death and was dead himself a few months after.

More than a quarter of a century after Benjamin Nathan had been consigned to his grave another story brought "a beautiful Spanish woman" into the case. Up in a small town in New Hampshire Irene Macready died. It was in her house on Fourteenth Street that Washington Nathan had dallied with Miss Clara Dale on the momentous evening. The Macready woman was said to have told her nieces that she had knowledge of how "the beautiful Spanish woman" had a key to the Nathan house and had been there until 2 or 3 o'clock on the morning of the

murder and had started to talk of certain harrowing happenings when Irene Macready gave her the advice to keep her mouth shut.

And then the *Gazette* had a theory of its own.   Here it is:

> In business circles there is a theory on the Nathan murder entertained
> to this day which we may as well give place to while we are upon the sub-
> ject.   Many who know him believe that Benjamin Nathan was in possession
> of papers of great value to some man of his own station with whom he
> stood in business connection.   He was, as we have said, a silent man in his
> affairs.   His own wife never knew what he had in his safe or what he car-
> ried in his pockets, save as he chose to tell her, consequently, he may have
> possessed documents of untold importance without the knowledge of any
> one but those whom they concerned.
>
> At any rate, the theorists hold that he did own such documents, and
> that he was put out of the way by the person whom they concerned, who
> afterwards plundered the place in order to send suspicion on the wrong
> track.

And so the case of many clues is still, and probably will always be, an unsolved
mystery.

Part II

THE RICHARD K. FOX GAZETTE

(1876)

RICHARD K. FOX.

THE PALE PINK PICTURE PERIODICAL

I

RICHARD K. FOX, when he started as proprietor of the *National Police Gazette* in 1876, undertook his obligations as owner and editor with practically no more than an idea—but it was a valuable one. The idea being: "If they can't read, give them plenty of pictures." Within ten years he saw his weekly paper enjoying greater international vogue than any publication then in existence. It was being subscribed for in no less than twenty-six countries, and was even going to a part of the world that was then so remote it received mail from the United States but twice a year.

To the energy and genius of Richard K. Fox must go the credit, not only of turning the wreckage of the *National Police Gazette* into a weekly of exceptional importance in its own peculiar way, but also of being responsible, in the so doing, of revolutionizing not a few newspaper standards. For it was the Fox success that eventually made the heads of even the most conservative of daily papers appreciate the value of brightening solid pages of newsprint with attractive pictures, and, as well, of the circulation worth that was to be found in giving increased prominence to doings in the world of sports.

The late Mr. Fox was a live-wire, a man of ideas and enterprise, and an early go-getter. What is more, he was a citizen of power and authority in his particular field of endeavor for not a few years of his interesting life. Before going further into the history of the modern *Gazette* some space should be devoted to the guiding spirit of its pink destinies. Nothing will give you a truer impression of the man and the essential facts of his history than to set down what he permitted to be printed of himself in his own paper in 1885:

> Richard K. Fox was born in Belfast in the year 1846, of that com-
> mingled Scotch and Irish parentage which has contributed so much to
> American enterprise and energy. The solid grit of the one and the mental
> acuteness of the other are both equally represented in him. His first em-

SINS OF NEW YORK

ployment was in the office of the *Banner of Ulster,* the celebrated organ of
the Presbyterian Church in Ireland. After remaining with the *Banner* four
years, Mr. Fox joined the staff of the *Belfast News Letter,* the richest and
most powerful newspaper in Ireland. He remained with the *News Letter*
for ten years, rising to the second place in its counting-room service. He
arrived in New York in September, 1874. Although he had but a few shil-
lings in his pocket, twenty-four hours after his landing he found profitable
employment with the *Commercial Bulletin* of New York, a situation he
left to connect himself with the *Police Gazette*—then at a very low ebb of
prosperity, although the oldest weekly in America. Applying the most
dauntless courage and industry to his work the new owner of the property
which he had literally snatched from extinction, in less than ten years has
made the *Police Gazette* building one of the sights of New York. It
towers alongside the Brooklyn Bridge, and it occupies more space and machinery than any publishing house in America. The job printing office is a
gigantic affair and turns out the largest and most vivid pictorial work ever
printed in this country. To see the slender, almost boyish proprietor of this
wonderful business moving modestly and good humoredly through its
mazes, and to realize that he is barely forty years old, is to make one convinced that after all even Monte Cristo was a possible character, with the
difference, however, that Monte Cristo had his fortune made for him, while
Richard K. Fox forced fortune to smile on him by his own genius, good
judgment and indomitable energy of will.

This rather vainglorious estimate may be excusable to some extent in view of
the fact that Mr. Fox did, beyond doubt, occupy an important position in the community when the above was written, and that he had undertaken the ownership of
the *Gazette* under even greater handicaps than this self-applause revealed. The
Gazette had been transferred to him in lieu of certain monies due him and for a small
amount of cash and encumbered by not a few debts. Fox increased his obligations
by several personal loans, one to the amount of $500. borrowed from William Mul-
doon, who then had some prominence as an athlete at Harry Hill's sporting resort,
who had lately become a member of the New York Police Department, and who was
soon to become the wrestling champion of the world.

Hampered by lack of capital the extreme energy which Fox threw into his
property was at first slow in making itself apparent. From the first he aimed at
giving the public the foremost of illustrated papers, yet more than a year went by
before the make-up of the publication, which had been increased from eight to sixteen pages, was close to being typographically or pictorially what he had in mind.

[146]

But finally it appeared in its pink dress and really well printed, Fox giving special attention to his press-room and bringing in brand-new type to its fonts throughout by the end of 1878. And it was out of this property that he made a fortune which was close to $3,000,000. at one time. At his death, which came in November, 1922, his estate was valued at more than one and one-half million dollars, even though his fortune had been taxed by some lean periods for the *Gazette* in his closing years, by a heavy losing suit, some dishonesty in his employ, and other misfortune. And, too, in addition, it is estimated that he must have given away fully one-quarter of a million dollars in medals, prizes, stake money, and other expenditures in the popularization and promotion of sporting events; also he had been very liberal in his charities.

What he made of the *National Police Gazette* was something that grew even beyond his own conception, and it is not to be wondered at if Richard K. Fox took himself and his paper overseriously.

II

In an early editorial, stress was laid on the fact that the paper was radically different from the old *Gazette* under its new management.

> Under its present management, no illustration and not a line of printing of immoral tendency is suffered to appear in its columns. So far from pandering to vicious tastes its object is to delineate vice in its proper odious character and to further the end of justice by every means of exposing the personality and doings of the criminal classes, and by giving wide-spread publicity to transactions of the courts of law.

Which would make it seem very much after the pattern wrought by Messrs. Wilkes and Camp. And so it was in the first two or three struggling years of the Fox régime, being little more than a chronicle of criminal doings and a paper with a more liberal display of illustrations than its rivals. Later on it was claimed: "When Mr. Fox acquired the proprietorship of the *Police Gazette* he had but one policy. This was to make his paper the greatest journal of sport, sensation, the stage and romance in existence."

Sensational, it surely was, from the outset, and it was as an arbiter of sports news that the *Gazette* came into world-wide prominence. But it was not until late in 1879 that it gave over a regular column to sports items. And it was a little earlier in the same year that attention was first called to its newest feature, a theatrical news department. Until then only a few random paragraphs gave space to doings in the theatrical and athletic world; actors at first only got their pictures in the *Gazette*

FENCING SCENE IN THE BLACK CROOK.
THE DESPERATE ENCOUNTER BETWEEN STALACTA, THE QUEEN OF THE FAIRIES, AND THE BLACK CROOK, THE DEMON INCARNATE.

through some unsavory escapade like Nat Goodwin's emulating John L. Sullivan in the Hoffman House. As for romance, its fiction features were nearly all second-rate serials. When it came to general news, its accounts were practically the forerunner of our "Untrue Story" magazines, except that the imagination generally dealt with real people and actual facts in a too personal way in the Fox paper.

Even when it was yet shy of the sports and theatrical features in which Mr. Fox was to take so much pride, it is only fair to admit that, by the middle of 1878, distinct gains had been made in circulation. Samuel A. Mackeever, who wrote easily and attractively under various names, among them Paul Prowler and The Old Rounder, and of whose work we shall in due time give some interesting examples, found many new readers through his series of articles. Particularly, "Glimpses of Gotham" and "Midnight Pictures." What is more, his graphic pen pictures of the town's fast resorts had the effect of stirring the police into action and led to a number of exciting raids on several "noted dens of vice."

Mackeever was also one of the few to volunteer for the first planned trip through the air across the Atlantic, which was to have been by way of balloon— an idea that created much talk and excitement, but was not gone through with.

Still another part of Mr. Mackeever's editorial work for the *Gazette* was that of dramatic critic. Under the nom de plume of Marquis de Lorgnette he wrote a column of stage gossip and provided the photos of actresses. I don't aim to "dish any dirt," but the picture of Miss Pauline Markham appeared three times in one year in his department.

Another early feature was a serial by Bracebridge Hemyng, which was a work of fiction on altogether different lines from his famous Jack Harkaway stories for boys, as can be judged by the title, which was, "Left Her Home, or the Trials and Temptations of a Poor Girl."

Another department, which had considerable early popularity, was one given over to paragraphs on "crimes and passions of the period," which were run together under the singular headline of "Homicidal Horrors." In fact the head- lines which graced the various news items were a distinct feature by themselves and told a story that was liable to excite one's interest, as can be understood from the samples presented. (See page 150.)

In the matter of headlines the *Gazette* in the early Fox years went in for effects that were as execrable in taste as they were gruesome. "Human Hash" topped the story of the Boston railroad horror in 1887, and "Roast Man" headed the story dealing with the Richmond hotel fire in Buffalo in the same year. How- ever, before condemning the *Gazette* too harshly it is well to remember that one of

SNARED BY A SCOUNDREL.

An Innocent Country Beauty, on her Travels, Encounters her Fate in an Adventurer

OF THE WORST TYPE.

His Easy Conquest of the Unsophisticated Girl Through a Grand but Diaphanous Yarn,

AND HER SUBSEQUENT SAD FATE.

St. Joseph, Mo., January 30.—Mattie Smith is seventeen years old to-day and for one so young she has had a bitter experience in the ways of the world. She was seated alongside a city employe last night in the ladies' waiting-room at the Francis street depot. A brunette of much beauty, long, black clustering hair, with great dark eyes that seemed to plead for sympathy, she attracted the attention of the itemizer at once, and soon it was learned by that method only known to reporters, that she had been the victim of a most cruel fate. Knowing the man with whom she sat it was an easy matter to get an audience with the girl, and in a few minutes a thrilling story of love, adventure and shame was being poured in the reporter's ears, which was drank in with eagerness. Three months ago Mattie left her parents at their cottage home in the pleasant little town of Pleasant Hill, this state, and started alone to visit her grandfather, James McLean, who resides at Hamilton. She was young and inexperienced, and had traveled but little. It was necessary to change cars at Kansas City in order to reach her destination, and in stepping from the cars to the platform she was approached by a well-dressed man, who kindly offered to assist her and see that see that she took the right train for Hamilton. He spoke kindly to her, flattered and talked a little love,

HOMICIDAL HORRORS.

Of Sufficient Number and Variety of Atrocity to Enable the Craving of the Most Exacting

TO FILL TO SATIETY.

A Sickening and Sanguinary Recital of the Murderous Tendency of Mankind. Which Should Afford

A FIELD FOR THE HUMANITARIAN.

WIFE MURDERER HANGED.

San Antonio, Texas, December 23.—Green Johnson was hanged at Menardville to-day for the murder of his wife in June, 1876.

THE BESSIE MOORE MURDER TRIAL.

Marshal, Texas, December 23.—Arguments of counsel in the Rothschild-Moore case closed to-day, and the case is in the hands of the jury.

MURDER IN THE FIRST DEGREE.

San Antonio, Texas, December 23.—The trial of Feliciana Cardoba, one of the Robert Tremble murderers, was concluded to-day, a verdict of murder in the first degree being rendered. The prisoner was twenty-one years old at the time of the murder.

A FATAL LOVE AFFAIR.

Cleveland, O., December 22.—The coroner's jury has rendered a verdict in the Rice-Angier shooting case, as follows: "The death of Dr. George W. Angier was caused by a pistol wound resulting from a shot fired by John B. Rice." Dr. Angier made an ante-mortem statement to the effect that Rice was jealous of him on account of alleged intimacy between Angier and Rice's wife. Rice is in jail awaiting examination on a charge of murder. Rice and Angier had been life long friends, and the former claims that the shooting was entirely accidental.

the great dailies of Chicago, which is very proud of its eminence in the newspaper field to-day, headlined a hanging story, "Jerked to Jesus."

Even though the improved *Gazette* did run a department for a time devoted to "Religious Notes," it is to be feared that the Fox weekly was a scandalous and sensational sheet. For its religious department was devoted only to the mistakes and misdemeanors of the men of the cloth, and even the ringing of the church-bells was condemned for their "hellish annoyance of the ill." While the proprietor found it a

THE FIENDS OF RELIGION.

HOW THE BROOKLYN HYPOCRITES TORTURE THE SICK AND DYING WITH THE HELLISH CLANGOR OF THEIR SUNDAY CHURCH BELLS.

source of gratification that commendations of his efforts were often had from contemporaries, and were even extolled by the Y.M.C.A. branch of Fort Shaw, Texas—which felt that its pictures on the career and death of the Magdalen, Nellie D. Camp, constituted a moral warning—it is probable that he took even more pride in a letter from Sempronius, Texas, which he gave much prominence. It read and was signed as follows:

> *Have been on the move so much lately that I have not received the* Police Gazette *regularly. Please send me a copy here and oblige.*
>
> *Jesse James.*

THE STRANGE WOMAN—EPISODES IN THE LIFE OF A MAGDALEN, AS ILLUSTRATED IN THE CAREER OF NELLIE D. CAMP—A FEVERISH ROUND OF GILDED VICE AND HOLLOW GAIETY WITH THE REACTION OF DESPAIR AND THE WOOING OF THE WELCOME OBLIVION OF THE DREAMLESS SLEEP THROUGH THE MEDIUM OF THE FATAL DRUG—THE CLOSING SCENE PARADING THE EFFECTS OF THE DEAD WOMAN BEFORE A THRONG OF MORBID CURIOSITY SEEKERS—SOLD FOR THE BENEFIT OF THE PUBLIC BECAUSE—"FRIENDS SHE HAD NONE," NEW YORK CITY.—SEE PAGE 2.

While this may have been a hoax, the fact remains that those notorious train and bank robbers, the James Boys, did send their pictures to the *Gazette,* with autographs that were generally accepted as authentic.

(Incidentally, it was the lawmakers of the State of Texas who endeavored to impose a special tax on the sales of the *Gazette,* in 1882, which was finally ruled to be unconstitutional.)

It was hardly to be wondered at that the *Police Gazette* had its troubles at times with the New York Society for the Suppression of Vice, and that said Society effected the arrest of Mr. Fox on a couple of occasions, and in time forced the *Gazette* to pay the sum of $500. as a fine for what was termed indecent advertising. Yet in 1879 we find the editor replying in the following moral tone in his department devoted "To Correspondents":

> William Commons, Asheville, N. C.—Your letter in reference to informing you where you can obtain vile pictures and publications has been forwarded to Anthony Comstock, of the Society for Prevention of Vice. He may be able to attend to the matter as it deserves.

The *Gazette* was not immoral, Mr. Fox insisted. It was certain ones of the people who were immoral. Presenting a pictorial record of the day was strictly within the bounds of legitimate journalism, and the *Gazette* was merely an enemy of hypocrisy and cant.

However, there was another factor that had something to do with the gradual success that was being attained in those early days by the *Gazette,* and this was nothing less than a deal of genuinely excellent reportorial and newspaper work. One might turn his eyes away from Mr. Fox's weekly with a contemptuous glance, but in doing so he was missing much in the way of artistic workmanship in many of its drawings and some exceptionally clever writing as well. There was a reason for this last fact.

III

Being a high-class newspaper man in the very early Eighties seemed to include a weakness for liquor. And many of the star men of the most important metropolitan dailies came to work for the *Gazette* in this unusual fashion: After they had finished with their labors on Saturday on the various papers with which they happened to be engaged, and had gambled or drunk their way into low financial state, they knew where and how to pick up a ten-dollar bill and to have free lodging and plenty to eat until the following Monday. They could stroll over to the *Gazette* offices, 2, 4 and 6 Reade Street and later 183 William Street, and find their way into a room the door of which would not open outward for the time being. And here they would find a well-stacked lunch counter, enough whisky to keep

THE NATIONAL POLICE GAZETTE PUBLICATION OFFICE, 183 WILLIAM STREET, CORNER OF SPRUCE, NEW YORK CITY —SEE PAGE 3 FOR DESCRIPTION AND HISTORY OF THE LEADING ILLUSTRATED PAPER OF THE WORLD.

[154]

their fires of inspiration burning, but not dimmed, and comfortable couches on which to take their rest. And in this period of incarceration they worked editorially for Fox and the ten-dollar bill that was given them upon their release Monday A.M. Going back through the *Gazette* of fifty years ago you find its pages studded with many a gem in the way of newspaper composition.

Take, just as one example, the story of Miss Lizzie Winsweiler, who appeared in Justice Paulin's Court in Newark, New Jersey, against Samuel Kellum, "a black-walnut-colored gentleman of thirty-five or thereabouts" in the matter of the paternity of Miss Lizzie's curly-headed baby with a dark nut-brown complexion. The description of the antiquated courtroom with its sagging floor and its judicial bench wedged up to a level so that the down grade of the floor would not "affect the hearing of his honor," is not only picturesque in its wording but also slyly humorous in its description, telling how "the walls are decorated with an oil painting of Queen Victoria in her younger days and an old map of New Jersey."

Unfortunately the story is too long to be given here in its entirety, though not a bit overwritten. But it gives a graphic picture of the odd court characters and of a free-and-easy atmosphere where the majesty of the law seemed to be meted out with more justice than dignity. There is quite a comical dialogue when the alleged father insists that the shade of Miss Lizzie's baby is due to the fact that it has been raised on black tea, and then the nut-brown baby is sent for and His Honor is shown how naturally the infant takes to its bottle of cow's milk. Upon which Justice Paulin hints to the lawyers that if it is true that only cow's milk had been given the child, then the suit had not been properly brought, and that the action should have been against the cow. And the examination of the witnesses is also made into a hilarious business.

Here was the work of no petty scribbler. No indeed. What was possibly a rather offensive news incident picked from out of everyday existence was turned into a masterpiece of narration, one to touch the risibilities of even the majority of exacting readers.

One can well picture this gifted man of the pencil at work under a flickering gas-jet at his littered desk weaving his story from the rather drab details of a vulgar business of miscegenation that make the report of the local paper. His eye is agleam with the creative glow, though the good liquor provided by Mr. Fox may have had something to do with the gleam. And you can fairly hear him chuckling to himself as he adds some new embellishment to the yarn which he is building in a round flourishing hand.

We are told that even Com. William K. Vanderbilt smiled over the story under the heading "Vanderbilt's Velocity," that related how the railroad magnate's dashing cutter pulled by his "lightning pair, Lysander and Leander," collided with the family sled of Patrick Sheedy, liquor dealer of Second Avenue and Eighty-third Street. Mr. Vanderbilt drove on gamely, according to the story, until his pair was under control, and then informed Mr. Sheedy he would be responsible for all

WILLIAM H. VANDERBILT, WITH HIS CELEBRATED TEAM, LYSANDER AND LEANDER, COLLIDES WITH A FAMILY SLEIGH, NEAR GABE CASE'S HOTEL ON CENTRAL AVENUE, NEW YORK CITY.—See Page 7.

damages. "Sheedy boasted of having passed Mr. Vanderbilt, but expressed the hope that they would both be going the same way should they meet again."

Another cleverly handled story which was titled "The Tale of the Torrid Wave," told how two society damsels attempted to keep up a fashionable appearance during the "heated term" by rigidly closing the front of the house and camping out on the back roof at night, and how their pleasant fiction was spoiled by two overinquisitive male acquaintances.

Make no mistake, there was expert writing aplenty within even the very early pages of Mr. Fox's weekly. And in no very great time he had assembled the finest staff of artists that could be found in the vicinity of New York. Among them were George E. McEvoy, Matt Morgan, Charles Kendrick, Paul Cusachs, George White

A TALE OF THE TORRID WAVE—HOW TWO CHARMING SOCIETY DAMSELS, WHO ATTEMPTED TO KEEP UP A FASHIONABLE APPEARANCE OF BEING "OUT OF TOWN" DURING THE HEATED TERM, BY RIGIDLY CLOSING THE FRONT OF THE HOUSE AND CAMPING OUT ON THE BACK ROOF. AT NIGHT, HAD THEIR PLEASANT LITTLE FICTION SPOILED BY TWO OVER-INQUISITIVE MALE ACQUAINTANCES; NEW YORK CITY.—SEE PAGE 2.

and others. For all the progress we have made in modern newspaper pictorial achievement, there is nothing finer in its way than some of the woodcut effects produced by the Fox artists; there was a perfection in the shadings, for one thing, that can only be had through the work of master woodcut artists. Fox procured the best of them, and they displayed imagination as well as talent.

Mr. Fox apparently placed no restrictions upon his clever staff. They were no respecters of person or position, or of the power of wealth or recklessness of character. Owney Geogheghan, Bowery dive-keeper, stormed the Pearl Street offices because he resented something that was written about his resort, and came flying down a full flight of stairs. Lorillard, the great tobacco merchant, gave a ball to rival one given by the Vanderbilts, and the *Gazette* "society editor" reported the occasion and had a lot of lively comment on the sayings and doings, even giving a description of an imaginary Lorillard coat-of-arms which was "a cuspidor *couchant,* with two cigars and a plug of tobacco rampant."

At times the comment on personalities was thinly veiled. Most every New York reader knew that Barney O'Shane was the particular alderman on whom the paper pinned a story that once had much popularity. It seems there was talk of an appropriation for the purpose of importing one dozen gondolas to ornament the lake in Central Park. The alderman referred to was very Irish and always very strong for economy and the following words were put in his mouth:

"Gintlemin, the idea is a good wan, but—I would make an amindmint. Why should we buy twelve of thim gondolas? I make a motion we buy two of thim— a male wan and a female wan. Thin, gintlemin, let nature take its course."

Naturally, there was much going to law seeking compensation for damage to reputations alleged to have been inflicted through the columns of the *Gazette*. This worried Fox so little that he devoted the good part of a page to a story in which he gave an itemized account of suits brought against his paper over a course of six months during 1885, with an invitation to try to collect—which nobody seemed to succeed in doing. The total amount of the suits threatened was for $3,120,000., which included a demand on the part of Lillian Russell for $20,000.

IV

It was in 1880 that the new *Gazette* made its first tremendous circulation leap, and it was a prize fight that sent one of its issues of June of that year clear up to the 400,000 mark, a record, indeed, a half century ago. The match in question brought together Paddy Ryan and Joe Goss in a battle that had at stake the American fistic supremacy. Prize fighting at this time was still regarded as a most sinful and

"OPPOSITION IS THE DEATH OF TRADE."

HOW MODERN SCIENCE REVOLUTIONIZES THE LAUNDRY BUSINESS—YOUTH, BEAUTY AND THE TROY STYLE AGAINST MAIN STRENGTH AND FLAT IRONS!

brutal business in the way of entertainment, though the matching of Goss, then the recognized champion, and Ryan, the Collar City Giant, had the country greatly interested. Still, it was given only minor attention by the newspapers and it remained for Fox enterprise to show the way.

Mr. Fox never pretended to be a sports fanatic himself, but he had just added a sports department to his weekly, and having a fine sense of advertising values he was desirous of drawing notice to his new feature.

It is probable he was also inspired by the fact that George Wilkes, of the original *Gazette* and while owner of the *Spirit of the Times,* had covered the Heenan-Sayers prize fight in England in 1860 and had disposed of a special edition of 100,000 copies of his paper in this country that had been printed abroad. Anyway, to cover the Goss-Ryan match, Fox detailed Arthur Lumley, one of his editors, several artists, and William H. Harding, who had charge of his new sports department.

It proved a long and an expensive assignment, but got the results; the Fox presses were kept busy printing their special fight issue for weeks after the contest to satisfy orders from every part of the United States and many places abroad. The battle was first arranged to be fought in Canada, but the contestants and those interested were chased from the scene by an array of redcoats. Many weeks went by before the two finally fought it out on the turf with bare knuckles at Collier's Station, West Virginia, under a gold and purple sky shortly after daybreak of a beautiful June morning and close to the scene of the bloodless pistol duel between James Gordon Bennett and Frederick May. At the end of eighty-seven rounds, that lasted one hour and twenty-four minutes, Paddy Ryan became the new champion. Soon afterward the *Gazette* brought out its special edition with the only full account of the fight that could be had and with ringside pictures in addition. The demand for the issue was astonishing to rival editors, who were giving most attention to the Garfield-Hancock presidential campaign, which got some attention from the *Gazette* as well.

From then on the *National Police Gazette* came into its tremendous vogue as the one organ which no one claiming an interest in sports could afford to be without. Its files were kept in hand in practically every saloon throughout the land, and certainly no barber-shop made any pretense of being up-to-date unless the latest issue of the "Barber's Bible," as they called the Fox *Gazette,* was conspicuously at hand; it was as essential a part of the appointments as the rack containing your individual shaving mug with your name thereon in letters of gilt. Forty and fifty years ago, and even less, the barber-shop was the congregation place in every town, community or neighborhood from Coast to Coast where the weighty questions of the athletic

SINS OF NEW YORK

world were discussed and decided. The proprietor, through pronounced loquacity and his opportunity for protracted study of the *Gazette* pages, was usually the authority whose opinion decided all arguments pertaining to sports. And when in doubt, then the "Answer to Correspondents" department of the Fox weekly was depended on.

In an indirect way, the Ryan-Goss fistic event was responsible for Richard K. Fox becoming the champion medal, belt and trophy giver of the world. Following the Ryan-Goss fight the *Gazette* proprietor then became known as the backer

TWO CYPRIANS, WITH AN EYE TO THE INTERESTS OF NO. 1, TAKE ADVANTAGE OF A POLITICAL PROCESSION TO ADVERTISE THEIR PREFERENCE AND CHARMS; NEW YORK CITY.—See Page 10.

of the new champion and he matched the latter for $5,000. for a contest with John L. Sullivan, of Boston, who was just then beginning to attract some renown.

Sullivan had been brought to New York by William Muldoon in March, 1881. Muldoon, while on one of his early tours as wrestling champion, made an appearance in Boston, where John L., who had gained some local prominence for his fistic prowess, was brought to Muldoon's attention. The wrestling champion sponsored Sullivan's appearance at Harry Hill's resort and the Boston boy's quick knockout victory over Steve Taylor was attended with so much acclaim that John L. was

[161]

hailed as the coming champion. Through the efforts of Fox and wide publicity through his *Gazette,* the match between Paddy Ryan and Sullivan was arranged. It was fought at Mississippi City, Mississippi, February, 1882, and Fox's champion, Ryan, was vanquished in eleven minutes—a happening that was not without significance to the future of the *Gazette,* and that reacted to its prosperity, though to some dissatisfaction for its owner. It furthered a long-standing enmity between Fox and Sullivan and led to the *Gazette* owner introducing the first of his great array of sporting trophies, the *Police Gazette* diamond belt for the heavyweight boxing championship of the world.

This donation was followed up by that of two belts valued at $1,500. each, one of which went to Jack Dempsey, the Nonpareil, as middleweight boxing champion, and the other to Jack McAuliffe, as peer of the lightweights. Then came the featherweight championship belt: cost $1,000.; holder, Ike Weir, sometimes known as the Belfast Spider.

Another $2,500. diamond belt that proved a valuable advertising medium was the "Richard K. Fox Six-Day-Go-As-You-Please Trophy." Sir J. Astley, a British sportsman, had presented a belt for pedestrian racers in 1878, which was won by Daniel O'Leary at Agricultural Hall, Islington, London, and lasted from March 18 to 23, during which period a distance of 520 miles, 2 laps, was covered. It was an international affair, and the second race for the belt was promoted in Gilmore's Garden in December of the same year. Edward Payson Weston went to London the following year, after an English walker had captured the Astley Trophy, and brought it back to this country. Then Fox put up his belt, which was far more valuable, and six-day walking was converted into the go-as-you-please foot racing and this form of athletic endeavor had a considerable vogue under the *Gazette* sponsorship.

So much valuable advertising came to Fox and his *Gazette* as a result that he followed up with a veritable deluge in his offerings of belts and trophies and medals. Two of the holders whose names still mean something were Gus Hill, winner of the club-swinging medal, who later became rich and renowned in the theatrical world, and Annie Oakley, whose medal pronounced her the female rifle-shooting champion. All descriptions of memorials for victors were presented, for rowing, wrestling, weight lifting, foot racing, fencing and every other branch of sport. One of the events Fox promoted, a swimming race across East River between Butler and Sundstrum, got the publisher in trouble with the police—because it took place on the Sabbath.

THE GREAT WALK FOR THE ASTLEY BELT, AT MADISON SQUARE GARDEN, NEW YORK CITY—EXCITING SCENE OF THE START OF THE THIRTEEN ASPIRANTS TO PEDESTRIAN HONORS AND EMOLUMENTS, AT ONE O'CLOCK ON MONDAY MORNING, SEPTEMBER 22.—[SKETCHED BY GAZETTE ARTISTS. SEE PAGE 6.

The offerings were not confined to athletic prowess. The champion singer was favored, so were champion dancers of various styles, and the avalanche even included the champion rat-catcher, one-legged dancer, oyster-opener, steeple-climber, and almost everything imagination could conceive. Medal contests that made for much interest and hilarity were those where the rewards were bid for by the champion claimants among the bartenders and the barbers. The one to decide the champion mixer of drinks was a pronounced success, only that bids for the positions of judges to pass on the virtues of the various concoctions were so numerous they almost drove Fox and his assistants to drink. Even then, it was hard to find a judge who was able to give a calm and unbiased opinion as to the most pal-

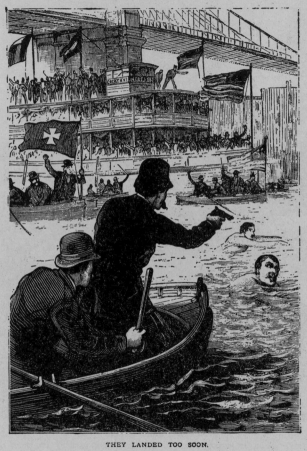

THEY LANDED TOO SOON.

BUTLER AND SUNDSTROM ARE PREVENTED BY THE POLICE FROM SWIMMING ON SUNDAY.

atable mixture of the bartender's art after the connoisseur had put in a couple of earnest hours at his task. A man could not be expected to be "as sober as a judge" under the conditions.

And the hair-cutting tournament had its drawbacks as well. Those on whom the tonsorial experts were permitted to display their speed and workmanship had the inducement of free admission to the contests and a hair-cut gratis. The use of clippers was not permitted during the operation, and only the regulation scissors could be used under the rules. But when the barbers came dashing with implements bared toward those ready to make the hirsute sacrifice, in more than one instance the man in the chair made a hurried leap from the platform and made his exit with a yell of dismay. The winning performance was done inside of thirty seconds, so maybe the person having his hair cut was taking something of a chance.

Mr. Fox's liberality as a donor of trophies and a backer of athletes drew the attention of all manner of cranks in no time and things got so annoyingly bad in

ON THE HALF SHELL.
THE GREAT OYSTER OPENING MATCH AT CLARENDON HALL BETWEEN FRANK BARRETT AND JOHN GILLEN OF NEW YORK.

this way that the *Gazette* owner, in an interview for the New York *World,* said he was seriously thinking of starting a crank's carnival.

One chap wrote from Chicago: "I propose to walk seven hundred (700) miles in one hundred and thirty-four (134) hours, covering this distance by walking around an ordinary flour barrel four thousand one hundred and ninety-eight (4198) laps to a mile." All Fox had to do was to pay the rent of Madison Square Garden for one week and stand all training expenses and "please send $50." He would furnish

SINS OF NEW YORK

the barrel. The *Gazette* publisher was inclined to favor this proposition providing the sport from Chicago would guarantee to do his walking inside, instead of outside, the barrel.

Try to figure this one out. Fox could not. It was a letter from Baltimore, dated February 28, 1882, and read as follows:

"me and george Kassidy an dan Kollyer is willin to bet $10. that you ain't got the nerve to back me for $50. that I don't cut the hart out of any man that says I can't walk from Baltimore to N. Y. without swimmin."

A party from Washington, D. C., desired backing to fight any man a duel at forty yards with buckshot. "The toughest man in the world" wrote from Norfolk, Va.: "I have been kicked three blocks just the same as if I was a football, had three ribs broken, and lost one eye, yet ten days after I was around better than if I was new." From Leadville, R. O. Tuttil requested backing to meet any man in the world: "I am the man that fought 48 hours with his throat cut and then his heart near broke because his sekonds would not let him fight 48 hours longer." Promptly on receipt of this the proprietor of the *Police Gazette,* so we are informed, sent Tuttil a ton of coal in an envelope. Maude de Viere, P. O. Cincinnati, desired backing as a pedestrian, having had much experience as a member of several disbanded barnstorming troupes. She was advised to join another company that made longer jumps.

When Sullivan knocked out Ryan there came a deluge of offers from would-be pugilists. "Nibsey" Guff, of Denver, stood ready to bet "his insides" he could do the trick of besting the champion. But the prize proposition came from John T. Errotin, Baltimore:

"Now that Sullivan has defeated your representative I suppose that you are thirsting for satisfaction. I can show you how to get it. You remember that after the fight between John C. Heenan and Tom Sayers and the former was skinned out of the belt he was to receive, Heenan offered to take Sayers by the hand and jump off the top of a house together. I am prepared to jump off the top of the *Police Gazette* building with Sullivan, provided you agree to my terms.

"1st—You must give me $2,500. to leave to my family.

"2d.—You shall print my picture on the front page of the *Gazette* with the line 'Champion Jumper of the World' beneath."

[166]

V

In a little more than five years from the day Fox had made his modest start as an editor, the *National Police Gazette* had become such a pronounced success that even the spacious quarters of the six-story building at 183 William, corner Spruce Street, had been outgrown, and in 1881 he saw the foundations laid for a new building, seven stories high, on the corner of Pearl and Dover Streets, which signaled the fact that the *Gazette* was now to have a home of its very own. Mr. Fox was a very proud man when he moved into the Richard K. Fox building shortly after the New Year, 1883. Its cost had gone beyond the quarter-million mark in dollars, a considerable fortune at the moment.

As he stepped into his private offices Mr. Fox knew that he was standing above historic ground. For the earth beneath had once been the site of the private cottage of another great editor, Benjamin Franklin, in whose honor the adjacent elevated railroad station had been given the name of Franklin Square. Looking through the windows to the opposite corner he could see the spot where the first mansion ever built for a president of the United States had stood. Where George Washington had once made his official home a tremendous gray column of stone had arisen, the anchorage of the new Brooklyn Bridge, which marvelous engineering feat was close to completion.

The gigantic span that made the first foot passageway between New York and Brooklyn was very soon to provide the *Gazette* with a news and pictorial feature that made for one of the prize numbers of the paper. On Memorial Day, 1883, two days after the bridge had been officially thrown open to the public, and while the structure was black with people, a panic was started by a couple of pickpockets and there came frightened cries that the suspension bridge (which many considered a fool undertaking) was giving way, and in the mad rush and confusion that followed twelve persons were fatally injured. From the roof of Mr. Fox's building his artists were able to get views of the horror that gave much work for their able pencils and added considerable to the realism of the pictures they gave to the world.

Undoubtedly the Fox Building was one of the landmarks of New York City almost half a century ago. It was one of the tallest then thrown against the skyline, also a not unimposing example of architecture, and the adornments of the exterior structural ironwork which portrayed athletes in action drew their share of

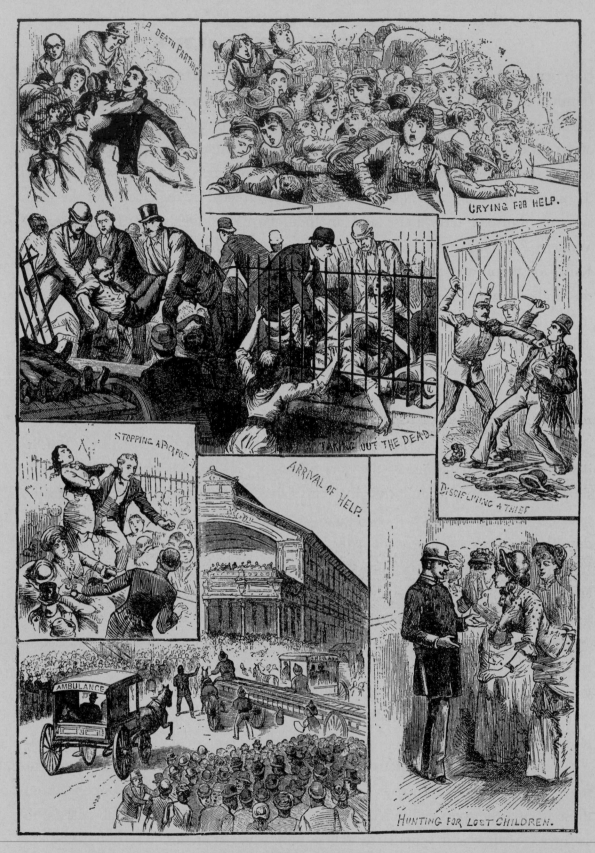

INCIDENTS OF THE BRIDGE HORROR.

THE STRUGGLES OF THE CRUSHED AND FRANTIC CROWD, THE EFFORTS OF THE RESCUERS THE WORK OF TAKING OUT THE DEAD, AND THE OPERATIONS OF THE PICKPOCKETS.

comment and observation. In addition there was one other feature that made it familiar to countless eyes and that added to its prominence: on the Dover Street side of the building was a clock that overlooked the bridge and that was an object of no little fame. At one time there were four prominent timepieces on the Manhattan river fronts by which the day of a vast number of people was regulated. Those passing along the North River side were greeted by the clock over the Pennsylvania Railroad ferry-house and another above the Delaware, Lackawanna & Western Railroad depot. On the East River shore the dial on the Long Island Railroad station and that on the home of the *Gazette* could be scanned. Back in the Eighties, when such a great percentage of the daily human traffic was diverted in the direction of the Brooklyn Bridge, the *Gazette's* illuminated clock was probably the best known of all. One day it chanced to be a few minutes behind time and indignant letters of complaint came to the Fox offices "by the hundreds" from those who had been made late to their work, and care had to be taken from then on that the clock should be kept correct to the second.

One flight up through a spacious entrance and a wide-staired hallway finished in oakwood with landings of the new tile composition, the whole being nothing short of elaborate, we came into the offices, reception parlor, and general business quarters of the publication. Its appointments were described as better fitted to some dignified banking institution than the editorial sanctum of a newspaper. "All its furnishings," we read in the *Gazette,* "are befitting a palace, the walls and ceilings are finished in rare and costly woods, while the chandeliers which illuminate this scene of business splendor are marvels from the hand of the skilled artificer in metals and glass-work. The furniture in the main office was imported and is modeled on rare old articles in the Louvre . . . everything is rich and costly yet restrained within the bonds of the most rigid taste."

Mr. Fox was "putting on the dog," as the slang-slinging element would put it to-day.

And here was the spacious room that had been arranged into a sort of museum for the display of the numerous Fox trophies; a place that was the mecca of not only those having the sportive interest, but of countless other visitors from all parts of the country. Such was its popularity that a uniformed attendant was stationed at the door to make one welcome and to give such information as might be desired concerning the various prizes and unique objects and pictures on display. The walls were hung with paintings in oil of the new fistic wonder and champion, John L. Sullivan, of Buffalo Bill, and of the other heroes of the day; Richard K. Fox, of course, was also in this gallery. Set against stands of plush or velvet there was on view the collection of medals and prizes about to be donated to the winners of some new contests projected by the progressive proprietor. The fighting colors of all the ring notables were suspended about and conspicuous space was given to the huge *Police Gazette* dumbbell, which was said to weigh one thousand and thirty pounds, and on

L. D. COPELAND,
THE INGENIOUS ATHLETE WHO HAS INVENTED AND UTILIZED A STEAM BICYCLE.

which numerous strong men had tested their muscular ability in attempts to raise it a record number of times. The new "steam bicycle," forerunner of the motorcycle, was exhibited here for a few days. Here all the noted ones of the sports world were wont to assemble, and here through at least two decades practically every important match was arranged that touched on the interest of the athletically inclined.

There is no question but that the Fox Building was the sporting center of the world, and that this fact, together with Mr. Fox's annual trips abroad, had much to do with making the name of Fox and his *Gazette* internationally famous. The man had a genius for advertising, or "selling himself," as we would put it now. He had a uniformed corps of newsboys whose regalia was patterned after that of the members of the metropolitan police force. There was a baseball team known as the Fox nine which took part in contests all about the vicinity. He paid Jim Keenan, the Boston sportsman, $10,000. for his fast trotter and changed the name of this equine beauty from Emma B. to Police Gazette. On the window of your place of business you were liable to find a sticker pasted which advised you to "Read this week's issue of the *Police Gazette*"; you were even liable to find such a sticker on the sweatband of your hat when you removed it from its peg in the place where you chanced to dine.

VI

And yet, for all its leaps in circulation and the furore its pink pages created, it was in very little demand as an advertising medium for quite a few years. Even after the *Gazette* had established itself in Franklin Square, not more than one of its sixteen pages was taken up with advertising, and, what is more, a full column and a quarter of the four columns that made up a page was devoted exclusively to bringing your attention to the publications of the Fox offices. In the fifth year of the Fox régime most of the *Gazette* features had been accorded literary distinction by being put into book form. There were then over twenty of these books in circulation, with four more titles promised for early circulation, the "Mysteries of Mormonism," "Folly's Queens," "Paris by Gaslight," and the "Assassin's Doom" being in preparation. "Glimpses of Gotham," to which reference has already been made, and which was described as "the best and cheapest book ever published," was soon in its fifth edition and had already a sale of 150,000 copies. The price was thirty cents by mail.

Though one of the advertisement columns had the heading, "Amusements," and the *Gazette* made some pretensions to being a theatrical organ, not one of the so-called legitimate playhouses bought space here, which could be had first at fifty and now at seventy-five cents per line. Owney Geogheghan's paid notice took up the most prominent position and ran thirty-five lines, telling of his new summer garden, 105 Bowery, which was described as "free and easy." Attention was called to its boxing and wrestling hall equipped with three regulation rings. McGlory's Variety and Dancing Hall, 105 Hester Street, claimed to be "the liveliest resort in

RICHARD K. FOX,
Editor and Proprietor.

NEW YORK, SATURDAY, JANUARY 27, 1883.

VOLUME XLI.—No. 279.
Price Ten Cents.

SHE HAD BEEN THERE HERSELF.

A LAST PAGE FROM THE HISTORY OF AN ARTIST'S MODEL; HOW THE BRUSH OF GENIUS AWAKENS MEMORIES IN A FORGOTTEN SOURCE.

Gotham." Harry Hill's was advertised as the rendezvous of all the champions and featured a grand sacred concert every Sunday night. Cremorne Gardens, 104-108 West 32nd Street, laid stress in capital type on its "fifty beautiful lady cashiers." Seven other similar places were mentioned, including "The Old Wooden Rocker," and the "The Old Basket," which were in the Bowery vicinity and also called attention to their "lady cashiers."

Not even one entire column was then devoted to "Medical" advertisements, a type which was later so prevalent in the *Gazette,* and which was to be the means in time of getting the paper into difficulties with the postal authorities. Several patented compounds which promised to cure very personal male disorders. including "Dr. Fuller's Youthful Vigor Pills," invited attention to their wares. J. C. Allan Co., though avoiding all mention of what their medicine prescribed for, promised "No. 1, will cure any case in four days or less. No. 2, will cure the most obstinate case, no matter of how long standing." Which was as far as their numbers apparently needed to go.

Under "Miscellaneous" there was a message "To Ladies Only," which had to do with the "Magic Beautifier" dispensed by Mrs. M. B. T. Gouraud, 48 Bond Street. H. O. Brown, Salem, N. H., recommended that his "Secret Helper" be sent for, providing "you want to win at cards. It will beat old sports." If you sent thirty-five cents to W. Fox, box 33, Fultonville, N. Y., you were privileged to see the picture of your future husband.

In all, not more than forty persons or concerns advertised through the pages of the *National Police Gazette* in 1883. Take a look a couple of years later!

Now, two entire pages were given over to advertisements and only two or three were concerned with Fox offerings. And advertising rates had jumped to one dollar per line. *Gazette* books now had but slight mention, but Fox's "cabinet size, exquisitely finished photographs" monopolized a column and listed for ten cents each the likenesses of prominent sporting men and actresses "in tights" or "otherwise"; that is to say, in costume or bust pose. There were fully one hundred each of the photos of pugilists and baseball players. Among the pugs were Sullivan, Jake Kilrain, Charley Mitchell, Billy Edwards, Peter Jackson, Prof. Donaldson, Mike Donovan and a few old-timers like Yankee Sullivan, John Morrissey, John C. Heenan, and a couple of the newcomers, James J. Corbett, George Dixon, and also Miss Alice Jennings, the champion female pugilist of New York.

Of the ball players Adrian Anson, Mike Kelly and Dan Brouthers are probably names still on the lips when the so-called national game is in discussion; though Darby O'Brien, Mickey Welch, Billy Nash, Mike Tiernan, Buck Ewing, Roger Connor, and such company, are names that ought to be still green in the memory of all lovers of the diamond. Also among the ball players we find John K. Tener,

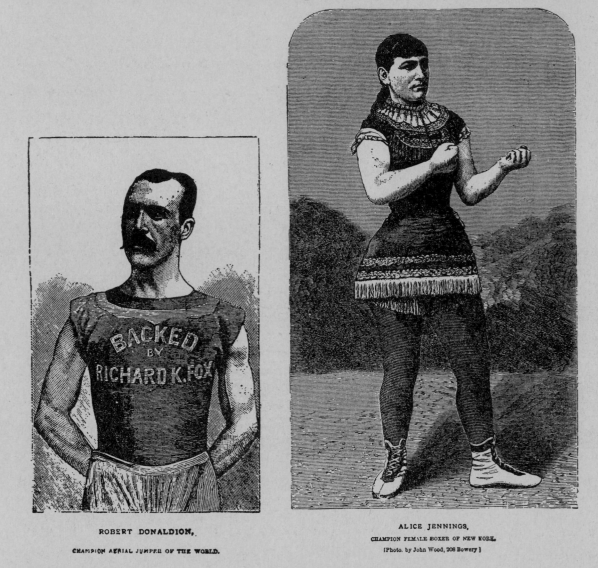

ROBERT DONALDION,

CHAMPION AERIAL JUMPER OF THE WORLD.

ALICE JENNINGS,

CHAMPION FEMALE BOXER OF NEW YORK.

[Photo. by John Wood, 208 Bowery]

who became the Governor of his State, and Charles Comiskey, now a major league magnate; also Billy Sunday, then referred to with more dignity as William A. Sunday.

William Muldoon headed the list of the twenty wrestlers pictured, and Fred Taral that of the jockeys. Jacob Schaefer and George Slosson still carry significance to the cue wielders, but mostly through the achievements of their namesakes. As to

POLICE GAZETTE'S GALLERY OF FAMOUS SPORTING MEN

FRED ROLLINSON,   JOHN S. PRINCE,

WHO RODE IN THE GREAT HORSE VS. BICYCLE RACE AT BOSTON.   CHAMPION BICYCLIST OF AMERICA, WHO WON THE GREAT RACE AT BOSTON.

[Photo. by John Wood, 208 Bowery]

AN AQUATIC MARVEL.

ASTOUNDING NATATORIAL ACHIEVEMENT OF MARQUIS BIBBERO, THE "POLICE GAZETTE" CHAMPION WHO SWIMS THE EAST RIVER, N. Y., WITH HIS HANDS AND FEET TIED.

[175]

the then noted among the bike champions (male and female) and the pedestrians, swimmers, oarsmen, runners, fighting dogs and fighting cocks, and such others as were given place in this photographic Hall of Fame, few, if any, of these names count to-day.

THE POLICE GAZETTE'S GALLERY OF FOOTLIGHT FAVORITES.

M'LLE SARA BERNHARDT.

For authentic history of this famous actress' life before and behind the footlights, with handsome portrait in her world-renowned impersonation of "Hernani," see FOOTLIGHT FAVORITES. Sold by all Booksellers. Price 20c

Under the head of "Miscellaneous," though hardly to be counted as prominent sporting personages in all cases, we find that the pictures were to be had of Rev. H. W. Beecher, Rev. T. DeWitt Talmage, Chief Inspector Byrnes, Henry George, P. T. Barnum, Abe Hummel, Bob Ingersoll, General Sheridan, President Harrison, W. E. Gladstone, William H. Cody, Steve Brodie, and Queen Victoria.

Every other week the actresses were listed. In costume: Lillian Russell, Mary Anderson, Rose Coghlan, Mrs. Kendal, Marie Wainwright, Modjeska, Ellen Terry, Sara Bernhardt and one hundred others. Some of them, like Lotta, Pauline Hall, Clara Morris, Sara Jewett, Camille D'Arville, Marie Halton, Marie Jansen, Kate Claxton and Lydia Thompson, ought still to be remembered. Actresses, showing bust: Corinne, Ada Rehan, Letty Lind, Mrs. Langtry, Minnie Maddern, Ida Siddons, Marie Tempest, Rosina Vokes, Cora Tanner, Fanny Janouschak and La Belle Fatima. Actresses, in tights: Pauline Markham, Anna Boyd, Annie Summerville, Fanny Rice, Nellie Farren, Vernona Jarbeau, Laura Burt, May Ten Broeck and several scores of others who could fill the requirements, if you know what I mean. Five Spanish dancers were also pictured, including the Señoritas Carmencita and Otero.

Only forty-one photos of actors were listed, of which, just to mention a half-dozen or so, we note Edwin Booth, Neil Burgess, Digby Bell, J. K. Emmett, Gus Williams, Tony Pastor, Lester Wallack and N. S. Woods—do you remember N. S. Woods, the youthful actor who used to stir the gallery gods in "The Boy Detective," and "The Streets of New York"?

Richard K. Fox also advertised other wares in which he was interested. The firm dealt in boxing-gloves and also in magic lanterns. About the latter, which ran in cost from $15. to $100., we will quote just a few lines from the advertisement: "To heighten the joys of the family fireside, nothing excels the advantage offered by our Magic Lantern, Dissolving View Apparatus, or a Stereopticon with appropriate slides offering a charming, sociable evening entertainment, combining amusement and instruction. As a money making business . . . only make an intelligent public aware that you are prepared to give such entertainments and you will have little difficulty in procuring engagements."

Let us look a little further through the advertising page. Miss Flossie Lee, who could be addressed at Augusta, Me., concedes, "I am the acknowledged belle of my own city, and have beaux by the score, but wish to extend my acquaintance over the whole country." She offered full-sized cabinet pictures of herself and one dozen photos of "charming young lady friends, sweet bewitching girls, making in all 13 exquisite pictures for 25 cents."

F. B. Teel offered a photo of your future husband or wife for six cents; of course, one could not expect too much for six cents. Under "Agents Wanted" the

Standard Silverware Company, Boston, offered a horse and buggy free to their representaives. The Standard Card Co., Oswego, New York, through the "Sporting Goods" notices, offered "readers and strippers for all games, fine holdouts, loaded dice, crap ringers, etc." The Pedine Co. advertised a remedy to make the feet smaller among "Toilet Articles," and another medical concern described the efficaciousness of a cure, in language that indicated that the word halitosis was not then part of the dictionary.

An important notice at the top of the advertising pages called attention to the fact that the *Gazette* would not under any circumstances publish advertisements of a "lewd, obscene or fraudulent character," and then added a line: "The proprietor will not hold himself responsible for the advertiser's honesty."

Despite these assurances we discover that this form of advertising constituted more than fifty per cent of the *Gazette* advertising notices. There were more than a half-hundred charlatans apparently finding it profitable to utilize the expensive Fox pages, some to the extent of a quarter of a column or more. They dealt in the main with exaggerated promises in the cure of venereal diseases, and with libidinous pictures and reading matter.

"Do you want to know all about it?" queries the Universal Publishing Co., Box 156, Moorehead, Minn. "Then send 50c. for the illustrated and handsomely bound 'The Mysteries of Marriage,' very choice and piquant perusal, giving more information than you could obtain in ten years of married life."

Through the Climax Publishing Co., 55D, Chicago, an advertisement advises that a lady who admits to having a turned-up nose and who is likewise "plain looking" wants a husband who must be good and affectionate. Such a mate will collect $5,000. and "one year later, if we are living together, I will give him $10,000. and $20,000. in real estate." The paper recommends itself to ladies and gentlemen "for Amusement or Matrimony."

"Marriage and its results with 14 vivid pictures," photo of your future husband or wife, together with a "teasing love letter" and 15 valuable secrets, could be had for 25c. for the lot, by addressing the West Supply Co., St. Louis, Mo.

Of the half-hundred advertisements that dealt with cures for venereal diseases and with "sexual invigorants" and the like, the wonder is not only that the *Gazette* managed for so long to evade a legal knockout for the things they put in print in the way of advertising, but that these advertisements should find so many gullibles to part with their money for such fraudulent promises, as:

"Dr. Sanden's Electric Belt, cures Nervous Debility, Seminal Weakness, Impotence, Lumbago, Rheumatism, Kidney and Bladder Complaints, Dyspepsia, Malaria, Piles,"—and might have added "what have you" if the phrase had then been in vogue. "We positively guarantee it to cure or money refunded. Beware of imitations. Our $5. belt contains 26 degrees of strength; our $10. one four times stronger." Sanden Electric Co., 822 Broadway, N. Y., or 169 La Salle St., Chicago. Dr. Sanden had opposition in the same line from Dr. W. Young, 146 E. 19th St., N. Y., and Dr. Owen, 191 State St., Chicago, but Dr. Young did not promise anywhere near as much in his catalogue of cures, and Dr. Owen's cheapest contrivance was $6. and offered only 10 degrees of strength.

"Weak Men whose Vitality is Failing, Brain Drained and Exhausted will find a perfect and reliable cure in the French Hospital Remedies . . . free consultation (office or mail) with six eminent physicians Free. Civiale Agency, 174 Fulton St., N. Y."

Sexual power positively and permanently increased by "delicious MEXICAN CONFECTION. . . . Restores Vigor, Snap and Health of Youth. Address San Mateo Med. Co., P.O. Box 481, St. Louis, Mo."

Youthful Indiscretion (self-abuse or excess) resulting in loss of memory, spots before the eyes, "defective smell," nervousness, weak back and quite a few other ailments, should get in communication with Dr. Jas. Wilson, Box 156, Cleveland, O., mentioning this paper, for an "instrument worn at night, and this never failing remedy" will enable one to affect a cure without a doctor. This advertisement points out that "all men, young and old, suffering from above afflictions lead a life of misery." We should think they would, particularly from "defective smell."

Something for nothing can be had from J. H. Reeves, P. O. Box 2320, N. Y. He promises to send victims of youthful imprudence a simple means of self-cure which he has chanced to discover "after having tried every known remedy in vain. FREE to fellow sufferers."

Married Ladies or those contemplating marriage, send 10c. for postage, &c., for a sample package of Hart's Celebrated F.P., particulars regarding a "Boon to Woman" and information to every lady. Union Specialty Co., New Haven, Conn.

From these excerpts one can form a good idea of what was once a very profitable source of revenue to the *Police Gazette* and can be regarded as a sign of the times. To-day this type of advertising, even if passed by the censor, would hardly receive the same space allotment. Have we become more moral, or less gullible? Or both? A nice question for the historian and sociologist.

Anyway, that was one distinct phase of the *National Police Gazette* in its heyday. Before going into more detailed review of the various Fox features in the way of reading matter and pictures, and as bearing on the sinfulness of the metropolis, we must mention one other feature that had to do with its popularity. Each week the leading barber, saloonkeeper, or hotel proprietor of some little community had his picture presented in a special column along with a few lines which made the reader acquainted with the basis of his fame. Here was renown indeed, to be thus singled out above your fellow man. For example:

> The above portrait is that of George W. Mann, the baseball playing barber of Birmingham, Conn. Mr. Mann is well known in the Nutmeg State as a skillful tonsorial artist and an excellent ball player. He is pitcher of the "Clipper," whose success is due to his good work.

> Frank Class, whose portrait appears in this issue is proprietor of the Track Hotel, Pine Brook, N. J. His place is the resort of all the sporting fraternity of Paterson and Newark. Mr. Class is also the champion pigeon shot of his State and has issued a challenge to shoot any man in New Jersey or Pennsylvania.

What proud days for Mr. Mann and Mr. Class! And what prosperous ones for Mr. Fox!

The *National Police Gazette* had a half-million circulation. Richard K. Fox had his first million dollars.

GLIMPSES OF GOTHAM

Peregrinations and Perceptions of Paul Prowler

BUT let us go back on Sixth Avenue and drop into saloons like the "Strand" and the "Idlewild."

The Strand has a bar in front and then there is a long room in the rear, dotted with tables. If you are taking a female acquaintance in for a drink you enter by a hallway made by a screen and are therefore not seen by those standing at the bar.

The Strand is democratic and beer is the most fashionable tipple. The tables are all wet with it. Waiters are constantly running about, twenty glasses in their grasp, filling orders. Fifty or sixty young women are in the room. Many of them are intoxicated—one or two very much so.

It is easy to perceive that another world has been reached by walking the few blocks, one that is considerably lower in tone than the other. The young man at the piano is playing "Where was Moses When the Light Went Out," and as you pass through the chattering throng you hear *double entente* remarks on the whereabouts of Moses that have the merit of being vulgar, however much they may lack in wit.

While the song is in progress there is a fight in the bar, much swearing and the breaking of glass. No one seems alarmed. It is something that Sixth Avenue on a Saturday night is used to. Perhaps a young girl comes in after the row is over and tells her friends that it was Ikey Somebody punching So-and-so's head.

"About Liz, wasn't it?" one of the party addressed asks.

"Of course."

"I thought so—but what'll you have?"

"Give me beer."

And the girl, who is not more than seventeen, slips nonchalantly into a chair and waits for her beer, which will be the tenth she has had since she started from her boarding house, while she rolls a cigarette.

Away up in a Connecticut valley, just at this hour, while the smoke floats lazily over the suffocating room, and the young man at the piano is singing

"My Mary Ann's a teacher
In a great big public school,"

there is a light streaming from the window of a farmhouse.

SKIPPING THE TRA-LA-LOO AT A FLASH HOP.

MIDNIGHT SCENES IN GOTHAM—WHIRLING IN THE MAZES OF THE GIDDY WALTZ AT THE EXPENSE OF EMPTY-HEADED NOODLES—THE SHOP-GIRL OF THE PERIOD AND HER MODES OF ENJOYMENT—SILKS AND RIBBONS AT THE DANCE, vs. POVERTY AND CALICO IN THE NINTH STORY OF A TENEMENT HOUSE—THE ROAD TO RUIN, WITH THE MANY TEMPTATIONS ON THE WAY DESCRIBED ON PAGE 11.—[SKETCHED FROM LIFE BY GAZETTE ARTISTS.

Let us approach in imagination over the crisp snow and peer in as Enoch Arden did when he looked upon his misery.

There is an old lady reading a Bible—a white-haired old lady, but when you look more narrowly you see that she is not so old. Gazing more intently the lines of sorrow in the face explain the white hair and the bowed form.

Still in imagination enter the barroom of the village tavern a mile distant. Young country sports are carousing. The applejack has made them talkative. One handsome, dissipated-looking fellow is leaning against the bar and is answering a question.

"I don't know what's become of Katy," he says as if it were a horse he was speaking of. "I think she's in New York."

Katy is the daughter of the white-haired woman in the farmhouse beyond in the valley. The handsome young man in the village tavern was Katy's sweetheart.

We know where Katy is. She is in the Strand, rolling a cigarette and waiting for her beer.

It was simply astounding the abnormal gifts of divination and observation possessed by Paul Prowler. The highly endowed Mr. Prowler, who was in real life, as already revealed, Samuel A. Mackeever, was so unusually prolific of pen that one is inclined to ask, how could he have had so much time in between all his duties of authorship to see so much of the night life of the great city; of its immoralities, foibles, frailties, depravities and oppressions.

In January, 1879, when he started the series, "Glimpses of Gotham," from which we have lifted the excerpt heading this chapter, Mr. Mackeever had the following features running weekly in the *Gazette*. He was the author, Colonel Lynx, of "City Characters"; of "Midnight Pictures" under the pen name of Old Rounder; and under the nom-de-plume of Marquis of Lorgnette, regularly contributed his theatrical notes. And at the same time under his own name he had a serial running, which was entitled, "The Phantom Friend; or, The Mystery of the Devil's Pool. A Romance of New York City."

Samuel A. Mackeever was only thirty-two years old when he died. He had been a contributor to various magazines during his early literary life and previous to his three years of service with the *National Police Gazette* had been an editor for the Frank Leslie publications. He was the author of the "History of the New York Tombs," and several other tomes, and in addition had collaborated on the play, "Nathan Hale," which is said to have made a marked hit at the Bowery Theatre during the Seventies.

But it was as the author of "Glimpses of Gotham" that he had his real vogue. These sketches of metropolitan life added thousands and thousands of readers to the *National Police Gazette,* and when published in book form by Richard K. Fox, shortly after the death of the author from consumption, the sale went close to a quarter of a million copies.

Scanning through articles that made up this series one gets the feeling that it was of the stuff fashioned to appeal to a gullible and ingenuous reading appetite. Its humors, situations and depictions are all so transparent as to be cause for wonder

PRETTY PETTICOAT POOL-PLAYERS.
THE PASSION WHICH HAS BEEN RECENTLY DEVELOPED AMONG NEW YORK DAMSELS—THEIR PROFICIENCY AS WITNESSED IN THE BACK-ROOM OF A BEER SALOON.

that they could be accepted as true pictures of the time and place in which they were written—New York City as the Seventies were melting into the Eighties. But they were accepted as true to life, particularly by those readers who looked on the great city from a distance. And under the overdramatic naïveté and the artless jocularity of vein in which he wrote there was a revealing and at times gracefully penned picture of the crude and captious times in which he lived and reported. In the *Gazette* obituary that marked his passing were the following lines:

In point of fact, Mr. Mackeever had a deep and thorough knowledge of the life 'mid which he lived. He was familiar with the sumptuousness of Fifth Avenue and the squalor of the Five Points, with the boudoir of the great actress and the cell of the condemned man. His intelligent eye photographed all phases of existence and stored his fertile brain with a wealth of knowledge which he poured forth to his numberless readers in a flood of literary gold, bright as his sunny nature, sterling as his own warm heart.

So let us roam about the streets and alleys of New York in the company of Paul Prowler. And at the same time let the sophisticated reader, ere he scoffs too openly and knowingly at these literary impressions, take a glimpse at the news-stands and turn the pages of some of our tabloids of the moment and go over the content of some of our "Untrue Story," "Gay Gangster," "Wild West," "Movieland Mirrors," "Lovelorn Lassies," "Aerial Antics," or others of similarly disguised titles and learn something of their considerable sale and imagine how a percentage of us will look to the student of our times fifty years hence. But, let us off with Paul Prowler on his rambles, and along with his simple friend Charley, who usually went with him and listened and learned about the undercurrents of a great city from the lips of the perspicacious Prowler. Let us take the steamdrawn elevated train and get off at Fourteenth Street Station, making a few stops and observations along the way ere we come to the Strand, where Katy was left rolling her cigarette and waiting for her beer.

"This is a remarkably lively avenue," comments Charley, "especially on Saturday night."

"This is one of the most remarkable avenues in every way that the city possesses," I [Prowler] answered. "It has a distinct character and an atmosphere peculiarly its own. Now on Seventh Avenue you perceive a characterless condition of things. It seems given over to stables, and piano factories. Third Avenue has a life of its own, and so have Second and Eighth—the former reveling in beer saloons and old-time Dutch families, and the latter in millinery stores, markets and retail emporiums of all descriptions. Here are the shopping avenues of the metropolis."

In this vicinity Prowler indicates several, what he refers to as "sub rosa private drinking parlors," which do a thriving business during the day, for "it is unpleasant to relate that no inconsiderable number of society dames and damsels have a great hankering for the exhilarating champagne, the bracing cocktail and the seductive cobbler, sometimes with sad results."

"What is the peculiarity of this thoroughfare," asked Charley, turning to watch two pretty girls who had passed us laughing up Sixth Avenue. "You have just begun to perceive it. From Fourteenth to Thirty-fifth

INSIDE SECRETS OF FASHIONABLE SHOPPING IN THE METROPOLIS—"IF YOU DON'T SEE WHAT YOU WANT, CALL FOR IT."—THE SPECTACLE PRESENTED BY A NOTED SOCIETY BELLE IN A "SPECIAL CUSTOMER'S," ROOM OF A WELL-KNOWN TRADE EMPORIUM, AS A CONSEQUENCE OF CALLING TOO OFTEN FOR THE INVISIBLE; NEW YORK CITY—SEE PAGE 2.

Street it is the rendezvous of the fair but frail, the sidewalk of the *lorettes,* the stamping-ground of the well-undressed unfortunates—"

"Why do you call it the stamping-ground?"

"Because it is the promenade of those who are looking for 'stamps.'"

At Twenty-third Street the avenue began to present a most animated appearance. The windows were all ablaze with gas-jets. An electric light (that newest of wonders) from a vast drygoods establishment threw a pale, bluish imitation of day upon everything, making the street lamps burn feebly and with a sickly glare.

The groups of young ladies became more numerous; here and there one walked alone; some had companions—I am speaking, it must be remembered, only of those who laughed loudly, who sometimes talked with

THE GENIUS OF ADVERTISING COULD NO FURTHER GO—AN ENTERPRISING PROPRIETRESS OF A BAGNIO PLACES A PHOTO-LITHOGRAPH IN HER WINDOW SETTING FORTH THE CHARMS OF THE INMATES; NEW YORK CITY.—SEE PAGE 3.

a very *broad* accent, and who, by some indescribable wearing of the seal-skin saque or the jaunty hat, gave the impression that they were of the half-world where dwell most of the heroines of your modern French dramatist and romancer.

Honest people there are on Sixth Avenue, Saturday and other nights. Husband and wife out shopping; a young girl hurrying home from her work, and hearing perhaps, at every corner something that makes the hectic flush on her pale cheeks deepen into the rose tint of shame.

And, besides, was I not there?

Between Twenty-third Street and the Aquarium (a well known resort at the Thirty-fourth Street corner) these "fast women" were to be found in great number, for, we are told, not only the avenue but all its side streets were "the abiding places of the Crimson Sisterhood. Some of the enterprising bagnios even had pictures of the charming inmates in their windows." Laughter is constant. Not the "joyous, ringing laughter of a healthy, innocent country girl at a frolic, but it has a hollow cadence; just as the trumpet suggests the color of scarlet, so does the sound seem to bring before you the painted cheeks and the sunken eyes of these revelers."

One, in particular, who stands under the gas-lamp of the street catches the observing eye of Mr. Prowler and he pauses to sketch the unconscious damsel.

A blonde who has been very handsome. Even now she is handsome, but you can readily perceive that her beauty is but a recollection, a shadow thrown behind that which is gone.

There are lines about the mouth and the eyes that glitter too far back beneath the tracing of black cosmetique. There is too much rouge upon the cheek and too much powder shading it.

Her dress is very rich, and the diamonds glitter as she turns. The poor shop girl, with insufficient clothing, with thin and broken shoes, and a faded shawl that does not keep her warm, turns to look at the luxurious coat with the fur about the throat, and the expensive hat with the trailing feather.

And mayhap, when she goes home, she takes the lamp and looking into the little mirror that hangs upon the wall of her cheerless room, says:
"I am as fair as she, and why shouldn't I dress as well?"

Who knows but what Mephistopheles whispers to her in her dreams that night?

And who knows but what, when we next visit Sixth Avenue, we may see her wearing furs and diamonds, the merriest of the merry.

You must remember that it was the jewel-case, after all, that gave Marguerite to Faust.

And then he related the moral tale of the downfall of one of these handsome working girls whom Heaven did not protect from an evil employer. After which we are given a glimpse of her haunts and those of her kind. And we follow, not unwillingly.

These gaily plumaged birds have places on Sixth Avenue where they congregate in flocks—places like the semi-circular bars of the Alhambra

TEMPTATIONS OF HANDSOME NEW YORK WORKING-GIRLS.

HOW THEY ARE CORRUPTED AND LED FROM THE PATH OF RIGHTEOUSNESS THROUGH THE MACHINATIONS OF SENSUAL AND
HEARTLESS EMPLOYERS—THE DOWNWARD CAREER AND USUAL SAD RESULT.

Theatre, London. In these bars fast young men of the town come to drink between the acts. Women from the Haymarket below, elegantly dressed women, the majority of whom have their own broughams and live in royal style at St. John's Wood, loiter about, but never enter the theatre.

In our Haymarket district there are theatres and dance halls also. One has been called the Haymarket Theatre out of very deference to the similarity of the localities. Its Thespian career was not an over-success-

NEW YORK'S DEADLY DIVES—SCENES AT THE HAYMARKET, FORMERLY THE OLD ARGYLE ROOMS, ON A GALA NIGHT—SHADOW DANCES IN WHICH THE SYRENS OF SIXTH AVENUE TRIP THE LIGHT FANTASTIC IN COMPANY WITH THE FAST BLOODS OF THE METROPOLIS—[SKETCHED BY OUR OWN ARTISTS. SEE PAGE 15.

ful one, and it is now the delight again of the fair promenaders who enjoy the shadow dance better than they do the farce, and who would rather take part in a free-and-easy quadrille than sit out the best play ever written.

Within three doors from Sixth Avenue, going to the west, you can find the Cremorne Gardens, built and conducted on the London plan, and giving now a mélange of acting and dancing. On a pretty little stage there are performed light sketches interlarded with songs by stout women in very low-necked dresses. On the floor below the "mazy" is continually going on.

It is a nicely waxed floor. The music is good and lively, and everything is very pleasant.

"You don't mean to say," my friend asks in a whisper, "that these well-bred, well-dressed women—"

"Hush! They may hear you. They are very sensitive."

How gracefully they dance, how thoroughly they melt into the music! There is more style here than you will find in a thousand "Germans." It is not strange that it should be so. To dance well—to captivate their partners—is part of the business which began with the flirtation two blocks away.

On another platform opposite the stage are round tables at which there are drinking and eating parties. The air is bluish with the smoke of cigarettes which men and women both indulge in. No loud talking or laughing. It is decorum itself.

In the street there is a line of cabs, their lamps lit. At three and four in the morning the thoroughfare will be filled with the rattling of the wheels over the cobblestones, and virtuous people, turning in their sleep, will say, in a dreamy way, "The Cremorne's out."

Farther to the west we have the Buckingham Palace, a dancing place exclusively. It is more elegant in its appointments, and the waxed floor seems to have a more resplendent sheen.

Benches run around the room. There is a card up announcing that a "schottische" is the next dance. As you stroll along you see familiar faces among the fringe of gentlemen.

I am present on business and, of course, it doesn't matter to me. The Rev. T. DeWitt Talmage and Paul Prowler, Esq., have a perfect right to go where they choose, although I do not believe that the Brooklyn sensationalist visited the Buckingham or any place like it. To judge from his sermons he must have frequented places like the "Sailor's Return" in Oliver Street, where Madden was killed.

You will find scores of solid business men at the Buckingham, and oceans of young fellows of nobby attire, such as you see at Jerome Park or a billiard match. There are a great many drummers taking country customers about. A young gentleman with an undisguisable agricultural overcoat and a general get-up which seems to suggest Pittsburgh, Pa., is talking to a pretty brunette in a black silk dress, over which a long gold chain trails like a yellow serpent.

The man from Pittsburgh (a place, according to the humorous Prowler, "that is so smoky that frequently a gentleman has to kiss a dozen ladies before he discovers by the taste which is his wife") and the brunette with a gold chain, who proves his downfall, appear frequently through the series, and serve not only to connect the articles, but as a moral warning of what happens to gentlemen from Pittsburgh who start out in iniquity on Sixth Avenue and then sink lower and lower as a result.

There isn't quite so much drinking in such places as the Buckingham and Cremorne, we are told. The women frequenting the halls are not naturally of a bibulous turn of mind, and when they are it is champagne they call for.

Charley and his guide, philosopher and friend, Paul Prowler, find the sights along Sixth Avenue so diversified that they are unable to exhaust its entertainments in one evening. That most risqué of terpsichorean activities, the French can-can, whose energetic twirling and high-kickings permitted such an intriguing glimpse of limb and lingerie, called for a word and a look or two. Besides, Mr. Mackeever found it advisable to save some of his material for the issue of the following week, when, after some light chatter they continue sailing along the animated roadway, and this is what they see:

Around in Thirty-first Street is a French café, much frequented by the daughters of *La Belle France* who belong to the midnight world of Sixth Avenue. There you go for dinner, for black coffee, for cognac, for absinthe. It is always crowded late at night both on the ground floor and in the supper-rooms above.

Every one is talking French; every one is drinking, for the latest diner has been satisfied long ago. This is still another phase of the Sixth Avenue street-life that we have been depicting, for it is so near it, and a very unique one. Formerly the café was on Sixth Avenue, between Thirteenth and Fourteenth Streets. That is years ago. It was during those days——or nights, rather—that frequently the door would be closed after business hours and genuine Mabille can-can given for the delectation of a few privileged visitors. The girls who danced were true children of the Boulevards and there is no doubt that their execution of the somewhat excessively lively dance was as artistic as can be witnessed at the score of gardens in Paris.

Occasionally they would get upon the tables and there would sometimes be sad havoc made of glassware, but there was always some one to pay for it, and the proprietress never cared.

There is nothing like this now in the new café. There are can-canners at every table, and at nearly every alternate table there are young men who would like to see it danced in all its pink-stockinged beauty; but morality has increased as money has vanished, and the matter is a little difficult. We take our erotic pleasures now in a subdued way, and instead of frequenting French cafés on Sixth Avenue to see the dance with closed doors, we buy tickets for a theatre where a Parisian play is all the rage and see that and a great deal worse in the company of our wives and daughters. All along the avenue there are free and easy beer saloons in full blast. The door swings open and you catch the chorus of a darky song, with the clatter

LADY'S DAY IN · NEW YORK.

THE ANNUAL OCCASION ON WHICH THE BELLES OF GOTHAM ASSERT THEIR EQUAL RIGHT WITH MAN TO THE ENJOYMENT OF· A RACKET.

of the bones and the thump of the tambourine asserting themselves through the plantation melody.

This hiring of minstrel bands by big beer saloons on the avenue is a regular feature. The players, who are genuine "darkies" from Sullivan and Thompson Streets, get all the beer they want, and are allowed to take up a collection at stated intervals.

It was from a Sixth Avenue beer saloon that Horace Weston graduated on to the concert platform and thence to the "Uncle Tom's Cabin" company which Jarrett & Palmer have in Europe.

At the plaza formed by the crossing of Broadway, which is brilliant with the lights of the Standard Theatre, we cross over and strike Sixth Avenue again opposite the Armory. In this block there are several more that are much frequented by the *pedestriennes* in question and on the Broadway block there is the place where Joe Coburn kept his free-and-easy, from which he issued to have the altercation with the police officers— a foolish artillery practice that jailed him for ten years.

Close by is the "House of All Nations." Here the male rounder could enjoy feminine society from all parts of the universe—girls not only from England, France, Germany, Spain, Italy and Russia, but even from China, Japan, Arabia and other parts of Asia and Africa, as well as South America, could be had for the asking and, of course, the paying. It is the boast of not a few young sports that, while they may not have traveled extensively, they have managed to see a lot of the world in one night.

No mention is made of there being an Indian maid among the inmates of the "House of All Nations," so it is to be presumed there was no keen desire on the part of the visitors to see America first.

Ere giving Charley a glimpse of the low dives in the vicinity of the waterfronts, a look into the resorts along the Bowery, and a peep in Bottle Alley of the Five Points environment, Paul Prowler first makes his companion acquainted with the wine-rooms attached to the variety theaters. His article is a strong tirade against this form of licentiousness, which he insists should be abolished.

"Jac" Aberle, who converted a church building on St. Mark's Place into the Tivoli Theatre, was inventor of the "wine-room curse." After commenting as to how Aberle had reconstructed the one-time house of religion into a "glaring monster of white paint with lime-light eyes" he congratulates the proprietor sarcastically on the diplomacy which has secured for him an immunity that was not enjoyed by the "Hail Columbia" Opera House on Greenwich Avenue.

The "Hail Columbia" must have raised something of a disturbance. The goings-on here resulted in its proprietor, Jake Berry, doing a stretch on "The Island." There was strong contention that Berry had been unjustly convicted, and his eventual release by the Governor was commended, even by Prowler himself. The "Hail Columbia," which later on became the Folly Theatre, before its transformation boasted not only a "wine-room," but what was known as a "French box," as well. We will let Prowler tell about his visit:

We advance to buy our tickets.

"Do you wish a French box?" says the gentlemanly clerk.

"What is the advantage of the box?" we reply.

"Oh," he answers, shrugging his shoulders, "it is so much more private. Some gentlemen object to being seen in our establishment, although I assure you that no legitimate theatre in the city could be more proper."

So we take a French box, and, once in it, soon discover its many advantages. We have a full view of the stage, for instance, where some vulgar revolving statues are being illuminated by lime-light, and are in close proximity to the wine-room, which occupies the front of the building over the lobby.

As we sit conning our programme there is a rush of skirts and the sound of laughter in the narrow passageway outside the box door, which is at length slyly opened, revealing two ballet girls in pink tights, one of whom says:

"You look lonely, birdie." And, saying this, they both incontinently enter and take possession of the two remaining chairs.

"Now if you are going to treat us," remarks the one who has the least on and the most to say, "you must be quick about it. We've only got ten minutes, because we go on in the next dance."

The easiest way out of such difficulties is to buy the drinks. So I call a waiter, saying at the same time, "What'll you have, girls?"

"Brandy mash," says one.

"I'll take a quarter instead," whispers the other.

In this way we get rid of them, and, fearing similar visitations from others, we get up and stroll out into the "wine-room." It is an apartment with a long bar, behind which pyramids of fancifully arranged tumblers glitter in the gaslight. There are many round tables scattered about the room, at which sit the ballet girls dressed just as they are upon the stage, talking to their various victims and drinking all that they can induce them to buy.

I will not repeat any of the conversation. It is low and vile where it is not flash and cheap. In every instance it has but one tendency, and that to induce the besotted fools toying with these painted hags, to prolong the acquaintanceship for a few fleeting hours after the performance.

In one corner is a senile, gray-haired old fool making love to a bestial blonde, while in another you will see the fast young man, just entering upon his metropolitan career of midnight dissipation. He has thrown a gold chain and locket about the greasy neck of his inamorata and the authoritative manner in which he orders another bottle of wine shows that he is well-known at the bar. And in a little while he will be well-known at the bar of justice, for he is just the kind of empty-headed youth for whom the surroundings have an undeniable charm. The popping of the

A NEW BLACKMAILING RACKET.
HOW UNSUSPECTING AND INNOCENT OLD GENTLEMEN ARE INGENIOUSLY AND PHOTOGRAPHICALLY COVERED WITH CONFUSION.

champagne corks blends with the music of the distant band, and there is a glamour of gaslight over all in which the faded creatures of the ballet loom up advantageously. Every minute while we are in the room, other ballet girls come rushing in like fantastically costumed wolves in search of prey. After the performance the drinking goes on until, as frequently occurs, it becomes an orgy. Then the women scream, police arrive, the lights are turned out.

While on the reminiscent tack, I may as well state that Robinson Hall in its palmy days was a variety establishment which, while not possessing any distinctive wine-room, afforded every facility for fools, young and old, to part with their money. You could have the most private tête-à-têtes

PARIS IN NEW YORK.—THE SHAMELESS ANTICS AND CONTORTIONS INDULGED IN BY THE LIVELY DAMSELS OF LA BELLE FRANCE, AT THE CERCLE DE L'ORPHEON MASQUERADE BALL AT THE ACADEMY OF MUSIC—FREE CHAMPAGNE AND OFFENBACHIAN MUSIC PUTS LIFE AND METTLE IN FEMININE HEELS, THAT GYRATE IN AIR WITH WONDERFUL DEXTERITY; NEW YORK CITY.—See Page 2.

[197]

with the ladies of the ballet, and entrée behind the scenes was always accorded to swells who could afford to pay for it. And, not infrequently, as the victim of some blackmailing racket they paid heavily.

Perhaps, after all, that was the real "lum tum" idea for the fast young man. Drinking with his girl in a more or less public bar was all very well, but not to be compared with the exquisite pleasure of having her sipping champagne as she sat upon his knee in the green room, from which he could catch glimpses of the gas man in his shirtsleeves pouring beer out for the fairy queen in spangles.

The sinful ways along Sixth Avenue could, of course, lead but in one direction—the Police Court. And so we are taken to the Jefferson Market hall of justice on a Sunday morning. And Charley went along. "No minions, bound in blue and brass, like a volume of cheap poems," escorted them, Prowler hastens to assure us. They went voluntarily. It was this way:

Having an hour which he did not know what to do with just before church time, Prowler happens in Sixth Avenue where by chance he runs into Charley. Charley was for putting in the morning playing some billiards, but Prowler promises him a more interesting hour and so we find them in the Jefferson Market court looking on while the magistrate deals with hope's outcasts in the shape of vagrants, prostitutes, and the drunk and disorderly. It makes a curious scene, we are told.

Especially on the Sabbath morning, when the church-bells are ringing outside, gayly dressed Sunday-school scholars are tripping along, and the more serene and sedate fathers and mothers are walking with that ill-concealed expression of content which comes from a knowledge that they are in the path of duty and their best clothes.

And then there appears before the bar one who is recognized with dramatic suddenness by both Prowler and his companion as the gentleman from Pittsburgh whom we had seen fall into the wiles of the brunette with the gold chain. "Pittsburgh," as this character was known, had betrayed the confidence of his employer and was forced to go back into a dungeon cell in default of bail to the amount of $5,000.

Charley thereupon decided to go with Prowler, being sure, after seeing what he had seen, that church was just the place for him. And furthermore, he intimated with no little firmness that it was his intention not to play any more the alluring game of billiards on Sundays.

Who says the *Police Gazette* was not a moral journal?

UP HILL'S AND DOWN THE ROAD TO McGLORY'S

With Stops at the Bal Mabille, the Bowery Bastile and Other Nice Places

"AFTER the lamplighter had gone his rounds," expounds the erudite Paul Prowler to his ingenuous friend Charley, "seeing the jungles of a great city has always been a favorite amusement with those sportsmen who combine a keen desire to hunt the elephant and yet have a natural disinclination to do their gunning too far away from the comforts of home. There are other hunting grounds beside those that make up the wilds of Sixth Avenue."

Prowler thereupon takes Charley on a pilgrimage further downtown. "Hunting the elephant" was the common phrase for slumming during the late Seventies and early Eighties and the quest of the metropolitan elephant was frequently more dangerous than the stalking of the pachydermatous mammal in the wilds of Africa.

"We will begin with Harry Hill's place, or 'Arry 'Ill's, as he is called by his cockney friends," says Prowler, "for it is the best of the worst places. And I mean exactly what my words are saying. For one thing, your pocketbook is perfectly safe here, even rolling the lush [rifling the pockets of a drunk] being here strictly forbidden, which is more than I can say for some of the resorts to which I am about to lead you. It is 'Arry's boast that no one has ever been robbed or killed in his place, which, strange but true, seems to be a fact. No matter how inviting the opportunity, any attempt on the part of a fair patron to lift the watch or bankroll of a male companion meant, if caught in the act (and ' 'Arry 'ad a h'eagle h'eye'), the guilty one was barred from ever showing her face in Hill's again."

Prowler apparently had a sincere liking for the proprietor of the Hill rendezvous, which is not surprising, for his was a very tolerable infamy. Visitors from the four quarters of the globe who chanced to come to New York usually made it a point to find their way through the doors of this irregular cluster of two-story buildings at Houston and Crosby Streets, that had been combined into the theater and house of entertainment of which Harry Hill was the dominant proprietor. One historian refers to Harry Hill as a dive keeper, something that will be resented

NEW YORK'S GAS-LIT LIFE—MIDNIGHT PICTURES OF METROPOLITAN SIGHTS, SCENES AND CHARACTERS—INCIDENTS AND ACCIDENTS OF A NIGHT AT HARRY HILL'S.—[SKETCHED FROM LIFE BY GAZETTE ARTISTS.—SEE PAGE 15.

by those who have an unconfused memory of the place he operated. Even the Rev.
T. DeWitt Talmage, when he crossed the bridge to gather sensational sermon enlightenment, through a slumming tour, for the Brooklyn Tabernacle churchgoers,
conceded that the Hill resort was the most orderly he had visited.

If a "dive," to follow the dictionary definition, is a place where "drunkards
and harlots consort," then Hill's was not precisely referred to. Its feminine clien-
tèle, to be sure, was made up of what was known as the *demi-monde*. But the
pleasure-seeking male was required to treat them as ladies, even if they weren't.
Prowler finds fault with a contemporary print which pictures a dancing scene here
in which a man is shown puffing on a cigar the while some terpsichorean measure
is being stepped. Paul points to a sign on the wall which reads: "Gentlemen will
not smoke while dancing." And the wall signs here exacted obedience, or the proprietor saw that they did. Drunkenness, loud conversation, or disorderly conduct
is something not tolerated here. Let Prowler show you what the place was like,
and with the assurance of one who was once in the Hill employ in its heyday, that
this is a truer pen picture than some of the highly colored ones that have been given
from time to time.

We buy our tickets—twenty-five cents apiece, ladies free—at a little
window downstairs and pass upward to where the laughter and applause
proclaim that an amusing song or farcical "nigger" sketch is in progress,
or the Punch and Judy box may be providing amusement. The room is
ablaze with light and heavy with smoke. The stage is occupied by a
young lady in a wig the color of "yellow-jack molasses candy," and a pair
of pink tights. Her cheeks are bright with excitement and paint, while
each energetic gesture accompanying the topical song she is singing displays her bosom lavishly.

When the song is finished there is a chance to look about. There
is a gallery overhead and a wine-room to one side. There is a long lunch-
counter well stocked with food of an excellent quality. You can also get
piping-hot coffee and tea. Singularly enough, Harry Hill's is more discussed and made much of in the country than anywhere else. There is
hardly a young man who comes up to "York" but takes in Hill's, just as sure
as he gets taken in later by some siren on the Bowery. Two such young
grangers sit at the table with Charley and I, and will have an interesting
experience to tell back in Punkton or Rushville of two young ladies in
seal-skin saques who sidle down beside them like a couple of birds going
to roost.

"Won't you buy me a drink, dear?" says one.

"You'll treat me, pet, won't you?" remarks the other, and without waiting to discuss the matter further the beautiful creature waves one of the waiter girls, who are flitting about like bees, to the table. Of course, the young men are equal to the occasion, even to standing a treat for the plump little woman who brings on the beverages. They get very sociable with the two young ladies, who live in furnished rooms on Crosby Street, and at 2:30 A.M. the four depart in a rather tipsy but orderly condition.

When the stage performance is not in progress there is an open space at the head of the stairs where the dancing is done. The orchestra strikes up and the quadrille begins. These girls dance very nicely (decorously, we might say, if the propriety of this pleasure is conceded), gliding through the figures with genuine grace. "No lovers wanted!" is the suggestion from one of the terse wall signs.

Suddenly there is a crash and a table is upset. One man has struck another in a quarrel about a girl. In any other place there would be quite a little scrimmage. Glasses would be thrown about and the gathering would be in a panic. But not at Harry Hill's. That ubiquitous gentleman, who has the frame of a pugilist in constant training and a grasp of iron, has already seized the man at fault and conducted him to the stairs, which he finds to his advantage to descend. The dancers hardly pause and the orchestra goes on merrily.

Nothing very out of the ordinary here, you will say. And yet no contemporary resort enjoyed the prestige or success of Harry Hill's. Its regular patrons included notables from every walk of life, of whom mention might be made of the son and namesake of James Gordon Bennett, Thomas A. Edison, who had the assistance of the proprietor in making "Harry Hill's Electric Light Hall" one of the first public places to install this newly perfected method of illumination. Richard K. Fox and P. T. Barnum, who was then the landlord of the property, dined there quite regularly. Oscar Wilde (who was the target of many *Gazette* darts) and others of name and degree who visited the city came often to the Hill place. And this condition of affairs existed even when the center of New York's night life had started to shift to Sixth Avenue and the latter district offered showier attractions to those seeking a lively evening.

Possibly the comeliness of the sixteen carefully picked waiter maids was part of the attraction. Also, the entertainment furnished here was somewhat superior to that provided in opposition houses of call. Billy Scanlon is said to have charmed audiences here with his sweet voice when little more than a boy; Maggie Cline and other talented entertainers are understood to have been given an early start by Hill. Quite possibly, the factor that had so much to do with bringing so many through the portals which were ornamented by a sign-board telling the world of—

Punches and juleps, cobblers and smashes,
To make the tongue waggle with wit's merry flashes—

was that here one was likely to get an earful of the very latest in the way of sporting chatter. For a quarter of a century, until that distinction had been usurped by

TOO, TOO, UTTERLY UTTER!

REMARKABLE EFFECT OF THE APPEARANCE OF OSCAR WILDE, THE APOSTLE OF ÆSTHETICISM, ON THE STREETS OF 'NEW YORK CITY.

the offices in the new *Police Gazette* building, here was the sporting center of the United States. All the noted men of the ring, Jem Mace, Joe Goss, Joe Wormald, came first to Hill's. Every important match was made here, and Harry Hill usually officiated, no matter where a contest was settled on this side of the ocean, and often, if the affair was of commanding importance, he traveled abroad. John L. Sullivan was brought here by William Muldoon to make his New York début in the ring in Hill's place and made himself so nationally famous by knocking out Steve Taylor in two rounds that less than one year after this feat the Boston Strong Boy was privileged to beat Paddy Ryan for the heavyweight fistic championship of America. Herbert Slade, the Maori, boxed here and married one of Hill's sweet-

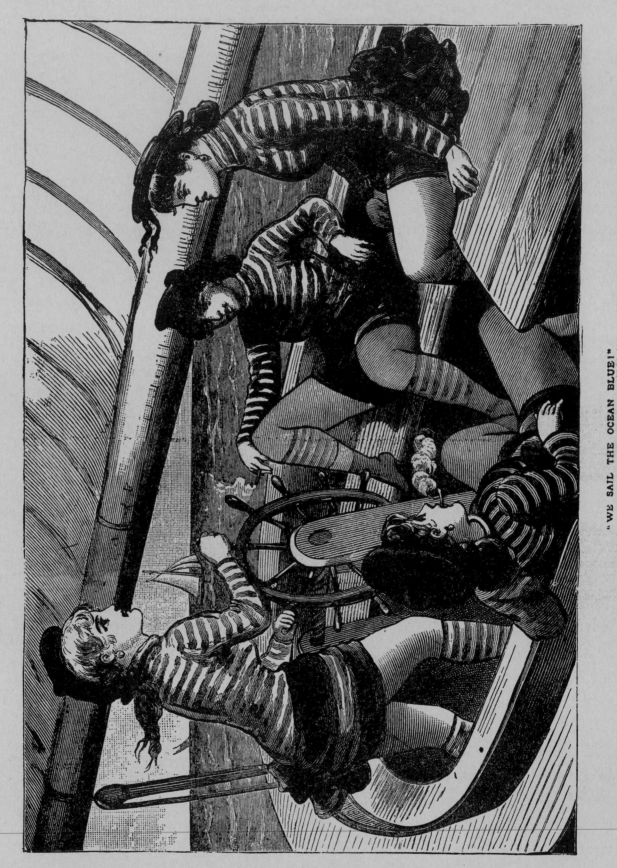

"WE SAIL THE OCEAN BLUE!"

A PARTY OF NAUTICAL DAMSELS FORM A YACHT CLUB AND TAKE AN EXPERIMENTAL SAIL OFF SANDY HOOK.

faced waitresses, Josephine. Jack Dempsey, the Nonpareil, was among the many who exhibited his skill of fist on the Hill stage; and William Muldoon, then a strikingly handsome young athlete, wrestled all comers.

The business integrity of Harry Hill had considerable to do with the popularity of his house. He came, we learn, from what was known as English "horse people," and was brought to this country by a wealthy Briton named Woolsey, of whose stables he had charge. Early in the Sixties he opened for business on the southeast corner of Houston and Crosby Streets. A small stable was part of his establishment and accounted for a sign over the Crosby Street entrance that advised of accommodation "for man and beast," which promise provided not a little amusement.

There was one evening in Hill's when his boast, that no one had ever met death in his quarters, came close to being an idle claim, 'Arry himself having a narrow squeak. Billy Edwards, a very well-known pugilist, became involved in some trouble with an underworld coterie from further uptown and they followed Edwards into Hill's with murderous intent. Harry gave them successful battle, though being so badly cut about the eyes that he came close to losing his sight. There was a woman mixed up in the trouble, none other than Maggie Jourdan, whose name came into much prominence for the part she played in effecting the successful Tombs escape, in 1873, of her lover, William J. Sharkey, ward politician, sporting man and murderer.

Harry Hill's went out of existence in 1886, presumably falling in the sweep of Mayor Hewitt's reform wave, though there is believed to be another side to the story, which has to do with 'Arry's refusal to submit to a too heavy shake-down burden. At the time of the Prowler visit he was rated a man of considerable wealth, with a fine country place near Flushing, L. I., and a reputation that no deserving individual, in genuine distress, ever went to him in vain.

"We will go a bit lower in our journey through the strata of New York night life," Prowler promised Charley the following evening, "and we won't have far to go. Only around the corner into Bleecker Street near Broadway, where 'The' Allen holds forth. But first, as it is still a little early for the night to be really at its height there, we will walk along Houston Street and I will tell you a little of its interesting history."

It would seem that Hill had, still had in fact, quite a number of interesting neighbors. For twenty years it had been a nest of hotel, drinking places, gaming palaces and dens, oyster saloons, dance halls, policy shops, brothels and other places of a sporting character and worse. On the same side with Hill's, across Crosby Street, in the short block extending to Broadway, where Reddy the Blacksmith, Matt Grace and a number of others had held open house, so many persons had met violent death in one way or another that this small walk had come to be known as "Murderers' Row," though possibly not quite as deadly as "Murderers' Alley," one-time Donovan's Lane, in the Five Points of the late Thirties. "Paugene" Mc-Laughlin was one of those shot to death in the "Row."

A little further down the street, toward the Bowery, was a Negro dwelling which, on account of the peculiar shape of the building and for other reasons, was known as the "Coffin House." Across the way on Houston Street for the several blocks leading from Broadway you could find one place after another where any type of excitement desired could be provided, including the fancy resort of which Madame Louise was the head.

And right in the midst of it all, almost across the way from Hill's was the somber convent of the Sisters of Mercy. From the walk the passers-by, including the "sisters of sin" and her brethren, could see the beautifully kept lawn where gray-and white-robed nuns paraded, intoning their prayers and oblivious of the wickedness without. Fixed to the gate was a box for the donations of the charitably inclined, and the investments in salvation were most generous.

But let us not linger, advises Prowler: "The" Allen's awaits us. The proprietor has been prominently before the New York public for more than thirty years at this time, though his face and figure do not hint as much. He has stood up well under the strain for one who has been close to death on a number of occasions and has been indicted for manslaughter and a number of other offenses, and who has figured in numerous precarious political schemes and enterprises, to say nothing of brawls and eye-gouging frays. He is still a well-favored man in appearance, lithe and gracefully molded as to figure and with features of an aquiline regularity. He must have been a really handsome man in his prime, and the tales of his escapades as a heartbreaker are easily acceptable. Were it not for a cruel gleam in his eye, it would be hard to believe that here is one of the most desperate and notorious characters in all Gotham. The cigar that invariably glows from between his teeth is a warning signal as to his savage nature to those who know "The" Allen well. The man, when aroused, would think nothing of jamming the lighted cigar point into your face as the first move of conflict. And once you were downed in a fight in Allen's he would think nothing of using the heel of his shoe on your face in a positively fiendish manner. This particular Allen, who had several brothers who were about on a par with him as undesirable citizens, first became an object of police attention in 1865 as the proprietor of the St. Cloud Hotel, at Prince and Mercer Streets, a hang-out for the criminal classes.

The "Bal Mabille," or Jardin Mabille, as it is now most generally referred to, and incorrectly so, was a music hall and ballroom after a fashion. It was then a few doors from the imposing Bleecker Street Bank. Originally a man named Hughes, whose time and capital had been frequently devoted to such abodes of festivity, turned the place into a rowdy saloon, but the Hughes administration, and that of his successor, a man by the name of Flynn, were not for long. Thus we learn from Prowler. Also:

It was a bare and unprepossessing structure when Allen took it in hand. He had it frescoed, architecturally beautified, filled with drinking counters and the ordinary paraphernalia of the concert hall. Upstairs free-and-easy singers discoursed popular or unpopular melodies as suited the taste or fancy. Downstairs a limited orchestra furnished dancing music, to which the youths and maidens in attendance footed it flatly; and in all possible places on both floors waiters with abridged aprons and spacious trays prevailed. Then there are special nights of festivity announced as Bal Mabille "soirée" occasions on which there are gaudy orders of dancing and ampler inducements of saltatorial exercise. This evening happens to be one of them. Young men in ulsters of various shades are ambling in at this orthodox hour, and women, with and without escort, are also strolling in; painted, bedizened creatures [the ladies(?), of course. We will get to the other kind later.]

The clinking of glasses keeps up a fitful accompaniment to the vocalization of the singers in the hall above, while down in the basement the dancers are rotating in the mazy. The lascivious waltz has become tame and the orchestra, catching the infection of the hour, strikes up the merry measures of Offenbach's can-can music. Lively feet keep time to the witching melody in all its lewd suggestiveness and dance themselves into an abandon till limbs of all shapes and sizes are elevated in dangerous proximity to male physiognomy.

This dreadful can-can dance! What made its gyrations, which would now be regarded as merely an acrobatic interpretation of music, something so extremely naughty? Well, it seems that the dancers wore pink tights beneath their lingerie and when they started flinging their limbs about glimpses would be had of these fleshings even above the knee at times. Was this not devilish?

Suddenly the doors were forced open and a clatter of footsteps broke in on the revels of the night. Captain Byrnes was on hand, and behind

NEW YORK'S DEADLY DIVES—THE TERPSICHOREAN ANTICS AND REVELRIES THAT FIND EXPRESSION IN THE HEELS OF THE HIGH-KICKING FAIR ONE'S ON A "SOIREE" NIGHT AT "THE" ALLEN'S BAL MABILLE—CAN-CAN DANCERS THAT RIVAL THE JARDIN MABILLE IN LEWDNESS AND INDECENCY. [Sketched by our own Artists.—See Page 15.

him drawn up across the entire length of the building, was a double file of the Fifteenth Precinct men. At once there arose a hubbub, in which women screamed and cried, young men uttered strong expressions and indulged in doleful witticisms, and anxious glances were cast in every direction for means of egress. But the captain had taken his precautions carefully and every exit was guarded. Theodore Allen was behind the bar, and he was notified to close the bar and regard himself under arrest. Then the painful part of the proceedings began.

The girls, several score in number, were handed out and placed in charge of the police to be taken off in relays to the station-house. Many of them brazened it out and laughed and joked as they went along, but there were some, too, who would be missed through the night from houses where their whereabouts were never guessed. There were not a few of them who seemed much affected and who sobbed as though their hearts would break as they were led through throngs of curious onlookers. By this time word of the raid had spread and a crowd was recruited from the district that skirted the line of march to the station-house. The males went off by the dozen, every pair linked with a policeman, and the whole of them aggregating several hundred in number.

CAPTAIN BYRNES SETS THE POLICE DRAG-NET, AND MAKES A HAUL OF FRISKY CITIZENS AND GAY DAMSELS AT "THE" ALLEN'S BLEECKER STREET BAL MABILLE ON SATURDAY NIGHT, JANUARY 17.—SEE PAGE 3.

Few of the men were of the ruffian type. Mainly, it was the young man released from his place in the counting-house or store counter that was best represented. And they were an aggrieved multitude. One young man with a white necktie was going to a ball and had just dropped in to get a shave. When it was pointed out to him that there were no lady barbers in Allen's and that his face was without whiskers, he remembered that he was wearing shoes and he wanted to get them shined. Even though a bootblack-stand did business on the premises, unhappily his plea was not entertained by the hard-hearted magistrate, nor was that of those who had just peeped in to see what all the disturbance was about. They were all marched off with the godly and naughty alike in pairs under police watch and ward.

The resources of the Mercer Street Station-house were tested to supply accommodations, but by a strict economy of space most of them were tucked away. Their registration on the blotter caused another scene, the uninitiated being at a loss to conceal their identity and the mendacious being quite ready with pseudonyms for the emergency. If there was one thing more marked than another about the list, it was the array of distinguished names it bore. Samuel J. Tilden was many times multiplied among the visitors, and of Charles McLeans there was quite an abundance. Beside Rutherford B. Hayes and Roscoe Conkling were there. All these distin-

THE NATIONAL POLICE GAZETTE'S SPORTING GALLERY.
OWNEY GEOGHEGAN, THE NOTED NEW YORK PUGILIST, POLITICIAN AND SALOON KEEPER.—SEE PAGE 10 FOR HISTORY OF HIS LIFE.

guished individuals, and a host of Smiths and Joneses who were nominally and physically quite ordinary, shared common cells and passed the night bewailing their hard luck.

A note should be added to the effect that Prowler and Charley did not round out their experience with a night in durance vile. It is hinted that the *Gazette* was responsible to some extent for the police activity on this particular night. It might also be worthy of note that "The" Allen was doing business full blast a night or two later and for many nights thereafter. Like many such police activities, it was probably only a gesture.

The following evening Owney Geogheghan's "Bastile on the Bowery," or, the Old House at Home, its actual name, was favored by the presence of Prowler and Charley, and after a short stay the latter intimated that the presence of the police was more desirable here than at Allen's. Prowler admitted that Geogheghan's had a bad name and was deserving of it. He added some facts about Owney's trouble with the police and other data concerning this rude character.

Captain Foley, before his dismissal from the police force, had Geogheghan in hot water occasionally. After Foley had been forced to step down his departure was celebrated by a unique wake here. A stuffed figure made up to represent the ex-police captain was placed in a coffin and the fancy male and female patrons of the place danced around the coffin in high glee for a number of nights. Several attempts have been made to kill Owney, but as he never drinks the liquor he or any one else sells, he is always on the alert, and while he has figured in numerous rough-and-tumbles and shooting scrapes his political strength has always enabled him to worm out of serious trouble up until now.

Geogheghan is a stocky, muscular individual standing five and one-half feet in height and his visage reflects his ruggedly callous disposition. He is given quite a prize ring reputation and at one time had challenged the world at 138 pounds and also laid claim to the middleweight championship. We are regaled with bits of his fistic career by way of revealing his cruel and cunning nature. One of his early fist battles after his arrival from Ireland, in 1849, had been fought in Kit Burns' place on Water Street. It was a desperate conflict with the buckskins with Ed Tuohey, who against many shining champions of the ring had proved that he was the "honeycomb." The stakes were only $75. a side, and the match was fought with only the seconds and a few others present. Geogheghan's hard-hitting and endurance won and gave him such a reputation that he was matched in May, 1863, for an important battle with Con Orem, the Pacific Slope Champion. It was fought at a place named Cheese Creek, Middlesex County, New Jersey, before a hard-looking gang, of which "The" Allen appeared to be the ringleader for the Orem supporters. Each side was armed with pitchforks, clubs and revolvers, but no trouble was generated after Harry Hill, who had conveyed a select party to the fighting ground, had made a plea for a square, stand-up bout with no interference or favors. Owney emerged the victor on a claim of foul after twenty-three minutes of fighting, though he should have been disqualified not less than a half-dozen times for

NEW YORK'S DEADLY DIVES—A BOWERY INFERNO—OWNEY GEOGHEGAN'S "HURDY-GURDY," WHERE THIEVES, PROSTITUTES AND BLACKLEGS HOLD NIGHTLY REVEL—UNADULTERATED DEVILTRY UNCHECKED BY THE POLICE—[SKETCHED BY OUR OWN ARTISTS.—SEE PAGE 15.

deliberately dropping to the turf. He also spat in his opponent's face and his conduct in general was not that of a good sport and a gentleman.

In a sparring match with an opponent known as the "Gas House Giant" the Geogheghan reputation as a knockout hitter was found to have been enhanced by the help of a horseshoe concealed in one of his gloves. The broadcast of some of

AMAZONIAN PRIZE FIGHTERS.

these truths in the *Police Gazette* had annoyed Owney to such an extent that he called at the *Gazette* offices to do bodily harm on the person of the publisher, and either slipped or was tossed down a full flight of stairs. Anyway, it is a known fact that, in a very dazed condition, he was led away from the Fox building by a couple of policemen and that he did not return again.

Taking various things into consideration, Owney Geogheghan was not nearly as tough as his reputation, but this does not apply to various places of business he operated from time to time. He had a sporting house at Third Avenue and Twenty-second Street, and was also for a time on Second Avenue, but the Bastile at 105 Bowery was the most celebrated of his places, until the Excise Commission revoked his license and his defiance resulted in his arrest and a thirty-day residence on Blackwell's Island. On his release he became ill and went to Hot Springs, Arkansas, where his unsavory career came to an end on January 29, 1885. He died quite well-to-do.

His Old House at Home occupied two floors and consisted of two long concert-halls eighty feet by forty. Flashy pictures of prize fighters and gaudy decorations abounded in profusion. Part of the area on the first floor was taken up with chairs and tables for the convenience of the cheap sporting and underworld element, whose main entertainment, when not drinking and dancing, was provided mainly by second-rate pugilists who battered themselves about nightly in a ring which had been raised on a platform at one end of the room. If the bruisers did not go about their efforts to the satisfaction of the crowd, their yells would bring

BILLY McGLORY,
THE NOTED NEW YORK SPORTING MAN.
(Photo by John Wood.)

on the scene an assistant with a gun in his hand, and he would take aim at the offending pugilist, and then "Bang!" he would let him have it. To be sure, the gun was only loaded with blank cartridges, but you should have heard the yelp when the discharge found the victim's bare pelt.

Female pugilists also mussed each other up and occasionally tested their man-handling abilities against male bruisers, but they were never "given the gun."

Easily the most depraved of all these licensed iniquities in the guise of concert halls, however, was the resort to which Paul Prowler led Charley on the following night, and which was conducted by Billy McGlory at No. 158 Hester Street, and known as Armory Hall. For sheer debasement and depths of degeneracy there was nothing lower than this, Prowler assures us, only excepting the under-cover dives of a few of the Bowery cellars and those which existed in the dark of some of the side streets or the shadows of the water-front.

It is eight or nine years since Kit Burns of Water Street rat-pit noto-riety [Prowler wrote this in January, 1880] and Johnny Allen, of the same locality, were running a neck-and-neck race for the unsavory distinc-tion of being the "wickedest man in New York." Both of these worthies were geniuses in their way, and plumed themselves on their ability to con-dense more deviltry into one day of their lives than ten ordinary sinners could manage in a lifetime. They stood alone in their unenviable posi-tions, with none hardened enough to contest their right to the insignia of infamy. "Every dog must have his day," runs the old proverb, and Kit and Johnny had theirs until they met their fate at last at the hands of a little band of moral crusaders, who assailed them fore and aft with a broadside of psalms, prayers and exhortations that finally attracted so much attention that their establishments were in time knocked into a worse condition than the traditional "cocked hat." Neither of them survived the destruction of their dives for long. Stripped of their power for evil, they lost their grip on this world and "Old Nick" foreclosed his long-due mortgage and sent them down below. Having thus taken care of his own, he set about securing some one who would maintain with equal credit the dignity of his earthly kingdom, and with that rare judgment which distinguishes his satanic majesty in every particular, he selected Billy McGlory.

Billy McGlory, we are told, was a spawn of the Five Points and had been a member and captain of the Forty Thieves and other desperate gangs. For all the grossness of his nature and the foulness to which he pandered, he had a penchant for subdued clothing and when dressed in his best black suit unconsciously took on a smug and sanctimonious appearance, which annoyed him considerably, as he rather gloried in the ignoble homage he commanded. His establishment was just what he aspired to. A resort for the lowest of pickpockets, street-women, thugs, and criminals and gangsters of every variety. A place of repulsive degeneracy rather than a gilded den of vice.

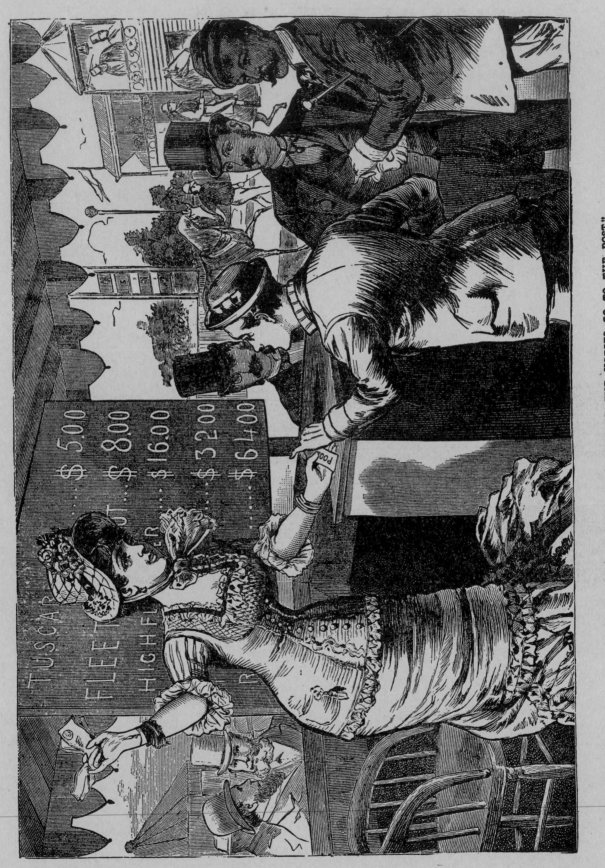

"PUT UP YOUR MONEY, GENTS, BEFORE THE HORSES GO TO THE POST."

THE POOL-SELLING MANIA (MIXED WITH CHAMPAGNE) TAKES POSSESSION OF A FAIR DISCIPLE OF PLEASURE, AND CAUSES HER TO MOUNT AN
AUCTION POOL-BOX AND SELL CHANCES ON A RACE: CONEY ISLAND.

SINS OF NEW YORK

Armory Hall was pitched in the center of a mean cluster of frowzy tenements that were overrun with thieves, prostitutes and similar underworld scum. The very entrance to his place was repelling, the doorway and passage being unlighted and having an unhealthy suggestion generally. There was something mean and cheap about the barroom and hall beyond. The plain chairs and tables had a greasy, fetid look, and the balcony which ran along the sides of the hall and which had been partitioned into small compartments was cut off by musty curtains. Only three pieces, piano, cornet and violin, made up the orchestra. A choice gang of cutthroats and manhandlers were stationed about to keep the ugly denizens in restraint, and the waiter girls who served the drinks were reinforced by a number of simpering males who were painted to resemble women and togged up in feminine raiment, and who in falsetto voices exchanged disgusting badinage among themselves and with the patrons.

This type of pervert was then something new, or at least did not bring its disgusting brand to attention. The "queers," as these abnormals among the male and the female are now known, have come to light of late as a reality that cannot be altogether ignored, now that books and plays have been written around them, but it remained for Billy McGlory first to advertise such moral deformity.

However, there was nothing squeamish about the McGlory stock-in-trade. Here is no pretense at modesty in either the singing or the dancing. As for the happenings in the curtained compartments, there is no limit to what may take place within these confines, only that the male occupant shall interrupt his diversions sufficiently long enough to put in his order for refreshments, and that the time between drinks shall be short. A visit to one of these boxes means that you will be without company for no more than the wink of an eye. Poor Charley was hardly seated before he and his guide and philosopher, Paul Prowler, were joined by no less than six bold brunette dames, who seated themselves as well as possible on their respective laps. Charley and Prowler may have preferred blondes, but no such blondes as these. They pleaded to have coins placed in their stockings. Not to make themselves overly conspicuous the investigating pair invested to the extent of one quarter to each lady, and while these ready-made banks had their attraction and the garter display was seductive, Paul and Charley excused themselves as quickly as possible, though the former cynically advised his modest young companion that he would be surprised at what those ladies would do for a dollar. But the blushing Charley said he wouldn't.

Prowler pointed out any number of the male and female company who had prison records and looked the parts. It was plain to see that aside from its underworld assemblage the visitors were out-of-town sightseers or seafaring men. They would be fortunate if they escaped being drugged or robbed, or both. Victims of a night at McGlory's were even said to have been left stripped naked in the very gutter, which may have been exaggerated reports, Prowler conceded, though he would put nothing past the McGlory place.

Shortly after midnight Prowler intimated that he smelled some fighting and blood-letting brewing and gave his opinion that it was high time to depart. Charley admitted, fervidly, that he had had enough for one night.

A few years later on, McGlory's became a "respectable tough joint." That is to say, it was made safe for the visiting sensation hunter. The orchestra was enlarged, and became known as Gaetano's Band Milita, and the resort became something of a show place for those who desired to have a look in on the underworld. And they were welcome, since they were usually good spenders and blew generously to champagne, or what was sold here as such. It became something of a hangout for many well-known newspaper men who were in search of what they called color, which was a good enough name for what they found. Billy was discovered to be something of a wit and his name often appeared in print in connection with various amusing stories.

One that was quite popular had to do with a relative of his, Barney Williams, who enjoyed some fame as an actor and who was renowned for his extensive wardrobe. The thespian died rather suddenly and when McGlory, who was his heir, was asked how he had fared, he replied:

"The only things he left to me that fit are his watch and his handkerchiefs."

In those "respectable" days, one of the attractions was a hard-visaged announcer know as "Poison Face," a blasé personage of grotesque humor and an English accent which carried his voice in a sing-song monotone, no matter the occasion or the interruptions. One evening his lugubrious voice announced:

"Miss Fanny Montmorency will now sing 'Love Among the Roses.'"

"Miss Fanny Montmorency is a ——" mocked a balcony occupant, who minced no word in telling just what he thought Miss Fanny Montmorency was, which was certainly no lady.

"Nevertheless," continued "Poison Face" without a glance upward, nor a particle of change in his monotonous drawl, "Miss Fanny Montmorency will now sing 'Love Among the Roses.'"

And she did.

VERACITIES FROM VICE'S VARIETIES

The Big Bandit and Yegg Men and Racketeer Stars of the Seventies

ONE did not have to be an especially heinous malefactor to be accorded a paragraph in the *Police Gazette* department known as "Vice's Varieties," and which, the subheading informed, was "An Assorted List of Evil Deeds and Evil Doers Collected by *Gazette* Correspondents in all Quarters." All one had to do was to get caught at what one should not have been doing and dishonorable mention was assured. But, unless you were a sporting character of prominence or a barber or barkeeper of parts, to be accorded picture space you had to be good—that is in a nefarious sense. Before going into any fairly extended mention of those who enjoyed real prestige in Mr. Fox's Hall of Ill-Fame, let us look rather thoroughly through just one copy of Mr. Fox's weekly and see what we shall see.

On the front page of the issue of January 25, 1879, for example, the lone illustration gives us a peep behind the scenes of the theater. What we glimpse of the stage from the wings leads to the belief that a violent drama is in performance, though accompanying details prove otherwise. A very wicked-looking customer with a knife of which the blade is fully a foot long, is apparently in the act of doing some deadly perforating of the person of a lady whom he has grasped by the throat. The foreground of the picture displays a female in tights and good health who is being attended by her waiting-maid the while she puts on the finishing touches of her make-up with which to "dazzle the anxiously expectant audience." It would seem that in those days even the ladies of the stage did their "making up" in private rather than public. The lady, we learn, is a belle of the burlesque stage. On page two there are twenty or so lines in explanation of the picture, which apprises us that we have not altogether misunderstood what the artist had intended to convey.

"Slight as the incident appears," we read, "it illustrates a by no means unimportant matter to the petted favorite of the footlights. No matter how elaborate her make-up and how much the care and taste bestowed upon it in the dressing-

WHEN WINE IS IN, WIT IS OUT.—A PURSE-HEAVY CITIZEN, OUT FOR A NIGHT'S FROLIC, WHEELS A DIZZY DISCIPLE OF TERPSICHORE THROUGH THE STREETS ON A WAGER.—SEE PAGE 2.

room by her attendant maid, she takes advantage of a waiting moment to indulge in a characteristic female 'postscript' by adding a few finishing touches before she bursts [we consider this word ill-chosen in conjunction with the generous pulchritude depicted] upon the expectant gaze of the audience she hopes to captivate, radiant with smiles and gorgeous in apparel."

[221]

Column one of the second page is taken up with answers to "Correspondents." The adjoining column and one-half is given over to editorial comment. The first article holds forth for more refined hangings, since a repetition of a bungling spectacle that had happened over in Camden, N. J., gives food for "crack-brained philanthropists to agitate against capital punishment." The editorial which follows also has to do with hanging and is the subject of illustration on another page and of a detailed story also. Then comes an editorial on the "murder record for 1878." The annual homicidal report is deplored, since it reveals that there have been 1,324 such killings, and no less than twenty-nine lynchings.

Several items follow which have to do with the various personages whose portraits chance to appear in this number. Richard Huntington, known as "Lofty Dick" and by several other aliases, is a forger who is now in the Ohio Penitentiary. "His little game was to affect piety, rent the best pew in the most fashionable church and make himself prominent generally in wealthy religious circles as a convenient cloak for carrying out his dishonest pursuits, which was to marry some well-to-do lamb of the flock, or fleece some gullible member, and decamp with the proceeds. He is said to have married at the age of fifteen. After this event he opened a cigar store in Elmira."

Then there is the sad tale of William Harney, whose likeness appears on page 13, and whose pathetic story "is exciting the sympathies of Bridgeport, Conn." William, we learn, is a waif of sixteen who had been abandoned by a hard-hearted father in infancy in Boston. The father utterly denied the relationship when the youth sought him out, so the latter thereupon decides to go to work, saying proudly: "If my father don't wish to own me, then I don't want to have him." Which seems strangely like David Warfield's dramatic outburst in "The Music Master"— "If you don't want her, I want her!"

Orlando Casler, convicted of murder in Seward, Neb., was another whose portrait and story appeared. Neither was interesting. Right after this come a few lines on the weekly feature, "Favorites of the Footlights," which has to do with the picture of Miss Minnie Palmer in her character of Dot in the play "Cricket on the Hearth." Completing this page is the department devoted to "The Theatres." It consists of but six items of three or four lines each. "An unapproachable bill headed by the great Tony" is offered at Tony Pastor's. The Tivoli presents attractive variety entertainment. Lester Wallack is offering "Ours," at his own theater. Harrigan and Hart are featuring "Mulligan Guard Ball" in the Theatre Comique, the burning of which was soon after to be pictured in these pages. At the Olympic another of the Charles Reade dramas, "Never Too Late to Mend," is offered "in a style that delights theater-goers of taste."

Page three is led with an account of "Toledo's Tragedy," which the subheads inform us is a "story of vice and dissipation." In this report a brakeman on the railroad making the run through Ohio takes time off to put a bullet through the temple

LAID IN ASHES.

BURNING OF HARRIGAN & HART'S THEATRE COMIQUE ON THE MORNING OF DEC. 23, AT A HEAVY LOSS TO THE POPULAR MANAGERS.

of his pleasure-loving wife with fatal results and also dispatches himself in like fashion. A shorter story from Germany tells an enlightening little tale. Two young students at Pesth have some trouble over a young lady and the insulted party demands satisfaction by means of a duel "after the American fashion." This, we are informed, involves a drawing in which the loser is bound in honor to blow his brains out within ten days. On the ninth day the winner informs that since he is very hard up he will sell the other the life that he is supposed to take and for the modest sum of five florins. The loser thereupon sells the revolver with which he was about to end his earthly existence and ransoms himself with the proceeds.

Next we have the story of a young woman who fell in love with a convicted bank-robber on her visit to the prison in Jefferson City, Mo., and was prepared to marry him upon his release. After a fond meeting at the prison gate at the completion of his term, the two were rudely parted when the law stepped in once more with another indictment.

An article picked up from an English paper deplores the tendency of youths of

A STRANGE EXPERIMENT.

THE TEMPERANCE CRANKS OF NEW YORK, LED BY MISS JULIA COLMAN, SET FIRE TO SOME SAMPLES OF COMMUNION WINE IN THE BROADWAY TABERNACLE.

good family to enter into marriage with women of the streets. "Frenchmen may gamble and spend all their money into the *demi monde,* but they do not marry into it; Americans may drink and indulge in eccentric and murderous exploits with bowie knives, but they do not marry Phrynes and Aspasias; Germans may drink to excess and beat their wives, but their wives are not weeds sprung from abomination and vice. Within the last few years ten men, all holding high social positions and bearing good names, have given their names and even titles to creatures whose names they would never under ordinary circumstances dare to mention before a lady. A marchioness, a duchess and the wives of two baronets have been recruited from the ranks of *les impurés.*"

Page four, which is mainly given over to pictures, depicts "the mania of a Negro reformer"—which was dashing into a faro room and shooting the dealer to death. His gambling reform is carried out in this startling manner at Jackson, Tenn. New York gets into the next picture, which has to do with an experiment by some female workers in the temperance cause; diligent search locates no associating story. Three other smaller pictures are reproductions of bust photos. Mrs. Kate M. Cobb, with her front hair all crimped, is shown in partial profile, also Welsey W. Bishop, both of whom are on trial in Norwich, Conn., for the poisoning of the lamented Mr. Cobb, the lady's husband. In between these two John Reilly looks bravely out in his regalia of member of the New York Fire Department. This gallant member of Engine Company No. 17 had been killed in a fire at Broadway and Grand Street, January 14.

There is also on this page a very small story of a New York police officer's heroism. Officer Michael Gorman dashed through the smoke and flame at 315 Delancey Street to the fourth floor and carried Mrs. Margaret Moore and her two children to safety. The metropolitan police get further attention in a story on this page of how Patrolmen Falvey and O'Neil pummeled each other in the Eighteenth Precinct Station-house; the fight as pictured elsewhere must have been a lively set-to. This picture and that of the Cobb trial monopolize the entire back page.

Pictures of the Misses Palmer and Richmond take up more than half of page five, which is not to be wondered at, as it shows a full view of these beauteous stage dames. One more picture on this page has to do with a census-taking incident; this occurs on a street-car and apparently is supposed to speak for itself, as there is no story to be found in connection therewith. Two items, the subjects of pictures elsewhere, are given space here. Out in Modesta, California, Miss Susie Jones, "who has only seen some fourteen or fifteen summers," shot a catamount, "one of the largest of his species." A few lines tell of the arrest by Detective Gallagher, of the Central Station, of Paulina Reinsch, who though but seventeen years of age, "has attained the distinction of being the boss shoplifter of Chicago."

Half of page six features the story of the shipwreck adventure of Captain Yates on the coast of Balize and, mostly in his own words, recites a lurid story of being buried alive by savages. Another long story hints at scandalous romance in the life of a certain nameless actress "very much in the public eye," and which the fair one indignantly repudiates. After going into details of her history it tells of her triumphs at the Union Square and other theaters and how all lovers were forced to admire at a distance. "As the snow-flake virgin, before it touched the ground was she, caring not for the gauds or the glitter of that which dazzles." Just what this means the reader may have difficulty in making out, but notwithstanding she

A CENSUS OF THE POPS.

HOW AN INVESTIGATION INSTITUTED BY A PASSENGER ON A NEW YORK STREET CAR BROUGHT A YOUNG WOMAN TO THE FRONT LIKE A LITTLE MAN.

was discovered in a compromising position and "unveiled charms" by the proprietress of a select apartment house where she resided and:

> *"Alas for the crown that the maiden erst wore,*
> *'Twas gone, it had perished, she had it no more,"*

Another account on this page, a short one, tells of the adventures in Chicago of Griffin Skinner, a New York drummer, who was taken advantage of while intoxicated by Belle Hamilton and Sarah Howard, a couple of light-moraled and light-fingered young women, who had been arrested as a result. Their pictures were shown on another page of the *Gazette*. Belle is not a bad-looker, in a hardened way, but these hussies look older than the twenty and twenty-one years they claim for their respective ages. On identical pages, both as to story and picture, we learn of what happened to a Williamsburgh, N. Y., miss whose mother caught her "rinking."

Page seven relates the end of the trial of the aforementioned Kate M. Cobb. Kate was pronounced guilty of murder in the second degree, to general surprise,

SHE CAUGHT IT HOT

THE DREADFUL CONSEQUENCE TO A WILLIAMSBURGH, N. Y., YOUNG DAMSEL OF 'GOING A RINKING WITHOUT HER MOTHER'S CONSENT.

after the jury had deliberated for five hours over the evidence as to whether or no she had been guilty of putting something in the tea of her husband that had resulted in his sudden demise.

The next little item has to do with the "swinging off" of Martin Bergin at Pottsville, Pa., "the nineteenth of the Mollie Maguire gang to be hung for murder in this State." In the last column a story picked up from the Cincinnati *Saturday Night* concerns "a pious toper's little game," which is the purchase of whisky as medicine for an alleged sick wife.

A BLACKSMITH'S DUEL.

THEY FIGHT A FEARFUL BATTLE WITH RED-HOT IRONS, FOR THE SMILES OF A RUSTIC COQUETTE OF PORT JERVIS, N. Y.

The entire eighth page is taken up with the gruesome depiction of a hanging at Mauch Chunk, Pa., with an insert picture of the murder for which the death penalty was paid. Three pictures take up page nine. Two of them have already been referred to; they deal with the fire-defying policeman and the lady nimrod, the one who shot the catamount. The third picture is of a fearful battle with red-hot irons between two blacksmiths of Port Jervis, N. Y., the duel being for the smiles of a rustic coquette.

All of the tenth and part of the eleventh page are devoted to the execution illustrated on page eight. From this story we learn that James McDonnell, alias "The Hairy Man," and Charles Sharpe, variously known as "Slippery Sharpe," and the "The Scraper," were among the most lawless who terrorized the town of Audenried, a mining town in Carbon County, Pa., when the Buckshots—predecessors of the Mollie Maguires—were at the zenith of their power. The Audenried colliery belonging to the Lehigh and Wilkes-Barre Coal Company was superintended by George K. Smith, and late in 1863 he was shot to death by a gang of the Buckshots, with McDonnell and Sharpe the apparent ring-leaders. The trouble was an outcropping of the Civil War draft, the colliery heads being ordered to coöperate with the government in the serving of notices on the drafted men who happened to be in the Smith employ. Manus Gull, alias "Kelly the Bum," and others made confessions and McDonnell and Sharpe fled and it took many years before they were finally run down by the Pinkerton detectives. More than fifteen years dragged by before the two were finally brought to their last account and then there was some question as to their guilt in the matter for which they were called on to pay the penalty. Both insisted that, while they had been guilty of many crimes, in this particular case their hands had not fired the fatal shots that ended the life of George K. Smith. No sooner had the death-trap been sprung than there was a violent knocking at the prison gate and in came a messenger with a reprieve for the two still quivering on the gibbet. Governor Hartranft had granted a five-day reprieve. His telegram from Harrisburg reached Mauch Chunk at 10:37 A.M. The execution had been completed at 10:42. The manager of the telegraph office had run all the way with the telegram personally and had come one minute too late.

Following this elaborate tale on page eleven a column is devoted to the recital of a brutal murder and the meting out of crude justice in the Alaska town of

Wrangel. From Louisville come three paragraphs on the death of a deceitful bartender who left behind him two grieving wives. Twelve miles out from Nashville, a farm had been the scene of a ghastly double murder: John Whittemeyer and his wife had been put to brutal death in their bed. A baby of twelve months and a little girl two years old were found beside the bodies. The details are most revolting. One more execution rounds out the page.

A POLAR EXPLORATION.

WHAT A JEALOUS WOMAN DISCOVERED IN A TENEMENT HOUSE BY THE AID OF A CLEAR HEAD AND A LINEMAN'S CLAMPS.

rour pictures take up most of the space on page twelve, three of which have already been referred to. The fourth picture, which is captioned "A Polar Exploration," illustrates how a philandering husband was caught "with the goods" by an ingenious and athletic wife. The story of this incident is followed by one in a light vein from Arkansas: of two men who dropped into a hotel and had left their wives without in buggies in the dark. Each drives off with the wrong wife. No serious consequences occur ere the mistake is rectified, though a quarrel gets under way in one of the buggies before the proper exchange has been made. One of the men gets so angry at the lady he supposes to be his wife that he says to her: "Give my teeth here; you shan't wear them another minute!"

A romantic tale from Kentucky runs over on the thirteenth page and takes up the space not used for picture cuts. Miss Addie Silver had been deserted on her wedding eve by Phil Hodge because he learned that she was still in love with Lou Foliet. Ten years later Hodge dies and Addie marries Foliet. Another story with picture, but no names mentioned, is captioned "Too Much Wet Goods in Dry Goods District." Some of our lady shoppers are imbibing too freely, so we are apprised.

Three columns of page fourteen are for the installment of the Mackeever serial, "The Phantom Friend." A reporter seems to be the hero of this narrative, which is described as a romance of New York. There is a chance meeting on Sixtieth Street with a beautiful girl who needs aid in mounting her horse. "The journalist stepped forward, raised his hat and offered his assistance with the unmistakable air of a gentleman." The young man studied with deep interest "the beautiful apparition vanishing down the street." Then he returned his note-book to his pocket and stood for a moment in deep thought.

"I think I'll have a kidney stew for breakfast," he said, and then suddenly turned into the store.

This ends Chapter IV. We won't go into Chapter V. The balance of this page is devoted to the "Glimpses of Gotham" series, to which we devote a special chapter.

Page fifteen has three columns of matter gathered together under the heading "Vice's Varieties." This is made up of forty-odd items of varying length, being from three to twenty-five lines and which concern murders, stage robberies, jail breaking, affrays with knives and clubs, adultery, embezzlement, swindling, abortion, etc.

One of the items has surprising interest. It tells of the scandal involving one who is a temperance apostle as well as deacon of a Presbyterian Church in Greenpoint, L. I., and a Sunday-school teacher. The deacon, a married man with a large family, had become over-intimate with the Sunday-school teacher, a spinster of thirty-five, as the result of which she was in what was even then described as "an interesting condition." The amours of this fond couple, it is charged, took place in this city (New York) at 58 Reade Street, "in the rooms of the National Temperance Society," where the man was employed as an agent and the girl friend as a book-keeper. Feminine bookkeepers must have been a rarity back in the Seventies and this only goes to show what comes of letting woman out into the world; anyway, carryings-on between the two were said to have extended over a period of six years.

BOOZY FEMALE SHOPPERS.

A DISGRACEFUL SCENE ON FOURTEENTH STREET DURING THE HOLIDAY SEASON—THE RESULT OF REFRESHMENT ROOMS IN FASHIONABLE STORES.

The pious man in the case must have been quite a lady's man, having been at one time a deacon in a Reformed Dutch Church, "where his name became associated with that of the pastor's wife in a rather unpleasantly notorious manner."

Jesse James and his escapades were given much attention by the *Police Gazette,* and Mr. Fox seemed to take not a little pride in the fact that the leader of the noted James Boys band was a subscriber. Jesse James sent little letters to the publisher quite often. Just before he was brought down by a bullet by one of his own gang, which was fired from behind his back while Jesse was in the act of hanging a picture, the *Gazette* of April 1, 1882, devoted an entire column to this interesting character.

We have received a communication from the grave. From a veritable corpse. Yes, a dead man. Not only a dead man but a dead man who has been riddled to hash by bullets and slashed to ribbons with bowie knives. That is, if we can believe the newspapers. The alleged corpse that has written us is none other than the remains or the ghost or what is left of the much-killed Jesse James, the terror of Missouri.

This famous bandit, train robber and desperado has beeen killed so often, however, in newspaper reports and has turned up safe and sound thereafter, that the people of Kansas have lost faith in his death. Every time he was reported positively defunct he would resurrect himself, board another train at an unexpected point, clean out the express packages and the passengers and then hie him away to the setting sun with many merry cuss words on his lips and his thumb pivoted on his nose and his fingers agitated in insulting suggestions to the minions of the law. Wasn't it provoking? The railroad companies thought it was. And unprofitable, too; so they made up a pool of $7,000. which they offered as a reward to the man who would capture or kill the desperado.

Then began a regular hunt in all quarters of Kansas. Every clerk who had a holiday and every tenderfoot who was out West selling tape and shoe laces shouldered his little gun and went out to capture or slaughter the famous bandit.

After a hunt of a month a party of detectives came up with his band and engaged in a desperate battle. Jesse himself retreated pell-mell and was pursued by a man named Shepherd, who, as we reported last week, returned wounded, with the bandit's pistol and bowie knife in his possession and gave other proofs that he had killed him. The $7,000. reward was paid over and he divided it with James and joined the band. Another grand laugh at the authorities. More despair among the citizens. Less confidence than ever in death.

Another hunt was started for the harlequin bandit who still played "hanky panky" with his pursuers. On the 8th ult. a very pale and broken-up man calling himself a deputy sheriff rushed into Moberly, Mo., and announced that Jesse James had been captured this time after a desperate battle. A sheriff's posse had surrounded him in a log cabin in a heavy-timbered district of Missouri and after a long and bloody siege in which he had been wounded and seven of the officers had been killed, he was obliged to surrender, owing to his ammunition giving out. This story was received with caution, for the public had been there before.

Of course the next day Jesse turned up miles away, safe and sound and as saucy as ever. And moreover he received his *Police Gazette* regularly, for his eye fell on our report of his doings and he occupied his leisure moments in inditing us a letter, of which the following is a photographic facsimile:

Mr Fox I write to you this: that Sheriffs Detectives & Scouts have been after me but It is of no use when I want to give up my Job. I will so people letme alone!

Yours Truly
Jesse James

As Mr. James by his own avowal will not be brought to justice until he is good and ready and as the authorities will only enrich him by offering rewards for his slaughter, the wise course would be for Missourians to boycott him, so to speak. Let them depopulate the State so he may have no one to kill; let them stop all the railroads so that he may have no chance to rob. Then when he grows weary of living alone he may, like Robinson Crusoe, have a hankering after civilization and may of his own volition come in and go cheerily to his dungeon cell as a variation to the monotony of his lonesome life. That is the only way to fix it. Jesse James says so himself and surely he ought to know. It is plain anyhow that he is the most knowing person in Missouri as far as we've got.

George Leonidas Leslie whom the *Police Gazette* dubbed the "King of Bank Robbers," and who was undoubtedly entitled to the cognomen, had his name more prominently in the Fox journal than any other criminal with very few exceptions. In the summer of 1884, when his partly decomposed body was found near a landmark known as "Tramps' Rock," located in the vicinity of Yonkers, the *Gazette* gave a summary of his doings as had been reported in that paper from time to time. Six years previous Leslie had been the master mind in the greatest of bank robberies,

COUNTERFEITING AS A WOMAN'S RIGHT.

THE MEANS AN INDUSTRIOUS MOTHER OF GIRLS ADOPTED TO PILE UP A BANK ACCOUNT WITHOUT TROUBLING THE MINT. AT BROOKLYN, L. L.

as a result of which the Manhattan Bank Building on Bleecker Street was cleaned out of $2,506,700. in registered bonds, $241,000. in coupon bonds, and $12,764. in cash.

According to the *Gazette* the robbery was planned at 861 Greene Avenue, Brooklyn, and was a three-year job. Leslie was the directing head, and was chiefly assisted by "Shang" Draper, though Jimmy Hope, "Red" Leary, "Banjo Pete"

Emerson, "Worcester Sam" Perris and others, along with Mother Mandelbaum, the noted fence, had a considerable hand in the conspiracy.

Leslie, who was by descent an Englishman, was well born, and his father, a prosperous brewer of Cincinnati, had enabled him to secure an excellent school and university education. He early displayed exceptional mechanical genius and an unfortunate penchant for the company of the criminal classes. He was barely of age when he decided to turn his fine mind to the hardest task of all, the making of easy money. He proceeded to lead a remarkable double life. Outwardly he was the associate of respectable society, a patron of art and the theater and a lover of good literature, which he in truth was. His appearance and upbringing aided him well and his clothing was provided by the most fashionable of tailors. Criminal records support all these facts; as well, that his was the cunning that planned with his associates 80 percent of the great bank robberies through the Seventies and early Eighties, and which was estimated to have amounted to around $7,000,000.

Eight years before the robbery of the Manhattan Bank, and while masquerading as an Internal Revenue Agent, Leslie became enamored of an attractive Philadelphia miss, Mary Henrietta Coath, who was then only fifteen years of age. He married the trusting girl and hardly was the honeymoon over when he engineered the robbery of the South Kensington National Bank, which netted more than $100,000. in cash. The marriage had gone into the fifth year before Mrs. Leslie came to know the true character of her husband. She clung to him, notwithstanding. Her trust was poorly repaid, for Leslie's fancy was a roving one and he devoted himself to the sister of Johnny Irving as well as the mistress of "Shang" Draper, his associates in many important robberies. This philandering is said to have led to his murder.

The rare ingenuity of Leslie was never better exemplified than in the Manhattan Bank job. The premises of the bank were surveyed until every inch of the place was known and the plans of the interior and surroundings would have done credit to an architect. After months of observation and investigation the name of the vault-maker was learned and a duplicate of the style of the combination lock was secured from the maker. Leslie experimented with the lock until he had discovered a method whereby the tumblers could be thrown out of gear. Then months more were spent in introducing a confederate into the service of the bank. Leslie was then able to get into the bank during the night and bore a hole through the indicator dial, which permitted him to manipulate the gears. But something went wrong with his workmanship and the safe could not be opened by the bank authorities the following morning, and the maker of the safe was called in and the lock was completely changed and many added months of work was required. In the end when the "job" was completed it was done with the aid of tools of the finest workmanship, several of which had been specially made by Leslie. Hope did most of the actual interior work. So expeditiously did the job have to be done that the compartments containing the great amount of cash which the burglars were really after could not be reached. The bank succeeded in replacing the registered securities, so that Leslie and his pals did not fare anywhere nearly as well as they had hoped. But with the ready cash stolen and the rifling of depositors' boxes the bank's loss was believed to have been in excess of $100,000.

While George Leonidas Leslie managed to steer fairly clear of the police, all of his partners were not so fortunate and every one of them knew the interior of a prison cell—but not for long, as a rule. Political connivance, legal brains, bribery, or daring and ingenuity in jail-breaking nearly always gave freedom. Two such escapes that startled the good citizens of New York deserve noting.

"Red" Leary is out again! The burglar who is famous for his exploits on two continents and who was about to be extradited to Massachusetts for the Northampton Bank robbery, took French leave of the Ludlow Street Jail about eleven o'clock on the night of May 7 (1879). Investigation revealed that rooms had been taken on the fifth floor of the tenement at 76 Ludlow Street, which immediately adjoins the jail. From here a passage had been burrowed with mathematical precision through five feet of wall into a water-closet set against the end of a corridor on the second floor of the jail, and when it was decided that "Red" should go to Massachusetts, "Red" decided to go next door, and did so.

Two years later, after some time abroad, Leary returned to this country and was recaptured in Brooklyn on February 4, 1881. The *Gazette* comment on the capture follows:

Since the memorable morning when "Red" Leary took French leave of Ludlow Street Jail the public has heard nothing of him. For a long time after the escape Kate Leary, his wife, was kept under espionage; but, aside from the fact that she wore a maroon-colored velvet dress and had her child's pelisse of the same material decked with bright steel keys as ornaments instead of buttons, the police discovered nothing. The woman seemed to have acquired some of the humor of the famous "Red," and those keys were doubtlessly put on the child's garment for the edification of the detectives. The watch on Kate was soon abandoned, for it was not thought possible that she would "make connection," as the police say, with "Red" in person.

It was known that Kate Leary was keeping Bob Scott's place in South Brooklyn, and for a time it was thought that "Red" might be there. An effort was made to "shadow" the house, but it was so exposed that this could not be done. They noticed several times, late at night, that a man muffled up came out from the house and entered a sleigh. The walk and general carriage of the man convinced the watchers that they saw no less a personage than "Red" Leary, but all efforts to get a look at his face failed. Sufficient evidence, however, was obtained to convince Detective Robert Pinkerton that the man was Leary, and on Thursday night he went over with Hiscock and joined the watchers, fully determined to accost the man should he appear. During all the cold hours of the night the watch was maintained, and about 3 o'clock patience was rewarded, for the jingle of sleigh-bells was heard and a sleigh came dashing along from the direction of Fort Hamilton.

At a signal the detectives concentrated and Pinkerton, jumping into the middle of the street, grabbed the horse's head, at the same time calling on the man in the sleigh to throw up his hands or take the consequences. Cornered on all sides, the man in the sleigh did as he was bid, and Pinkerton recognized the voice of the man he was looking for when Leary remarked:

"It's rather cold this morning, Bob."

The following day Leary was on his way to Northampton. Six year previous the *Gazette* had reported another famous escape from jail, that of William J. Sharkey:

On Sunday, September 1st, 1872, William J. Sharkey, ward politician and sporting man, killed Robert S. Dunn in a barroom at 288 Hudson Street. Dunn had been a professional gambler for fifteen years. Sharkey was the son of respected residents of the Ninth Ward, but he went astray early in life, and after a brilliantly notorious career of the crooked sort, bloomed out into a successful political adventurer. He was a power in the Eighth Ward primaries, had a club named after him, and belonged to every influential political organization in the Fifth Congressional District. Sharkey was found guilty of murder in the first degree, and sentenced to be hanged on August 15th, 1873. November 19th, 1873, found Sharkey still in the Tombs, an occupant of cell 40, on the second tier.

At ten o'clock of the morning of that day the murderer was visited by his mistress, Maggie Jourdan. The girl, who, since her separation from her first lover, Thomas Murphy, the pickpocket, had been a devoted companion of Sharkey, had beggared herself in order to provide him with funds for his defense. She visited him constantly in jail, and her quiet, modest demeanor had made her a general favorite. On the day in question she remained in conversation with him for two hours and a half, when she was joined by her friend, Mrs. Wesley Allen. At one o'clock Maggie Jourdan left the prison. At half-past one a tall, ungainly female, heavily veiled, handed a ticket to the doorman and went out. At two o'clock Mrs. Allen tried to pass out without a ticket, alleging that she had lost hers. An alarm was sounded, and Sharkey was found to have shaved his mustache off, invested himself in the attire provided by his mistress and her friend, and escaped. The ungainly female with the thick veil was the convicted murderer himself. The last trace Sharkey left was on a Bleecker Street car. George W. Matsell, superintendent of the police, took vigorous steps to trace the assassin. All the European steamers were kept under surveillance. Two thousand dollars reward was offered. The Eighth Ward was searched with a vigor that left no likely refuge unexplored and people who were known to have been Sharkey's intimates were closely shadowed. But all in vain. The flying man had managed to vanish and leave no trail.

Some years later the *Gazette* revealed that Sharkey had escaped on the schooner *Frank Atwood,* which also became famous as the means of Tweed's escape to Cuba. Sharkey was secreted aboard this boat and taken to Hayti. He did not like the looks of that country and continued on the boat to Cuba. In 1881 the *Gazette* wound up a story on the Sharkey career with this paragraph:

During his stay in Cuba the woman to whom he owed life and liberty made a voyage from New York to see him. He ill-treated her so brutally that the captain of the steamer which took her down was compelled to rescue her from his violence. Maggie is living in New York; a year or so ago she married and her present life is a happier one than her past ever promised to be. Not a bit happier, as the reader will probably agree, than her heroic devotion to her miserable lover entitled her to find it.

From her exile in Canada there came by a wearisome and circuitous route to the city of New York a corpulent matron in her sixties, who, though of a build and physiognomy that lent itself readily to caricature, had commanded rare iniquitous power in the very metropolis to which she was now returning in dread secrecy. This was a truly sad journey she had come these many miles and was made at the danger of long imprisonment, for it was inspired by the desire to have a last look upon the still face of the youngest of her four children, a young girl of exceptional beauty and tender years, who had suddenly died in the city from which her mother had been forced to decamp in disgraceful notoriety. The mother dared not even follow the beloved body to the grave. New York held no haven for this woman and she could do no more than send the funeral on its way and then hurry off in her bereavement and hoping only to escape unnoticed back to her enforced home in Toronto. She had fled New York in the closing month of the year, 1884, just in time to escape the fate of justice, which had finally trapped her for all of her cunning and power.

Though she looked only the part of a motherly Jewess with whom the years had dealt rather carelessly, this was none other than Fredericka Mandelbaum, "Queen of the Fences," and with such genius in her line that, though the police had been aware of the villainy of her business for a quarter of a century, she had thrived through all these years in an almost open defiance of the law. To break the criminal connections of this strange woman, her partnership with the foremost thieves and shoplifters of her time, that could only have prospered with the connivance of those who should have hunted her down, it was finally necessary for an earnest District Attorney to openly snub the metropolitan police department and call in the services and ingenuity of a private detective agency before the evidence could be gathered that in the end brought her in contact with the law.

A rare character was this Mother Mandelbaum, or "Marm," as she was better known. There was nothing of exaggeration in the résumé of her activities as revealed in the story which the *Gazette* published soon after her trip in disguise to New York, of which excerpts are here set down for the sake of brevity.

Fredericka Mandelbaum, born in Germany of Hebrew parents, arrived in this country with her husband sometime in 1849. Five years later the two opened a dry-goods and haberdashery store at 79 Clinton Street, corner of Rivington. This three-story structure, in what was then the heart of the German residential section and known as *Kleine Deutschland,* soon became the property of the Mandelbaums, as did the two-story wing which sprawled at a somewhat odd angle in the rear. On the shelves of the store was displayed the usual assortment of goods in keeping with its character and suitable to the needs of the neighborhood, and the trade in this line was more than an ostensible one.

Passing into the rear building there was a distinct change of atmosphere. It was mainly given over to lavishly crowded living rooms. Chairs of rare antiquity and other fine furniture, as well as carpets and drapes of most expensive character, together with costly silver and glassware and belongings, made this one of the most expensively appointed homes in the city. Here, it is understood, she entertained not

MOTHER MANDELBAUM TRAPPED.

THE FAMOUS FRIEND OF THE BURGLARS TAKEN BY A DETECTIVE'S STRATAGEM, SURROUNDED BY HER RICH SPOIL.

I.—"MOTHER BAUM." II.—BARGAINING WITH THIEVES. III.—SELLING STOLEN GOODS. IV.—OPENING HER JEWEL SAFE. V.—ARRAIGNED IN SILKS
AND JEWELS. VI.—THE CASTLE OF "MOTHER BAUM."

[241]

a few persons high in official circles, and, on other occasions, the shining lights of the criminal world. In 1874 "Marm" became a widow, a fact which in no way affected the success of her dealings, for her husband was a nonentity. She was the brains of this marriage, and in her heyday she had no peer as a receiver of stolen goods. She was a remarkable woman in many ways and it was only unfortunate that her efforts did not happen to be honestly directed. She was adept in business, acute in her acquaintance with the machinery of the law and its representatives, and uncanny in her association with the criminal classes.

It is claimed she never left a criminal her creditor and that she became a veritable "Bureau of Prevention of Conviction." While she drove hard bargains with the possessors of stolen property, she had a reputation for dealing honestly with these violators of the law and her adherence to criminal ethics gained her an absolute confidence among the guilty gentry. She paid at once and in cash to almost any amount and she even advanced money for contemplated "jobs." When in trouble with the police the apprehended rogues seldom appealed to her in vain and many a one had their escape through her financial assistance, or her ability to clog the wheels of justice. She is supposed to have paid a yearly retainer of $5,000. to the well-known firm of criminal lawyers, Howe & Hummel. Whenever her pets got into trouble she provided the bail and defrayed the expenses of their trial, for which she taxed them afterwards the amount of these expenditures; so she always had a fine array of lawbreakers in her debt and service.

Almost everything in the way of silks that was stolen for years went through her hands. This included the $30,000. worth of goods stolen from H. B. Claflin & Co., in 1876, by Johnny Irving and Billy Vaite, and the valuable stocks stolen from James A. Hearn & Son and Messrs. Simpson, Crawford & Simpson. She had rooms in different parts of the city, in Brooklyn, and in adjacent cities, where the stolen goods would be received in bulk and every bolt of silk or article that came into her possession was expertly examined and all labels and trade-marks removed or erased. All plunder was minutely gone over for obliteration of every possible mark of identification. It is estimated that she handled between $7,000,-000. and $10,000,000. worth of stolen goods. Occasionally she dealt in stolen bonds, but silks were her hobby, and it was a deal in this specialty that finally got her into trouble from which even she could not be rescued. Among the thieves with whom she had affiliation were "Sheeny Mike" Kurtz, Billy Porter, Jimmy Irving, "Shang" Draper, Johnny Dobbs, Charles Penan, George Leonidas Leslie (whose widow she assisted for

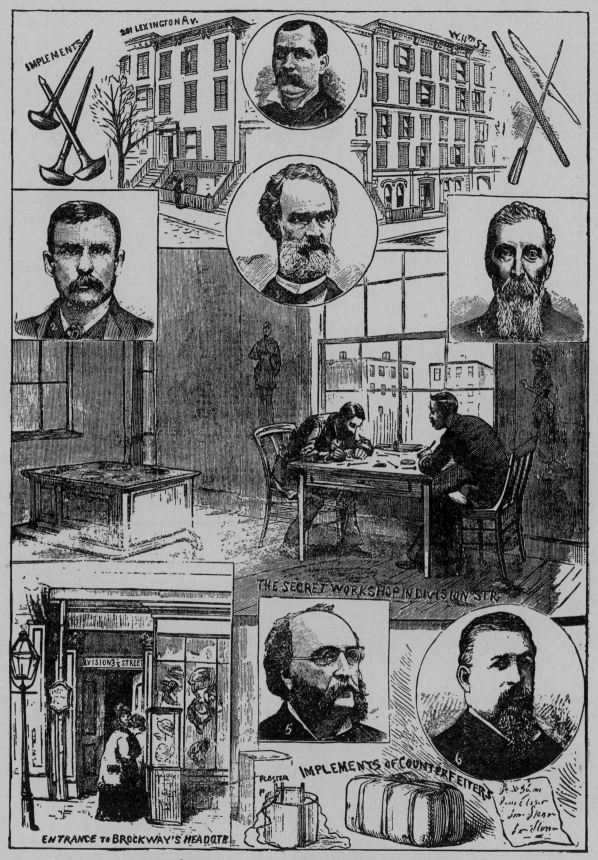

THE BREAKING OF THE COUNTERFEITERS' RING.

THE HEADQUARTERS, WORKSHOP, TOOLS AND IMPLEMENTS OF THE GANG OF NOTED FORGERS AND COUNTERFEITERS, WITH
PORTRAITS OF THE PRINCIPALS IN THE GREAT RING, BROKEN UP BY THE SKILL OF UNITED STATES AGENT DRUMMOND AND
INSPECTOR BYRNES OF THE NEW YORK POLICE. PORTRAITS: 1—INSPECTOR BYRNES. 2—NATHAN B. FOSTER.
3—WILLIAM E. BROCKWAY. 4—LEWIS B. MARTIN. 5—CHARLES H. SMITH. 6—JAMES DOYLE.

(From Sketches by Police Gazette Special Artists)

years) and many others almost equally infamous, and such feminine shop-lifters and worse as Sophie Lyons, Molly Holbrook, Black Lena, French Louise, Little Rosie, Lizzie Lancie, Polly King and various other customers only too well known to the police.

After several civil suits that saw "Marm" escape almost redhanded, Peter B. Olney, the District Attorney, spurred on by a number of prominent merchants, decided it would be a waste of time to depend upon the coöperation of the municipal police and he assigned the Pinkerton detective agency to the task of "getting the goods" on the "Queen of the Fences." After four months of persistent work, overwhelming evidence was submitted to Justice Murray and warrants were issued for her arrest. The Pinkertons had detailed special officers to visit her place in the guise of petty thieves and to gradually worm their way into her confidence. Finally they caught her with certain pieces of silk in her possession which could be positively identified as property that had been stolen. On complaint of George A. Hearn, Jr., of the firm of James A. Hearn & Son, of Four-teenth Street, the Mandelbaum woman was lodged in jail and released under heavy bail. By the time, December 4, 1884, when she was to face trial, such a strong case had been made out against her that her conviction seemed inevitable. Her flight to Toronto came as no surprise, though nothing was done to prevent it. There she was in a few days placed under arrest by the Canadian authorities, and was promptly released once her legal representative, the wily Abe Hummel, appeared on the ground.

Her fortune, once estimated at over one million dollars, is said to have shrunk to one-tenth of that amount, and while she is living in comfort and plenty in the scene of her banishment, she has been heard to say she would only too gladly sacrifice every penny that is still hers if she could breathe her declining days in the atmosphere of the Thirteenth Ward where she so long had her home. The *Gazette* was fully aware of the fact that she was secretly in the city for the funeral of her daughter. While it is conceded that her existence warranted a more extreme punishment than exile, we did not feel it our duty to intrude on the few hours of sadness that she spent in this city and we have refrained telling of her presence here until her departure, since it was immediate once the body of her daughter was on its way to the grave.

Space will not permit details on the ingenious capture of William E. Brockway, the "King of the Counterfeiters," and the other famous knaves whose deeds and fates were chronicled within the pages of Mr. Fox's journal—there were altogether too many of them. It was Brockway who, in 1865, counterfeited a $100. note that was so perfect and gained so large a circulation the Government was forced to withdraw the genuine bills from circulation.

THEY LET GEORGE DO IT

Hanging Artistically Performed, Satisfactory Work Guaranteed

THEY called him George, though his correct name was quite well known outside of official circles. He was also known as Monsieur New York. In private life he was regarded as an estimable neighbor and a worthy friend. Back in the Eighties he still resided with his family in Harlem in a modest three-story house close to the East River, in the vicinity of the 125th Street "L" station, and was a member of the Methodist Church. Very few, if any, among his associates knew that this quiet and rather portly gentleman with the ruddy, cheerful visage, and George, or Monsieur New York, the noted hangman, were one and the same person.

Early in the Fifties the sheriff of New York was drowning his perplexity in a glass of hot Scotch in Matt Gorderson's popular hostelry opposite the City Hall when he was approached by a pleasant-faced young man who remarked:

"Sheriff, I hear you are looking for a man to do that little job for you next Friday?"

"I am, indeed," was the answer.

"Well, I wish you would give me a chance to do that little job for you. I'll do my best, I assure you, Sheriff, and I believe I will give every satisfaction."

The little job in question was the hanging of a Negro prisoner. It seems that the man who had been delegated to attend to the execution of the condemned man had suddenly changed his mind and the sheriff was encountering much trouble in finding some one to undertake the duties of hangman. The sheriff was agreeably surprised when George called on him the day after the above conversation and made formal application for the post of common hangman.

George, it turned out, was a butcher's assistant in Washington Market and was then aged about thirty. He had read the autobiography of Jack Ketch, the renowned high-executioner of Great Britain, and had conceived the idea that he was called upon to emulate this historic character in his own city. Anyway, George was appointed a deputy sheriff, was conducted around to the tier of the condemned

[245]

in the Tombs and, looking the situation over generally, as it were, he thereupon entered upon his duties with great zeal and in quick time became a true connoisseur in his peculiar calling.

The Negro was duly hanged and the delicate operation was performed with such perfection that Monsieur New York, as he shortly came to be known, had his fame established at once. He soon was regarded as an authority in the science of inflicting death by means of the halter. His fame spread until his services were in demand all over the United States.

Until George became a specialist in his vocation the several hangings that had taken place in the vicinity of New York had been by means of what was known as the "trap gallows," and the dispatching of the doomed had been attended with much awkward work, and in some instances the business had involved gruesome torture. The visitation of death upon Angelo Cornetti was most horrifying. We read that "his terrorized clamor was like the barking of a dog as he was led to the scaffold, and his body was not sufficiently heavy to produce the requisite rebound to dislocate the neck, so that death came through strangulation in a way that sickened all onlookers."

George showed himself to be an artist from the very first. Even before the undertaking of his first assignment, he was inspired by a desire to excel in his work, and in his leisure hours he had given much thought and study to this business of hanging. His daily visits to the slaughter-house had made him familiar with the use of the windlass then in use for the hoisting of the cattle and he applied the principle of the windlass to the perfection of an apparatus for the "humane accommodation of the law-breaking community." With the able assistance of a carpenter named Joseph B. Atkinson, their joint efforts produced "a perfected gibbet" which came to be termed the New York pattern, and the inventors brought forth a species of machinery which, to use their own language, "was unsurpassed in simplicity and perfection of construction by any machine in the market." It was generally conceded that the invention worked so faultlessly that, if such a thing had been possible, the inventors would surely have boasted the possession of "testimonials from the nether regions."

George took genuine pride, indeed, in his work. He was not merely "the man who cut the rope and thus cut off the thread-life of the culprit." He was the master of ceremonies who supervised the erection of the gallows and the adjustment of the

SINS OF NEW YORK

weights, and the testing of the hooks, the ropes and the noose. "On the morning of an execution he bustled into the prison yard like the manager of a theater just prior to the first performance." The quotes and the information provided in this chapter are all culled from the illuminating work of Charles A. Mackeever, in the *National Police Gazette* and substantiated through other reliable sources.

In a way it was to be regretted that this artist could not have been "master of ceremonies" at the execution of Guiteau, the assassin of President Garfield, and which was featured with such detail in the pages of the *Gazette*.

The conscientious Monsieur New York, we learn, became a very prominent figure at practically all of the hangings of importance in his time. When the clergyman attending had signified that the doomed one was fully prepared for the last event of his life, this short, ruddy-faced, neatly dressed man, whose snowy white shirt was ornamented by a large diamond, appeared on the scene. He dropped quietly into the cell and from out of a little black satchel he took a neatly worked noose and slipped it over the head of the culprit with such dexterity as to be hardly noticed by the man. Next from the little black satchel there quickly appeared a black cap, and it was over the head of the prisoner and his arms were pinioned behind his back in a jiffy. George carefully avoided giving any needless pain, and his few words were so well-timed and intoned with such a fine sympathy as to "inspire confidence even in the victim himself." When the procession arrived at the gallows the noose was adjusted without the loss of a second. When the body was taken down, the pulley and pinioning ropes and the noose were returned to the black satchel and George was ready for the next job. One could not help but concede that the job was cheap at the price, one hundred dollars, and that it had been well done. Also one could readily excuse the glow of pride that was evident in the deportment of Monsieur New York when his thoroughness and efficiency through every detail were considered.

Monsieur New York helped many noted criminals out of the world and had some very interesting experiences in providing a "respectable taking off." In 1864 he was specially sent for by General John A. Dix, then in command of the Department of the East. George was called on to act as executioner of Captain Beale, on Governors Island, and of Captain Kennedy at Fort Lafayette.

Captain Beale was a proud-spirited Southerner, who died for the cause he had espoused and he maintained his pride to the very last moment. He turned his back on George haughtily with the remark: "Sir, I am a gentleman and desire to be treated as such." George said later that this particular job was the hardest one he had ever undertaken.

A month or so later came the hanging of Kennedy, who had been guilty of burning down a hotel. He had been an officer in the Union army and was a personal friend of the jailor, the commander of the fort. During the night before the hanging a carousal took place in the casement, and it is said that not only the prisoner and the commandant of the fort, but a certain man of the gospel, were raised to a more or less exhilarated condition. When George made his appearance on the scene and started talking in his blandest tones, the significance of his identity was not at first grasped by the hazy-headed prisoner. The caller's pleasant manner was found so agreeable that he was invited to have a drink and a cigar, but when George started to ask personal questions about the Captain's weight Kennedy wanted to know:

"Who the hell are you?"

George answered: "Oh, I'm just here to see that everything goes off all right."

George had to leave the casement in double-quick time. He said it was just another of the few unpleasant jobs he had experienced.

Such an enthusiast was George in his vocation, it is a matter of record that when in 1866 thirty Indians were to have been hanged, he communicated with Washington and offered to pay his own expenses to and from the State of Nebraska, solely for the purpose of demonstrating how, on a patent gallows which he had invented, thirty persons, to use his own terms, could be "worked off at once." This invention was secured by a caveat in the Patent Office. While George was waiting an answer from Washington, President Johnson granted pardons to nearly every one of the Indians, and thus the invention could not be practically tested, much to the chagrin of the proud inventor.

For all his enthusiasm George had a stubborn streak in his system. In 1869, after Harry Lazarus, who stabbed Barney Friery in a famous killing, and one Ferris, who had killed his wife with a hatchet in front of the St. James Church on James Street, had been sent out of the world by Monsieur New York, he refused positively for some reason or other to put his services further at the call of Sheriff O'Brien. The latter had to bring in another master of ceremonies and the departure of John Real was sadly bungled.

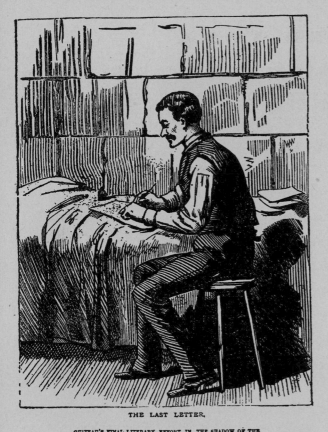

THE LAST LETTER.

GUITEAU'S FINAL LITERARY EFFORT IN THE SHADOW OF THE
GIBBET.

GUITEAU'S LAST BARGAIN.

HE SELLS HIS PHOTOGRAPH TO A LADY VISITOR AND ANNOUNCES THAT HE HAS GONE
OUT OF BUSINESS.

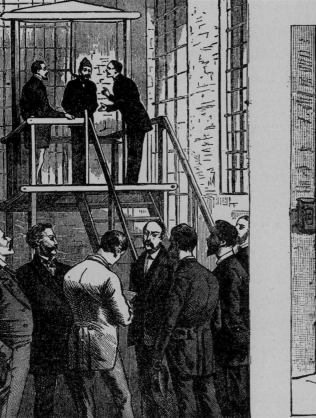

THE GIBBET'S PREY.

(FROM A SKETCH TAKEN ONE MINUTE AND A HALF BEFORE THE DROP FELL.)

THE ASSASSIN EVANGELIST.

GUITEAU READING AND EXPOUNDING THE BIBLE TO ONE OF HIS DEATH WATCH THE DAY
BEFORE HIS EXECUTION.

However, George was not without employment during the régime of O'Brien as sheriff, or even through the period when capital punishment was abolished in the State of New York. That law was made to cover the case of Mrs. Hartford, who had been guilty of doing away with an obnoxious mate in 1858. After the many killings of the Civil War the law resumed its right to take human life.

They say that, on more than one occasion, the demands for the fine handiwork of Monsieur New York were such that, since he could not appear in two parts of the country at one and the same time, the condemned ones had to wait on the convenience of the hangman. Possibly, if those who had need of his special attention would have had any say in the matter, they would have requested George not to hurry himself.

Only New Jersey, always behind the age, so we read in the *Gazette,* failed to recognize the talent of the New York Jack Ketch, though George had offered on a couple of occasions to work for mere glory. However, George was tendered the compliment of a pass to the execution in the jail yard at New Brunswick of Bridget O'Brien, who had slain her mistress, the wife of Dr. Corriel.

"Boys, that Jerseyman will make a mess of the job," was the first remark made by George when he got a sight of the gallows. Events proved that the affair was likely to be one of the most unskilful possible.

"What are you trying to do, you damned fool!" cried George, when he saw the Jerseyman handling the rope, and then, unable to restrain himself, the scientific stranger pushed his way through the crowd and saw to it that Bridget was sent out of this vale of tears in as laudable style as conditions would permit and the hand of an artist could assure.

July 13, 1860, however, was the big day in the life of Monsieur New York. This was the date of the hanging of Alfred E. Hicks on Bedloe's Island, and it stands out as a specially gala occasion in the history of New York. Never before had such a tremendous gathering been privileged to be onlookers upon the handiwork of the mysterious George. Water carriers by the hundreds, private and excursion, all heavily loaded hugged the island shore. The sail was delightful, the day balmy, and the law had provided something unusual for the seekers of a morbid thrill. And, George?—he was truly at his best on this day, and praise cannot well go beyond this. The crime for which Hicks was punished was the sensation of the day and the penalty was meted out with rare expediency, we are informed by the *Gazette*.

On March 16, 1860, the sloop *E. A. Johnson* left port for Deep Creek, Va., to procure a cargo of oysters. The company on board consisted of Captain Burr, two boys named Oliver and Smith Watts, and a man known as William Johnson. The captain had with him a considerable sum of money.

At six o'clock on the morning of Wednesday, the 21st, the small sloop was picked up by the schooner *Telegraph,* of New London, Conn., and subsequently towed to Fulton Market slip by the steam tug *Ceres*. Here she was boarded by Captain Weed, of the Second Police Precinct, and Coroner Schirmer, who at once proceeded to make an examination.

The sloop had evidently collided with some other vessel, as was indicated by the damaged condition of the bowsprit and cutwater. The sails were loose upon the deck, and everything denoted confusion and violence. The floor, ceiling, benches and furniture in the cabin were stained with blood, as were also the clothing, bedding and papers which had been scattered about on the floor. Marks of the dragging of some bloody substance from the cabin door to the sides of the rails of the boat were discernible, and the spectacle on board the sloop was ghastly and horrible. The small boat at the stern was discovered to be missing.

Within a short time after this discovery two men residing at 129 Cedar Street appeared at the Second Precinct Station-house and stated that a man who was believed to have been one of the crew had arrived at his home in the house where they resided and had appeared to have come into a fortune. By the time the man was sought he had already made a hurried departure with his wife and child. The suspected man was quickly traced to a place near Providence and he was transferred to the custody of Isaiah Rynders, now United States Marshal. Overwhelming evidence revealed that his real name was Alfred E. Hicks and that he was the guilty man sought. It took a jury only seven minutes to pronounce him guilty of piracy and murder on the high seas. While confined in the Tombs Hicks stated that he desired to make full confession before his departure from this earth, and before a large assemblage of officials and reporters the murderer stood with arms and legs shackled and told minutely and without sign of emotion of the gruesome happenings aboard the sloop *E. A. Johnson* on the night of his dreadful crime.

He described the affair as having occurred at 9:30 or 10 o'clock at night, when Captain Burr and one of the Watts boys were asleep in the cabin. He said he was steering at the time, and the other Watts was on the lookout at the bows. He had been shanghaied from a place in Water Street, he declared, and brought aboard while drunk. Suddenly the devil took possession of him, and he determined to murder the captain and the crew

SINS OF NEW YORK

that very night. Creeping forward softly, he stole upon the boy at the bows, and with one blow of an ax knocked out his brains. The noise attracted the attention of the other Watts, who jumped out of bed and came up the companionway to see what was the matter. Just at that moment Hicks struck him a heavy blow on the head and left him weltering in his blood on the deck. He then went down in search of the captain, and upon entering the cabin they at once came into conflict. The captain, who was a short, thickset, very muscular man, grappled with his assailant and there was a long tussle, during which the stove was upset. The Captain was beginning to master the murderer, when a well-directed blow of the ax felled him to the floor—another blow and he was dead. Hicks then went on deck, and taking up the bleeding and helpless man he had left there, threw him over the vessel's side. The man clutched at the taff-rail, but Hicks chopped off his hands with the ax, and the poor fellow dropped into the sea. The other bodies were then thrown overboard, the captain's money-bags were rifled, and Hicks headed the sloop for shore. He used the small boat to effect a landing.

Among the people who visited Hicks in the Tombs, following his confession, was P. T. Barnum, who sought a private interview. Barnum had a proposition to make—he was desirous of obtaining a plaster cast of the head and bust of the murderer for exhibition among the curiosities in his museum. The two came to terms, the price being twenty-five dollars, with two boxes of cigars tossed in after some haggling. Barnum then offered to give Hicks a suit of new clothes for those he had on. The transaction was agreeable to Hicks until the exchange had beeen effected, when the prisoner complained to the warden that the new clothes were not as good as his old ones. But now we will let the *Gazette* bring us to Monsieur New York's part in the proceedings.

At 6 o'clock on Thursday, July 12, the day preceding his execution, Mrs. Hicks took farewell of her husband, but neither exhibited the slightest emotion. It was more like parting for a few days than forever. At 11 o'clock he partook of a cup of tea and retired for the night. He was awakened at 4 o'clock the following morning and told to dress. He was perfectly unconcerned as to his fate, and manifested no signs of grief or penitence.

At 9 o'clock Marshal Rynders, Sheriff Kelly and others entered, when he quietly arose and saluted them. The marshal then read the death warrant, and told Hicks to prepare himself for the approaching execution. He did so by arraying himself in a suit of blue cottonade, made expressly for the occasion. He was driven in a closed carriage to the foot of Canal

[252]

Street, there to embark on the *Red Jacket* for Bedloe's Island, where it was arranged the execution would take place. About 1,500 persons, consisting of gamblers, politicians, pugilisits, reporters and medical men, were assembled on board at 10 A.M. and immediately started for their destination.

The marshal, finding that he had plenty of time to spare, and the *Great Eastern,* then lying at the foot of Hammond Street, having but recently arrived on her first voyage to this country, concluded to give his guests a view of that monster ship. The steamboat was accordingly headed up the river, whither it proceeded as far as Hammond Street, sailed around the *Great Eastern,* and then started for Bedloe's Island, where it arrived at 11 o'clock.

The pier was lined by a platoon of marines, under command of Capt. John B. Hall, and on the passing of the procession, they, with the troops from Fort Hamilton and Governor's Island, formed themselves into a hollow square all the way to the scaffold.

The scene was altogether a very imposing one—hundreds of boats, large and small, being within easy distance of the shore. For eighty or one hundred feet out the boats formed one solid mass, and again on the outside of these were excursion boats moving about.

The execution was witnessed by about 10,000 people. Hicks maintained his stolid air of bravery to the last. He never quailed beneath the glance of the crowd. Immediately on landing on the island he knelt down and silently prayed for a few moments, and then proceeded to the scaffold, which was within fifteen feet or twenty feet of the shore.

The fatal signal having been given, Hicks was executed at precisely 11:05. For three minutes he struggled severely, but after that exhibited no signs of pain. The body was allowed to remain suspended for half an hour, when it was cut down, placed in a coffin and borne back to the ship.

The remains were buried in Calvary Cemetery, but no stone has ever been erected to show the precise spot. Even if it did exist, it would be to little purpose, for the corpse was removed a night or two after the burial by some body-snatchers and sold to the surgeons for dissection.

CRIB DIES LIKE A DOG

How Pilot, the New York Brindle, Won the American Championship

I F only to point the refining influences of the years, it seems worth while that we should take note of how the now almost extinct pastime of the sporting gentleman, dog-fighting, was elevated in 1881 over the rude days when Kit Burns had his rat- and dog-fighting pit doing a flourishing business at 273 Water Street, where his house of prostitution was merely incidental to an evening's entertainment. It was here through the Sixties and Seventies that the rough characters who made up the denizens of the streets along the lower East River water-front took their diversion in watching rats the size of well-grown kittens, which had been captured from the nearby wharfs, in revolting contests with terrier dogs, and on special occasions, could wager on their favorite when the terriers had been pitted. There were many such places through the city of New York, and we merely mention Sportsmen's Hall (or Bandbox, as it was sometimes called), of which Kit Burns was the proprietor, because it happened to be the most noted.

Of course, the gentleman sport had his fighting dogs and his fighting cocks well back in the last century and even earlier in this country, but as a rule dog-fighting was rated an entertainment for the more debased element. Such contests are still being waged occasionally on the quiet in the vicinity of Greater New York. As a sports editor of a prominent metropolitan daily I have refused in recent years more than one special invitation to attend such matches. But in 1881, when the white brindle, Pilot, worried Crib, until there was no more life to shake out of his canine foe's body, thereby winning the American championship, this was an interstate contest for a stake of $2,000. which had an international tinge, was conducted with an extreme of ethics in its way, and was an occasion graced by not a few of the most prominent and respected among sporting personages. This was nothing short of dog-fighting de luxe. The challenge was officially filed through the *National Police Gazette;* its proprietor, Richard K. Fox, whose paper gave attention to both blue-ribbon and fighting dogs, proudly accepted the office of stakeholder; and he specially

DEAD DOG IN THE PIT.

SCENES AND INCIDENTS OF THE GREAT INTER-STATE BATTLE BETWEEN "PILOT" AND "CRIB."—GOING TO THE FIGHT; PREPARING FOR
THE COMBAT; THE LAST GRAPPLE.

[From Sketches by the Police Gazette Special Correspondent.]

delegated his editor of sports, William E. Harding, to the important post of referee. Louis Kreiger, of Louisville, had challenged the world on behalf of Crib, an

THEY WET THE RIBBON.

THE ASTONISHING WAY IN WHICH TWO MURRAY HILL BELLES NOTIFIED THE MADISON SQUARE GARDEN BAR-ROOM THAT "DEAR NEP" HAD COLLARED A PRIZE.

imported dog, to what was described as a "fair-scratch-in-turn" match for $1,000. a side. "Cockney Charley" Lloyd, of New York, took up the challenge published in the *Gazette* and backed his fighting dog, Pilot, an American animal. The preliminaries of the contest were quickly consummated, but it took some time before Pittsburg, Kentucky, was finally announced as the battle site. It was in this state, Kentucky, that professional fistic contests were long outlawed, and from Louisville that a certain well-known New York journalist brought a once very popular story when he returned from one of the very first bare-knuckle fights privately staged there, which non-parlor story is worth setting down for its significance in driving home the contrast in viewpoints.

It seems that, after the prize fight in question, this gentleman of the press was one of a New York delegation who proceeded to round out the evening by getting intoxicated and visiting the sporting houses of the city. At the final stop the newspaper representative got himself quite interested in one of the inmates and in the course of conversation his companion wanted to know what he was doing in her town. He volunteered the information that he had come on for the prize fight.

"Do you know," she answered, regretfully, "that I was fair crazy to see that fight. But my man, my man he says, that a prize fight ain't no place for a lady."

For the dog-fighting match between Pilot and Crib, some of the best-known sporting lights from New York, Chicago, St. Louis, Cincinnati, New Orleans and many other leading cities journeyed to Louisville, which was in close proximity to the scene of contest. Considerable sums of money were wagered on the outcome all over the country. The Ohio and Mississippi Railroad issued special excursion tickets to the fight, and the sporting delegation was met at the Louisville Hotel by Alderman Gifford, president of the Louisville Board of Aldermen, and by Chief of Police Adam Bly and other notables of the city.

POLICE GAZETTE OFFICE)
NEW YORK, Sept. 1, 1881)

Articles of Agreement entered into this first day of September, A.D. 1881, between Louis Kreiger, of Louisville, Ky., and Charles Lloyd, of New York:

The said Charles Lloyd, of New York, hereby agrees to fight his brindle and white dog Pilot, ears cut and tail on, against Louis Kreiger's, of Louisville, white dog Crib, ears cut and tail on, at 28 pounds weight for one thousand dollars ($1,000) a side: The said fight to take place on the 19th day of October, A.D. 1881, at or within a point of seven miles of Pittsburg, Ky. The stakeholder or the referee to name the place of fighting. The dogs to be weighed at 7 o'clock A.M. on the day of fighting, and to fight between 7 A.M. and 8 P.M., Richard K. Fox to be final stakeholder and to select the referee. The deposits to be made with Richard K. Fox, of the POLICE GAZETTE, the final stakeholder, viz: The first deposit of five hundred dollars ($500) a side on September 5, 1881, and the final deposit of five hundred dollars ($500) a side to be posted with Richard K. Fox, or his representative, on the 19th day of October, 1881, and on the day and place of fighting, Louis Kreiger to deposit five hundred dollars ($500) to Charles Lloyd's four hundred dollars ($400), there being an allowance of one hundred dollars ($100) for Lloyd's expenses to and from Pittsburg, Ky.; thus Louis Kreiger wagers one thousand ($1,000) to Charles Lloyd's nine hundred dollars ($900).

The said Charles Lloyd and the said Louis Kreiger do hereby agree that should the authorities in any way interfere or try to stop or prevent the said battle, that the referee shall have full power to name the next time and place of fighting. It is also agreed that the referee shall insist on the dogs being again weighed, and the said weighing shall be within thirty minutes before the time named by the referee for the fight to be decided. Should there be any after interference the dogs shall again be weighed day after day, and neither will be allowed to exceed 28 pounds in weight.

It is further agreed that the handlers shall each taste the other's dog and sponge them with wet sponge. The sponge used shall then be squeezed into each other's dog's mouth in order to prove there is no poison or pernicious drugs placed on them. After the dogs have been tasted neither of the sponges must be changed.

In pursuance of this agreement the said Charles Lloyd and the said Louis Kreiger do hereby agree to comply with the rules embodied in this agreement or forfeit the money now deposited with the stakeholder. It is also agreed that the battle shall be fought according to the POLICE GAZETTE's revised rules of dog-fighting.

Five A.M. on the morning of the contest, the roads leading to the battle-ground were crowded with vehicles of every description. Kreiger had Crib in a buggy, and Pilot was conveyed in a closed carriage. At 6:30 the party arrived at Garr's farm, six miles from Louisville. Six miles out of this pike was a rough-looking old barn, which the writer tells us "was as illy fitted up for a dog-fight as it would have been for a high-toned wedding." A pit thirteen by sixteen feet was erected in one end of the barn, and in this dilapidated old building the crowd was quickly wedged. Harding, the referee, however, was not satisfied with the conditions of the building interior, and every one was forced to go outside while the barn was cleaned up. Whether it would have then been fit for a "high-toned wedding" is not known, but Mr. Harding finally adjudged it suitable for the dog-fight. Before the would-be spectators were allowed to return " 'Cockney Charley,' who didn't propose to lose a cent," said that everybody would have to pay a dollar to get in and see the fight. Some did, but not a few climbed in through holes in the sides of the building.

It was around 7:15 when the dogs were weighed in. Pilot scaled twenty-seven and three-quarters pounds, being one-quarter of a pound heavier than Crib. Betting was "pretty lively even up" as the referee tossed up a silver, or what the report describes as a trade dollar, for choice of corners and washing. Kreiger won the toss and decided Pilot should be washed first. In Garr's farmhouse everything was ready for the washing. In the kitchen, in which were Mrs. Garr's two daughters and a baby, the washing was done in the presence of the referee. Pilot was placed in a tub of warm water and washed thoroughly, he was then washed in warm milk, and Kreiger tasted him to see if there had been any red pepper placed upon him. Pilot was then dried with towels which had been examined by the referee and then put in blankets. Crib was then "put through the same course of sprouts." And now the dogs were brought to the pit, which, we are given to understand, was surrounded by some of the most important men of Louisville.

Intense excitement prevailed when the dogs were placed in the pit. Chief of the Louisville Fire Department Hughes announced the desire of the referee that both handlers be searched. The handlers searched each other's clothes thoroughly, being solicitous that nothing was concealed that might cause injury to the opposing dog. When this ceremony was gone through with, the word was given at 9:20 to let go the dogs. Their blankets and muzzles were speedily removed and the dogs set at liberty. But let Mr. Harding tell the story in the words he reported in the paper of which he was the sports editor:

Both uttered low growls, and then, with one savage bound, Crib sprang to Pilot's corner and attacked his antagonist. He caught Pilot by the nose, but the brindle dog shook him off and grasped him by the right leg. Pilot loosened his hold upon Crib's leg to get a better one upon his throat. Crib succeeded in freeing himself, and once more caught Pilot by the nose, only to loosen it almost instantly and seize Pilot by the back of the neck and ear, throwing him down. While down Pilot got Crib by the breast and had a terrible hold, but being unable to retain his hold to any good advantage, let go and grasped Crib by the left ear. Then in turn Pilot loosened the ear-hold and got Crib's left front leg between his molars. As he pressed his jaws together the bones in Crib's leg fairly cracked. This terrible punishment seemed only to enrage the Louisville dog the more, for with one great effort he threw Pilot five times in succession with the ear-hold. Crib again seized Pilot by the nose, which, by the way, seemed to be his favorite hold, and once more downed the New York dog. As quick as a flash he let go Pilot's nose and went to chewing Pilot's front leg. With the fighting that Crib was now doing the Louisville people thought him a sure winner of the fight.

But it now came Pilot's turn to do some fighting, and the manner in which he viciously chewed Crib's left leg was terrible to behold. Crib, with a growl, broke loose only to be caught again in the same way. With another effort Crib once more gained his freedom, and for fully five minutes the dogs fought with ear-holds, until finally Pilot downed Crib and while holding him by the ear, bumped his head on the floor of the pit. Crib secured a hold on Pilot's throat, and although only fighting on three legs, succeeded in throwing his antagonist. This seemed to incense Pilot, for he threw Crib with a throat-hold and again with a hind-leg-hold. Crib returned with a leg-hold on Pilot, and then a bet of $100 was made that Crib would win the fight. The bet was promptly taken by "Cockney Charley," the owner of Pilot.

The fight had now lasted forty-two minutes. Crib succeeded in getting from under his adversary, but the poor critter's gameness was gone. He turned to the side of the pit and was in the act of leaping out when he was grabbed by the brindle dog and dragged back into the field of battle. Crib was a whipped dog at this moment, but Pilot, not content with the victory already achieved, determined to kill his antagonist while the opportunity of so doing was at his command. Crib once more turned to the side of the pit, and this time succeeded in getting outside, followed by Pilot, who seized the Louisville pet by the under jaw and, clinging on to him, refused to loosen his hold, necessitating the picking up of the dogs together and placing them again in the pit. Pilot threw Crib in the corner with an ear-hold and held him there. Kreiger fanned Crib vigorously with his hat, but did the dog no good, for he was fast failing. From this time on Pilot did nothing but endeavor to shake the little life out of Crib that still remained.

The fight lasted exactly one hour and twenty-five minutes.

Just as the winning party reached the depot to make their departure for New York, up dashed Kreiger and said to "Cockney Charley" Lloyd:

"I told you I would stand treat if I lost, and I'm here to keep my word."

And he kept his word. No getting away from it, the Louisville gentleman was a thorough sport. He amply proved this when he permitted his nearly dead dog to be dragged back into the pit by the conquering Pilot.

MR. SULLIVAN AND MR. FOX

How the Sport of Boxing Came to Be Big Business

The Fox may go to England
And the Fox may go to France,
But to beat John L., he can go to Hell,
And then he won't have a chance.

ON a gusty evening very early in the month of April, 1881, Richard K. Fox and his editor of sports, William E. Harding, came into Harry Hill's place on Houston Street to regale themselves with a plate of the proprietor's tasty prime roast beef. As the two took their chairs at the table that had been provided for them they noted that some person at the other side of the room was very much the center of interest.

"It's that young Boston fighter, Sullivan," explained Hill, who had come over personally to see that the wants of Mr. Fox and his companion were given special attention. Hill hazarded the opinion that this young man was destined to be the next champion of the prize ring. He then went into details of how the husky young fist fighter from Boston had cleaned up Steve Taylor on the stage in this very room only a night or two previous.

"Tell Sullivan to come over and see me," condescended Fox.

The message was delivered to the young pugilist. Flushed with victory and the applause of his surrounders, and possibly feeling the effects of several glasses of champagne, which was a brand-new indulgence for young Sullivan, he replied proudly:

"Tell Mr. Fox, if he wants to see me, to come over to my table. I'm here with friends and I don't intend to leave them."

And on so trivial an incident the seed was planted that was to see the pastime known as the manly art blossom, in future years, into big business boxing.

As a result of this affront to his dignity, a dignity which Mr. Fox had come to prize quite highly, the proprietor of the *Police Gazette* decided that he would see to it that the chesty youth from Boston should be taken down a peg. His endeavor to satisfy this desire prompted a world-wide search for an opponent who could humble John L. This search for a man who could beat Sullivan led to an expenditure of thousands and thousands of dollars, and each one of these dollars was returned many-fold to Richard K. Fox in the way of added circulation for the *National Police Gazette*.

A few weeks after the incident already related, on May 16 a barge was towed up the North River by the tug-boat *Sadie Ellis;* her sinking by the ferry-boat *Secaucus* was later graphically pictured by the *Gazette*. The barge came to a stop nearly opposite the then tiny city of Yonkers. On this barge, for a purse of $800.,

PERILS OF NEW YORK'S WATER HIGHWAY—COLLISION ON THE NORTH RIVER BETWEEN THE HOBOKEN FERRYBOAT SECAUCUS AND THE TUGBOAT SADIE ELLIS, RESULTING IN THE SINKING OF THE LATTER.—See Page 3.

which had been subscribed by a gathering of the sporting fraternity, John L. Sullivan and John Flood, a burly longshoreman, fought a contest with hard gloves. The Boston Strong Boy came through this test in a way that gave greater impetus to the trumpeting of the Sullivan valor.

Flood was no match for Sullivan, concedes the *Gazette,* which treated the world to the first artistic conception of John L. in action. The first blow the latter got in was landed plump on the side of Flood's jaw and completely demoralized him. He was groggy and no good from that moment. In the expressive language of a bulging-eyed and very much astounded New York reporter, who had never attended a prize fight before, "Sullivan hit Flood so hard in the neck that it swelled his ankles." After the contest the hat was passed for the vanquished man and a collection of $98 was made, of which amount the winner contributed $10.

Following this victory the *Gazette* blazoned an announcement that Richard K. Fox stood ready to back Paddy Ryan for a stake of $5,000. for the fistic championship according to Queensberry rules. Fox at once deposited $1,000. with Harry Hill, who was finally chosen stakeholder, as part of Ryan's half of the purse.

The match created an unprecedented interest in pugilism, but it remained for Richard K. Fox to take real advantage of the situation. The prominent newspapers of the country gave the Sullivan-Ryan match far more attention than was the case with the battle between Ryan and Joe Goss. Even against their will the leading editors were forced to take cognizance of the circulation harvest that the *Gazette* had reaped out of the prominence it had given the Ryan-Goss match the previous year. But Fox distanced all contemporaries in his handling of the meeting between Ryan, the American champion, and the challenger, Sullivan. Though the men did not come together until February 7, 1882, every issue for many previous weeks had several columns devoted to the preliminaries and the training.

The battle-ground, it was agreed upon, was to be located one hundred miles from New Orleans. Though it was secretly agreed it was to be pitched within the boundaries of the State of Mississippi, the lawmakers of that commonwealth soon got wind of the plans and the Mississippi legislature passed a bill which prescribed severe penalties for prize fighting. The training quarters were hastily shifted near to New Orleans and the preparations for the battle went on and for several weeks before the day set for the contest the sporting men from all over the country were gravitating toward the Crescent City. On January 28, a special train left Jersey City that carried so many from New York that "Gotham was depleted of her fancy element almost entirely." In spite of the action of the Mississippi legislature the ring was pitched in front of the Barnes Hotel, Mississippi City, Mississippi.

In its issue following the contest the *Gazette* added an eight-page supplement which was given over entirely to printed matter and pictures that had to do with the Sullivan-Ryan prize fight. On the first page was a picture of the gladiators shaking hands in the ring just before squaring off. Pages two and three gave fine display to the fighting colors of the contestants. Sullivan's colors, we are informed, were made abroad and nowhere nearly as attractive as those of the *Police Gazette Champion,* Paddy Ryan, which could be purchased through the Fox offices at $10. each, and less costly but beautiful ones could be had at $7.50 each.

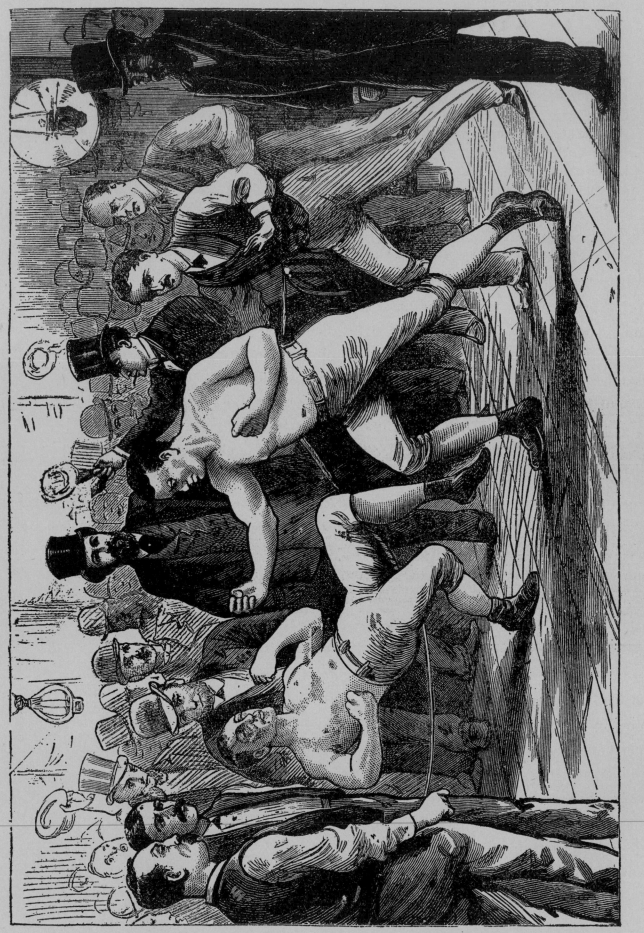

THE FLOOD-SULLIVAN PRIZE FIGHT

FOR A STAKE OF $1,000—FOUGHT ON A BARGE SIX MILES UP THE HUDSON RIVER, ON THE NIGHT OF MAY 16TH—SULLIVAN WINS
AFTER FIGHTING EIGHT BOUNDS,

Ryan's colors represent America, Ireland and New York. On white silk is a border of red, white and blue, representing our national colors. In the center is an eagle standing on a globe, the latter colored blue and dotted with stars. Beneath is the inscription, "Paddy Ryan, Champion of America." The eagle holds a scroll with the inscription, "Police Gazette, New York, 1881." In the left-hand corner is an Irish harp, in the right-hand corner is a golden sunburst, which is an emblem of the Fenian Brotherhood. In the lower right-hand corner "Excelsior" represents the seal of New York. In the lower left-hand corner is an American shield.

The fighting colors of the two men were on display through the country in practically every saloon of prominence, to say nothing of the barber-shops, both of which sporting centers usually had the complete files of the *Gazette* for the year on hand. The center pages of the special fight issue were entirely taken up with pictures. One page was devoted to bust photos of the pugilists and their backers. The other depicted lively scenes on the way to the battle-ground. The back page of the supplement was given over to the artist's conception of "The Battle of the Giants," as the picture was captioned. We see Sullivan and Ryan in the center of the roped space in the act of making threatening gestures toward each other. The spectators are standing many-deep around the ring and all appear tremendously excited. Apparently much money is being waged.

Although this special supplement edition was not to be had until a full week after the Sullivan-Ryan contest was fought there was such an avid demand for this number of the *Gazette* that the Fox presses were kept busy day and night to supply the demand. Though Mr. Fox's champion suffered an ignominious defeat, being unable to respond for more of the Boston Strong Boy's sledgehammer smashes after eleven minutes of bare-fist fighting, Mr. Fox's weekly profited handsomely.

Fox became the more determined to put John L. in his place, when John L. disdained to accept the Fox "dog collar," as he dubbed the championship belt. From Leicester, England, Fox brought a middleweight named Joe Collins, but better known as Tug Wilson, who had been recommended by Arthur Chambers, a well-known figure in pugilism of the time. Sullivan at first declined to take up the *Gazette* challenge on the grounds that the Briton was too small to make a fit opponent, but his backer finally agreed to wager $1,000. that Wilson could not stand up to John L. for four rounds in a contest with gloves. Fox snapped up the offer and the bout took place in Madison Square Garden, July 17, 1882. It was a sizzling hot night, but Sullivan had other reasons to be burning up. He failed dismally in his attempt to knock out Wilson, who dropped to the floor and hugged and worked all manner of artful tricks that baffled the American champion completely. The affair drew a packed house at an admission of one to five dollars and the gate grossed around $16,000.

So nettled was the champion over the outcome of this match that he accused his manager, Billy Madden, of double-crossing him, and the two came to the parting of the ways. Madden thereupon allied himself with Fox in trying to bring about the overthrow of Sullivan. With $5,000. of Fox's money, just as a starter, Madden went to England and promoted a boxing competition. Charley Mitchell came through the winner and on March 25 arrived in this country on the *Republic*. On May 14, of that year, Mitchell was sent against Sullivan. This was in Madison Square Garden.

There have been various versions handed down of this contest, most of them unfavorable to John L. The *Gazette* report may be of interest therefore, since, while it may have been biased in favor of the man backed by Fox, the report makes it look like Sullivan's fight.

After Al Smith (a noted sporting character of the Eighties with no designs on the presidency) called time, both pugilists went right to work. Sullivan, in his usual off-hand, rushing style, dashed in at Mitchell, as if to annihilate him, swinging left and right with tremendous quickness and determination, expecting to land a terrific steam-hammer blow on the English champion's neck and end the contest. Mitchell electrified the crowd in the first round by a series of new ring tactics, landing his left with terrible force several times on the "mark,' which must have made the champion feel anything but easy; and then when the champion would again swing his right, hoping to knock Mitchell out, the Englishman would evade the terribly dangerous blows and make a grand rally. Sullivan followed Mitchell up all over the stage, sending in tremendous blows, many of which landed but not on the spot intended, but he managed to knock the Briton down several times. Mitchell also knocked Sullivan down—clean off his pins, and it was the cleanest knock-down ever seen. The first round ended at the expiration of the specified three minutes without either having the advantage.

In the second round Sullivan knocked Mitchell around à la Tug Wilson, and fought Mitchell to the ropes, and knocked him down. Mitchell fell over the ropes off the stage, injuring his back, and his friends looked blue.

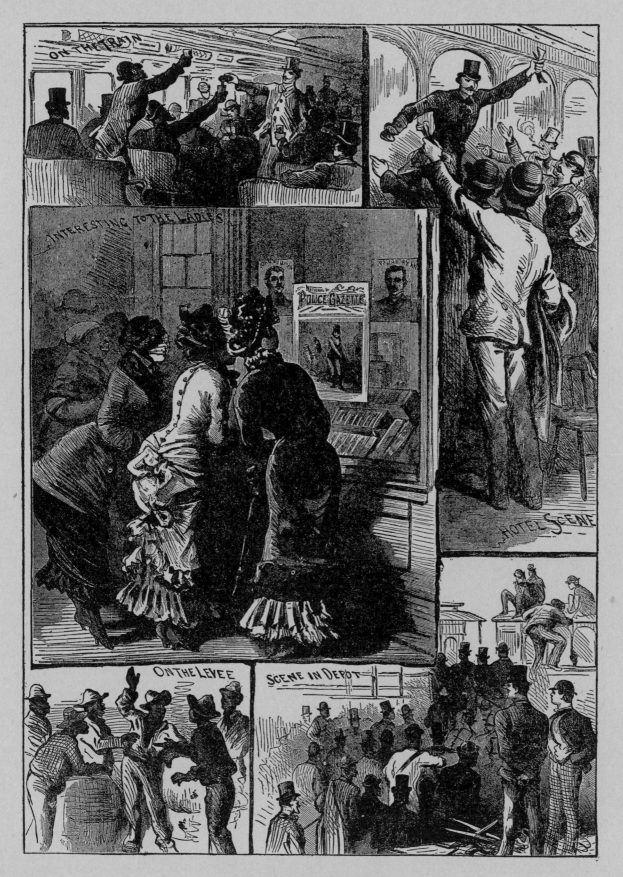

JUST BEFORE THE BATTLE.

SCENES IN NEW ORLEANS, AND INCIDENTS OF THE TRIP TO THE FIGHTING GROUND WHERE PADDY RYAN, THE "POLICE GAZETTE"
CHAMPION, AND JOHN L. SULLIVAN MET.

In the third round Sullivan forced the fighting and several times he floored Mitchell, but the plucky pugilist, who was overmatched, gamely faced the music. Finally after a grand rally and any amount of slogging [now termed slugging] Sullivan bore Mitchell to the ropes, fought him down and fell on top of him. Mitchell was apparently dazed when he got up, but was going to continue when Capt. Williams jumped on the stage and stopped the affair.

According to one who was associated with Mr. Fox in those days, the Mitchell investment stood the *Gazette* owner $20,000. in one way and another, but Fox thought the money well invested. He got much publicity for the *Gazette* by the manner in which he took up the cudgels for Mitchell, but more than a year went by before Sullivan was drawn into a return match with the Briton. Interest in the bout was tremendous.

Monday, June 30, was the date set for the contest and all the sporting houses through the city were thronged with visiting sportsmen, and the respective merits of the pugilists were apparently the one topic of discussion. Crowds from Philadelphia, Baltimore, Boston and more distant points had come on to witness the "great fistic display between the champion pugilists of the Old and the New World. At 5 P.M., fully four hours before the rival gladiators were to meet in battle array, a tremendous throng swarmed every street leading to the arena. Tickets were retailing at two dollars each, and they were sold like hot cakes to the sweltering mass of humanity. Soon the mammoth Garden, which will seat 13,500 persons, was packed to its utmost capacity."

The *Gazette* lists in fine print more than a column of names of those at the ringside. William K. Vanderbilt, from whom the arena was rented and who was then reputed to be the richest man in the world, was there; and Paymaster Cunningham, U.S.N.; Supervisor P. Pickett; Samuel Carpenter, Esq., General Passenger Agent of the P. R. R.; Coroner Robinson; and a lot of Aldermen, including Duffy, Cleary, O'Neill, Fitzpatrick, McCabe, O'Reilly, McLaughlin; and Judges Duffy, O'Brien, McCord, O'Rourke and Whalen; and Assemblymen Brogan, Cassidy, O'Donovan and Harrigan; and County Clerks Keenan, Cahill, Mooney and Maloney; Roscoe Conkling, Edward Stokes, Herman Oelrichs, and other notables had good seats, as did Fire Commissioners Purroy and Croker, Police Commissioners Nichols and Matthews, and Police Inspectors Thorne, Dilks, Murray and Burns; also Rev. Henry Ward Beecher and Rev. De Witt Talmage. The sporting notables were out strong and a quick glance noted Joe Goss, Billy Edwards, Harry Hill, William Muldoon, Jake Kilrain, Mike Donovan and a long list of others. It was a big night in New York.

Shortly after eight o'clock Billy Madden, who had charge for the real sponsor of the affair, Richard K. Fox, presented J. Hyland, master of ceremonies, and after a rattling setto between a couple of light-weights, Gus Hill, the champion club swinger, was accorded the stage, and a delegation of the uniformed *Police Gazette* patrol lifted the Richard K. Fox club, weighing 115 pounds, onto the stage and Hill gave a "first class" exhibition, after which came several more lively short bouts. Then came an annoying delay during which disquieting rumors spread through the gathering. Just as every one was on the border of restlessness the tall form of Sullivan was seen coming from the Madison Avenue entrance. He was followed by Police Captain Williams. Sullivan mounted to the ring with difficulty, and, taking off his hat, staggered to the ropes and said:

"Gentlemen (hic) I am sick (hic) and not able to box (hic). The doctor is here (hic), and this is the first time I disappointed yer (hic)."

The champion was drunk as a lord, and a very intoxicated one at that. The *Gazette* intimated that the beer-makers' strike had not had its effect on the champion, who had advanced beyond the beer-imbibing stage.

No, the crowd did not wreck the place or start a serious disturbance. There were hisses, groans and cat-calls, but that was all, though the box holders had paid as high as $25. for their places. Not a penny of the receipts was returned to the victimized patrons. The gate was said to have amounted to only $6,668., which would seem to have called for a lot of explanations.

Can you imagine any modern prize ring champion, even Jack Dempsey, living down such a fiasco? Yet John L. Sullivan was able to come back to New York not only as a fighter and actor, but as a public hero as well. It was soon after this that the song, the chorus of which heads this chapter, and which was soon carried all over the country, was first sung in Tony Pastor's music hall. Which was on the same night M'lle Zuila, one of the performers, had a perilous accident.

A few months previous to this bad break by the champion he had made short work of another of Fox's importations. Jem Mace, a former champion of the ring and one of the most scientific big men the game has ever known, brought from New Zealand, Herbert A. Slade, the Maori. The coming of Slade was made much of. He looked even taller than his six feet, two inches in height, had a tremendous shoulder spread and his fists were an enomous "pair of pounders." Slade was something of a sensation as he arrived at the *Gazette* offices. His skin was a coppery hue and his hair was black and straight as an Indian's; his burly form was encased in a huge buffalo-skin coat and on his head was a high sealskin cap. Crowds followed him everywhere. There was some trouble over securing a permit from the Corporation Council for a bout between Sullivan and Slade at the Garden. A warrant

PERILOUS SITUATION OF M'LLE ELLA ZUILA CAUSED BY THE BREAKING OF THE BALANCING POLE WHILE RIDING A BICYCLE ON A HANGING WIRE, AT TONY PASTOR'S THEATRE, NEW YORK CITY.—SEE PAGE 4.

was sworn out for the arrest of Richard K. Fox as instigator of a prize fight. Without waiting for the serving of this warrant Mr. Fox and his lawyers appeared at the Tombs prepared to do legal battle for the cause of boxing.

Fox's lawyers contended that, while prize fighting was prohibited under a legal act of 1859, this law did not affect sparring contests in which scientific exhibitions of the manly art were given with padded mits. Henry Bergh, who led the enemies of the sport of boxing, was charged in the *Gazette* with being soured against the sport because he could not get Sullivan and Slade to box for the benefit of the Society for the Prevention of Cruelty to Bald-Headed Men. The *Gazette* printed a long list of notables who condemned the arrest of Mr. Fox, which never actually happened, as an outrage. When Fox finally forced a hearing his lawyers made an excellent plea for boxing as an exercise and an entertainment. Well-known teachers of the fistic art were lined up ready to prove that their pupils included ministers, ministers' sons, deacons and doctors and men of high standing. Henry Ward Beecher, it was insisted, was quite handy with the gloves. When Judge Donohue handed down his decision it did not come as a surprise that it was to the effect that sparring was not necessarily an unlawful act.

It was a notable victory for Mr. Fox. It took an entire page to give expression to the messages of praise that came from various parts of the country, and the press of Gotham rallied strongly in support of the *Gazette* owner as was evidenced by a column of editorial comment culled from the *Tribune, Herald, Sun, Times* and other dailies.

The only unsatisfactory part of this victory, so far as Fox was concerned, was the outcome of the Sullivan-Slade bout. They met for four rounds in Madison Square Garden, August 7, 1883. The Maori was knocked out of time in the third round.

In 1884 Richard K. Fox brought another foreign contender to these shores in the person of Alf Greenfield, of Birmingham, England. Sullivan took him on in Madison Square Garden, on the night of November 17. The physical advantages were decidedly with the American, still the Briton showed pluck and boxing science that enabled him to make a commendable showing through the first round. The second round indicated that John L. was too strong for his opponent. The smaller man fought back with desperation but he suffered a severe cut over his left eye that soon had his face and chest crimson stained. Soon Greenfield was fought to the ropes, where he was being wickedly belabored. At this point Police Captain Williams leaped upon the platform and pushed the fighters apart.

The bloodstained men were loath to stop, but Captain Williams pointed in the direction of Superintendent Walling. It seems that the latter had come to the conclusion that the contest had ceased to be a sparring exhibition, that the passions of the contestants had been aroused, and that they were trying to knock each other out —which made it a physical combat contrary to the letter of the law.

Once again many notables outside of the sport and theater world were among those present. The gathering included quite a few members of the Union Club, many of them still wearing the apparel with which they had graced the Astor wedding that afternoon. In the boxes and at the ringside were Isidor Straus, Benjamin G. Arnold, Dean Sage, William B. Hilton, John J. Knox, Rev. E. W. Donald, Charles L. Tiffany, Henry M. Flagler, James B. Colgate, Cyrus W. Fields, James McCreery, Elihu Root, Abe Hummel and many others equally prominent.

Shortly before Christmas Day, 1884, a jury was empaneled to try Sullivan and Greenfield on the charge of prize fighting. Richard K. Fox was on hand with a fine array of legal talent. The *Gazette* report of the trial has some interesting points.

The first man called for jury duty was Felix Bohen, a bookkeeper in a liquor store. He said he didn't know Sullivan or anything about athletics. He was accepted. Thomas R. Bronson, a drug merchant, testified that he had read Roman history and knew about gladiators and such things. He was accepted as Juror No. 2. James M. Bulger would seem to have been excused by the District Attorney for no other reason than that his shoes gleamed, his hat was nobby and his clothes natty; anyway he was excused without a word. David Kirsch, a lace merchant, who admitted he was opposed to men like Sullivan, but thought he could be fair, was accepted. James D. Spraker, ship chandler who not only admitted having seen sparring exhibitions in Madison Square Garden, but seemed proud of the fact, was also accepted.

After several rejections along came William McBride, who admitted he did not approve of boxing to excess. To illustrate, he said he had often played checkers all night and considered that excess. When he said "checkers" the court room smiled right out loud and the checker fiend was excused. Alfred H. Thorn, an architect, caused something of a sensation when he looked calmly at the great John L. and told the court that he did not object to boxing, but he did object to Sullivan and many of his acts. It took over two hours and a half before a full jury was panelled. The others accepted were as follows: John Graham, builder; Joseph Swan, silk goods; Lippmann Toplitz, millinery; Julius Friend, another lace merchant; Ludwig Schwabacher, metal broker; Silas H. Rushton, who was employed in the same capacity as Juror No. 1, but not in the same line of business; John G. Gnadt, machinist; and H. A. Barclay, whose business, if he had any, was not given.

Police Superintendent Walling was called first and went into a description of the blood spilling. He admitted that Captain Williams had made the arrest under his instructions. Captain Williams, who came next, made a fine witness for the men under arrest. He admitted he had seen more blood and harder exchanges of blows in boxing bouts presented under the auspices of the Police Athletic Association. Inspector Thorne's testimony was also in favor of the defendants. He did not think there had been any evidences of passion shown by the contestants. Captain Clinchy came next and he was not of much help to the people. He admitted he liked to box himself and did not think the blows exchanged between Sullivan and Greenfield had been hard ones. The gloves were next passed over to the gentlemen of the jury. Mr. Schwabacher tried one on and so did Mr. Lippmann Toplitz, and Mr. Cohen and some of the others examined the gory stains.

Here the people rested and Lawyer Howe opened for the defense. Harry Hill was called and after kissing the Bible promised to tell the truth. Then he up and said that, without wishing to express anything derogatory to the character of either pugilist, he was prepared to say that nothing had been less ferocious than the exhibition which those two gentlemen, Mr. Sullivan and Mr. Greenfield, had given. With some trouble he was confined to the dry testimony about the rules of the Marquis of Queensberry. Quite a number of other qualified, but possibly not disinterested, judges were called. They all agreed that the blows struck were tame, bordering on gentle.

Alfred Greenfield was called next. Those who may have taken note of how small he appeared compared to Sullivan, probably wondered how large he looked beside Mr. Schwabacher and Mr. Lippmann Toplitz as he passed the jury box. He promised to tell the truth, as the rest had done. Assistant District Attorney Gove wearily requested him to merely tell the truth.

Greenfield identified the gloves he boxed with, and said the bout was only an exhibition to please the public. They fought under no rules in particular, and he didn't want to hurt Sullivan any more than Sullivan wanted to hurt him. In England he taught gentlemen how to take care of themselves, and he treated Sullivan as he treated any of his gentlemanly pupils. "The way we came to clinch," he said, "is this. 'E's a good judge of the bizness, and when I tried to 'it 'im 'e ducked 'is 'ed, and my arm slipped round 'is neck. We 'ired the 'all through our managers, just to make a little money. I 'ad no ill-feeling, and 'e had no ill-feeling. We do it in England all the time, but of course, I don't know whether it's allowed 'ere or not."

John L. Sullivan next testified. He was satisfied with Judge Barrett's decision, and had decided to be ruled by it. He simply sparred a friendly round of three minutes, and in the second round both received their scratches by ducking their heads to avoid blows. He had no intention of hurting Greenfield.

"Were you angry during the exhibition?"

"No, sir. I have never been angry in any of the engagements I have been in."

Sullivan showed a slight abrasion on his head, back of his ear, to the jury. He assured them that he had not been hurt by any of Greenfield's blows, and had reserve power to have struck his opponent much harder, but refrained from doing so. Though it was customary for even prize fighters to shake hands before a contest, he had shaken hands with Greenfield simply through friendly motives. The master of ceremonies, a Mr. Johnson, had stated to the audience that the exhibition was to be under the Marquis of Queensberry rules, but neither he nor Greenfield intended that they should be.

At the conclusion of the champion's testimony the case rested. Mr. Mitchell, Mr. Howe and Assistant District Attorney Gove made short addresses. Mr. Mitchell pitted the testimony of Captains Clinchy and Williams and Inspector Thorne against the impressions of aged Chief Walling, and drew the conclusion that when supplemented by the testimony of all the other witnesses there could be no question that Sullivan and Greenfield had taken part in nothing more than an athletic exhibition. Mr. Mitchell was followed by Mr. Howe, and Assistant District Attorney Gove closed the case, after which Judge Barrett charged the jury. He warned its members to divest themselves of sympathy with sparring matches and of any prejudice against boxing contests and determine if this was a fight or contention without weapons for mastery; "if it was a physical contention for supremacy, then the defendants are guilty under the statute."

The jury filed out, taking with them the gloves. When they had been gone out about eight minutes they filed back. The defendants stood up, stared at the foreman, and the foreman stared at them. Then he sang out in a loud, clear voice:

"Not guilty."

That this trial cost Richard K. Fox a goodly sum in coin of the realm is well known, though no specific amounts appear to have been charged on the books of the publication. Whatever it was he spent, the *Gazette* owner was well satisfied with the investment. Fox, and the sport of pugilism, profited, of that there can be little question.

By this time, however, Fox appears to have given up any hope of discovering a foreign fist fighter who could humble John L. Now he diverted his search through this country, and after looking over the field with much thoroughness he

Inscribed to the POLICE GAZETTE'S Champion, Mr JAKE KILRAIN.

OUR CHAMPION.

Words and Music by

As sung by America's queen of Vocalists, MISS MAGGIE CLINE.

M. H. ROSENFELD.
Author of "THE KENTUCKY GALLOPADE,"
"THE RED BANDANNA," and other popular works.

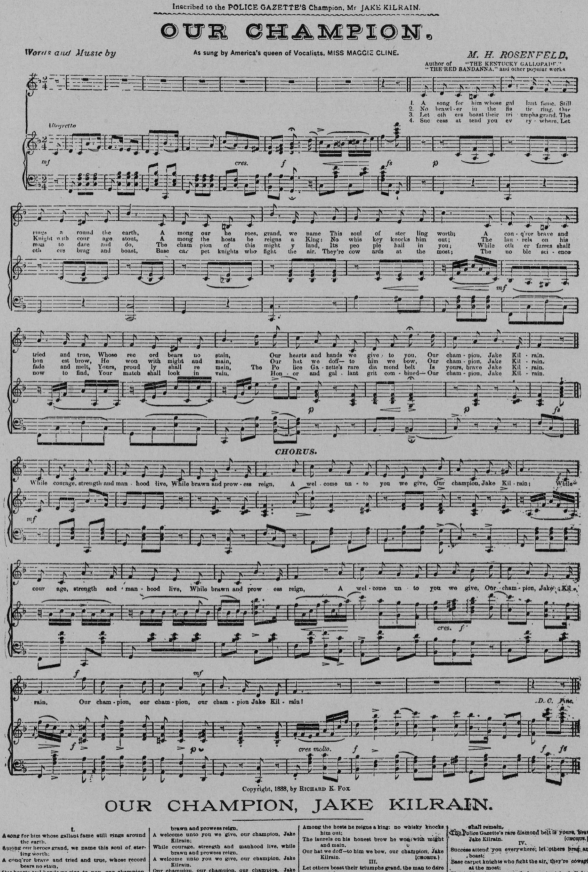

CHORUS.

Copyright, 1888, by RICHARD K. FOX

OUR CHAMPION, JAKE KILRAIN.

I.
A song for him whose gallant fame still rings around
the earth.
Among our heroes grand, we name this soul of ster-
ling worth;
A conq'ror brave and tried and true, whose record
bears no stain,
Our hearts and hands we give to you, our champion,
Jake Kilrain.

CHORUS.

While courage, strength and manhood live, while
brawn and prowess reign,
A welcome unto you we give, our champion, Jake
Kilrain;
While courage, strength and manhood live, while
brawn and prowess reign,
A welcome unto you we give, our champion, Jake
Kilrain.
Our champion, our champion, our champion, Jake
Kilrain.

II.
No brawler in the fistic ring our Knight with courage
stout.

Among the hosts he reigns a king: no whisky knocks
him out;
The laurels on his honest brow he won with might
and main.
Our hat we doff—to him we bow, our champion, Jake
Kilrain.   [CHORUS.]

III.
Let others boast their triumphs grand, the man to dare
and do.
The champion of this mighty land its people hail in
you;
While other fames shall fade and melt; yours proudly

shall remain,
The Police Gazette's rare diamond belt is yours, brave
Jake Kilrain.   [CHORUS.]

IV.
Success attend you everywhere; let others brag and
boast;
Base carpet knights who fight the air, they're cowards
at the most;
The noble science now to find your match shall look
in vain.
Honor and gallant grit combined—our champion, Jake
Kilrain.   [CHORUS.]

became the backer of John Joseph Killion, who attained ring prestige under the name of Jake Kilrain. This was in 1886. Mitchell was engaged as trainer and Kilrain was taken abroad the following year for a big international bout with Jem Smith, the English champion. It was called a draw after one hundred and six rounds of bare knuckle fighting that consumed two and one-half hours. The *National Police Gazette* and the American press were united in the contention that the decision should have gone to the American fighter.

When Fox brought his new "Police Gazette Champion" back home a broadside of challenges was fired at Sullivan, and when John L. was tardy, for various reasons, in taking up the defi, the title was claimed for Kilrain. The war of printers' ink went on for many months until finally, late in 1888, John L. took the position of challenger himself, and dared Kilrain to fight for a purse of $20,000. Fox called the bluff, if bluff it was, and signified his willingness to back his champion for $10,000. The battle did not take place until July 8, 1889. Sullivan's victory, which came after seventy-five rounds of fighting, was forecast by the kids on the street, who could be heard going about chanting:

Sullivan will KILLrain!
Sullivan will KILLrain!

DENIZENS AND DEPRAVITIES OF THE DEADLY DIVES

A Tour of the Five Points, the River Dens, and the Bowery
When It Was the Bowery

SHORTLY after the Reverend De Witt Talmage—this was in the late Seventies —came over from his Tabernacle in Brooklyn to "flash a dark lantern on the slums of New York," the *Gazette* did more than derisively intimate that the good pastor from over the river was a little late in his exploring and exploiting, and, what was more, had not looked where he really should have for his sermon material. For his better enlightenment he was advised to peruse the new *Gazette* series dealing with the Deadly Dives of New York. The promise held out was that it would afford a real insight into the underworld of the city as it had been and as it was now. Furthermore, the series would endeavor, as it went along, to bring out for his benefit some of the things that had been and were being done to bring about an improvement in social and moral conditions. And, Talmage had better confine his researches to the sanctimonious frauds of his own realm rather than waste his time among the lowly. The clerical investigator was advised to drop into the Academy of Music after midnight on the occasion of one of the ultra balls sponsored by the more or less socially elect. Take the Arion, Old Guard, Charity, Liederkranz and, in particular, the French ball of the Cercle Français de l'Harmonie!—

Long before the hour of one, when the programme would be at its height, the Academy was packed, Gilson's supper-room was overrun, the boxes were filled, the amphitheatre was entirely occupied, sleighing parties had come in from Central Park, the theatres had sent their quotas, and the smart young men in dog collars and an elaborate condition of friz as to hair were lending their social instincts to the general gayety. Delegations from Philadelphia and other provincial places added their scintillations to the general brilliancy. There was one noticeable improvement. Instead of having in the supper hall long tables at which men and women sit and fight for food, Mr. Gilson set the room with little tables at which parties were served decently if not in order.

For all the lively doings, it is a more decorous affair than a few

years back, when it was not unusual to see a lady dressed as a page, passed
down, head foremost, from one box to another, just for the sake of the

DOMINIE TALMAGE'S BIG CIRCUS REVIVAL.

STRATEGY OF A GIDDY COUNTRY DAMSEL DETERMINED TO WITNESS THE ACROBATIC RANTER AND HIS FESTIVE SHOW ON A BOSS
PROGRAMME NIGHT—HER NOVEL SUCCESS WITH THE ABLE ASSISTANCE OF HER CITY "MASH"

gallants who had requested a loan of her for the pleasure of treating her
to a glass of wine. But, if it is imagined that the stationing of officers all
over the hall has prevented the dancing of the can-can, then little is known

of ways and means. Necessity is the maternal parent of invention, although it has never been definitely ascertained who Invention's Pa is. No birth or marriage statistics throw any light upon the subject, and the matter is shrouded in the same gloom which envelopes the query as to why Miss Fortune should have a child. To return to the ball and the can-can. For the benefit of the bluecoats who say "can't-can't"—a bogus dance is started in one corner of the dancing floor. While the guardians of law and order have their attentions here engaged there has been elsewhere a pink-toed and lace-edged petticoat quadrille that would have evoked approval of the eye-glassed loungers of the *Mabille* in Paris.

Do not think that we do not award the palm of virtue to the hop in Wallhalla Hall on Orchard Street. Certainly we do. On one hand we have champagne and can-can, on the other, beer and beauty. Nor do we see at Wallhalla these disgusting new society dances, the "Racquet," the "Wave," and the "Telephone."

The Reverend Talmage would have found not a few of his pewholders taking part in the "cutting-up and mad capering" of the new dances. And by way of emphasizing the laxities of the churchgoer and in contrast to its pictures of the Bowery and the water-front thoroughfares in all their shocking sinfulness we are also made aware through the *Gazette* series of how certain pillars of the magnificent temples of religion degraded the existence of their employees. And this information came by means of dramatic examples like the following:

There is no place so admirable for a rendezvous as certain of our department stores along Sixth Avenue and Grand Street. Come with me [invites Paul Prowler] to any one of these bazaars. Let us depict a little play, which will illustrate:

Scene: A Sixth Avenue or Grand Street department store.
Time: The present [1880, in this instance].
Dramatis Personæ: Handsome married woman. Handsome man (no matter about his marriage, i.e., not in this play).

SHE: But really you ought not to come here so often *accidentally.* You know I *have* to come here to shop.
HE: Certainly I do; that is why I come here.
SHE: But people will notice.
HE: Never fear that; they are too busy with themselves, and beside, we are so eminently proper.
SHE: Why, of course, we are—what should we be?
HE: Friends instead of mere acquaintances.
SHE: But consider how we met—how impudent and horrid you were

GRAND BALL OF THE ARION SOCIETY AT MADISON SQUARE GARDEN, FEBRUARY 19—NEW YORK'S BEAUTY AND CHIVALRY JOIN IN THE WORSHIP OF TERPSICHORE AND BACCHUS—SCENES AT THE ENTRANCE OF THE COMMITTEES OF FINANCE AND ARRANGEMENTS, DRESSED IN THE COSTUMES OF THE EMPRESS KATHERINE OF RUSSIA AND CASSANOVA—A CHAMPAGNE-INSPIRED BELLE PROPOSES A TOAST.—SKETCHED BY SPECIAL GAZETTE ARTISTS.

SEE PAGE 2

to follow me from here and offer to carry my bundles.

HE: Never mind that now. It's ancient history. But let us go and have some lunch. You know you didn't come in here to buy anything.

SHE: I came in to look at that cloak, the $150. one. I'll dream of it to-night.

HE: What's the trouble? Price too steep?

SHE: It would swamp my husband's business if I bought that.

HE: Why not let me present it to you?

SHE: Heavens! You take my breath away. And why should you?

HE: Simply because it pleases me. Here, miss. [*He beckons the sales-lady.*] You have this lady's address. Send that cloak to it. Give me a receipt for the money. [*Throws down the filthy lucre.*]

SHE: But my husband—he will wonder!

HE: No, he won't. If he does, tell him it's really inexplicable how they get up these imitations. Then say, "Now here's a cloak I only gave $38. for. It's every bit as good as one I saw marked $150." Then he'll think what a provident, prudent wife he has. But come, I have the receipt, let's take the little lunch.

SHE: [*Sotto voce.*] But am I prudent?

Well, anyway, the modern gold-digger would say that this imaginary Talmage parishioner, knew how to "pick a live one." It was the poor saleslady who figured in the above scene who did not get the breaks. See what this poor white slave was up against from the hard-hearted owner of the store. (White slave carried a different meaning than in later years. And yet, there was not such a vast difference in the human bondage.) Here is what we learn about the young lady who had smilingly taken the order for that $150. coat.

But as a matter of fact the young lady is not happy. She is acting a part. She smiles because she will be fined if she does not. She is neatly dressed because she will be discharged if she is not. How she manages to dress so well God only knows, for her salary is but five dollars a week, the average of her weekly fines is fifty cents, and she has to contribute to the support of a mother.

But that is simply neither here nor there. We simply wish to consider facts, and what I want to insist upon is that the large firms in this city, whose towering stores [then five or six stories at most] are stocked with the richest fabrics of the earth, and all a-glitter with the ingenious baubles of the boulevards, are guilty of serfdom in the treatment of these girls just as much as the Czar of All the Russias was. The shop girls are the white slaves of the metropolis, and although they are not bought and sold in a market-place as are those Caucasian girls who are brought to the Constantinople shambles, they are just as much in bondage.

For what is the condition of our white slaves? The average salary is $3.50. and board is nowhere less than $4. The consequence is she has to keep house in order to take care of her mother. I cannot give the bill of fare at the tenement of the young lady who made the sale of the $150. coat. It consists, undoubtedly, if bought from the money earned in the store, of but a single dish.

Stew, at the utmost.

And then Reverend Talmage and the *Gazette* readers are told:

"The wickedest house on the wickedest street that ever existed in New York, yes, and in all the country and possibly all the world, was the building known as the Old Brewery on the street known as 'Cutthroat Lane.'" Cross (later, and even in this day, known as Park) Street was the actual name of "Cutthroat Lane," and 59 was the number on the building known as the Old Brewery. The house and the street and several of the surrounding thoroughfares, which are now taken up in part by fine municipal properties, made up the section known as the Five Points.

The dismal and repulsive alleys that made up this cluster of slums and whose ways were often ankle-deep in mud, are lined with crumbling tenements which have in many cases begun to sag out of shape, the foundations having sunk into what was originally a swamp land. It is a low-roofed darksome place that leads apparently into the infernal regions. Into these old rookeries had swarmed Negroes who had escaped the bonds of slavery, also the scum of early immigration from Great Britain and with a preponderance of Irish, but with nearly all nationalities represented and intermingled. Thieving, beggary and prostitution provided their vile existence, and the drunkenness and the attractions of the lowest of grog-geries their sole escape in the way of what they deem pleasure. The music that filters from these cheap dance dives is generally the blatant strains of a wheezy accordion. The noises that emanate from the houses are usually drunken cries and the odors the foulest of stenches. Here is vice at its lowest ebb, a crawling and fetid vice, a vice of rags and filth. The place was the terror of every officer, for it was all but worth one's life to go into the houses singlehanded.

In one survey of the Five Points, around 1850, which was made under police protection, the following conditions were reported in just one block: During five hours on the Sabbath two of the drinking dens were visited by 450 men, 445 women and 68 girls. Out of 916 adults in this one block 605 could neither read nor write; of 614 children, only nine went to school. Most of them carried too much vermin to be admitted to the public schools. Along this same block there were twenty of the vilest grog shops and dance halls and no less than thirty-three underground lodging houses, where most of them had bunks filled with decayed rags or canvas bags filled with rotten straw for beds. In the Old Brewery the tenants numbered over one thousand.

For a full score of the sixty years that this structure stood, the debasements within its confines were so utterly repugnant as to make any unvarnished relation of its putridity seem nothing less than the play of an unsound and exaggerated imagination. It had been erected as a brewing plant by a party named Coulter some fifteen years after the Declaration of Independence by these United States and was not demolished until our republic was ten years away from the internal throes of the Civil War. In 1837, when the one-time brewery had been converted for dwelling purposes, it had already reached an advanced age of dilapidation through a period of disuse and neglect.

Originally it had been only three stories in height, but one of the floors which had been high-ceiled to make room for the large brew vats had been made over into two floors and the attic beneath the peaked roof had been divided into another floor, so that in its days as a residence it was known as a five-story building. Including the cellar, which had been divided into small compartments, and those above ground there were close to one hundred rooms in all and to which windows gave to but few; fresh air or sunlight was denied to most of the occupants. Nothing had been done to improve its outward appearance with its transformation into a place of habitation. Its frame shell had been originally painted yellow but the rigors of time and weather now left only an unhealthy discoloration.

When the building was razed in December, 1852, to make way for the mission house sponsored by the Conference of the Methodist Episcopal Church, the wreckers carried out human bones by the sacks-full. The removal of the Old Brewery had been an achievement of twelve years of labor by the religious society, which had been the means of bringing to the Five Points the able and earnest reverend and humanitarian, Lewis Morris Pease, who with his equally sincere and godly wife, founded the Five Points House of Industry, an institution that had much to do with the reclaiming of the Five Points from its depths of sin and squalor. The Peases, for all their religious training, seemed to appreciate where education and employment could be even more efficacious than prayer in this work of regeneration. The Five Points Mission, which was also established nearby by the Methodist society, went in more for the industry of religion than the necessity of self-supporting occupation. Still, the Mission reclaimed its quota of lost souls.

Referring to its own columns the *Gazette* cited how in 1847, in just one month's issue of four numbers, its department headed "Police Items" recorded no less than fourteen notes that had to do with crime and misdemeanor within the confines of the Five Points. As these were taken from the station-house blotter and so had to do only with the wrongdoing that came to the attention of the police, the whole made up only a small percentage of the crime committed in that wretched district. By way of realistic illustration the *Gazette* reprinted a few samples:

DEATH AND DESTITUTION—The Coroner was called on Sunday to hold an inquest in the Old Brewery on the body of a female about forty years of age, named Mary Vieta, who was found lying dead in her room. It seems, from the evidence, that the deceased was a woman of intemperate habits, and whose husband a Portuguese, who is now on Blackwell's Island, had been in the habit of begging about the streets, exhibiting, for the purpose of exciting sympathy, a sickly child, of apparently only a few months old—but whose growth had in reality been prevented by sheer starvation! the poor thing being nearly as many years old as it seemed months! A few days ago the woman became deranged, apparently laboring under delirium tremens, and while in this state became so violent *that some of the dwellers in this vast charnel-house of wretchedness and misery actually nailed up the door of her apartment and left her to perish!* Upon opening the room yesterday morning, Mary was found dead and cold, with her child in the agonies of dissolution, upon her bloated bosom! Her ill-used offspring is probably by this time beyond the reach of human charity. Verdict upon the mother: death from delirium tremens.

ATTEMPT TO VIOLATE—Sunday afternoon a fellow named Mulligan was arrested on the Five Points for drunken and disorderly conduct. No sooner was Mulligan locked up, than two men, named James Campbell and Arthur Rogers, entered the basement of Mulligan, and made a desperate attempt to violate Mulligan's wife, Catherine. The offenders were taken to the Tombs by officer Rafferty and a detachment, and detained to answer.

HIGHWAY ROBBERY—Officers Connolly and Riley, of the Sixth Ward, arrested on Saturday two black fellows called Sam Rice and George Morgan, on a charge of knocking down Abraham Hummer, of Lebanon Township, Hunterdon County, New Jersey, while passing along Orange Street, Five Points, on Friday night, dragging him into an alley-way, and while there robbing him of eight dollars, and his coat and boots. The coat and boots were found on the person of one of the prisoners. Justice Osborn committed them both for trial.

JUVENILE DEPRAVITY—An interesting white girl, Ellen Amelia Walker, who about a week ago left home and took up her abode with some of the most depraved colored men and women at No. 51 Anthony Street, Five Points, was restored to her friends.

A TOUGH CASE—An English sailor, named Owens, while strolling about in search of the lions on Saturday night, stumbled upon a house of notoriously bad repute, kept by James Green, at No. 156 Anthony Street, Five Points. He became fascinated by the charms of a frail syren named Ellen Murphy, who had lodgings at the above address. After an hour or two spent in very agreeable intercourse M'lle Ellen expressed a wish for a slight draught—just the merest dust in the world of something or other to increase the joyous hilarity of the occasion—and Jack, nothing loth, also expressed willingness to splice the main brace, when, on feeling for his wallet, what was his consternation to find he had not a shot in his locker. He immediately bore away for the police office and entered a complaint and Ellen was placed under arrest and a portion of the money was recovered. The amount of which this land pirate had robbed him was $45, mostly in gold; and as Ellen could give no reasonable account of how she became possessed of the pieces found upon her she was locked up for trial. Owens was also placed in limbo as a witness.

SUPPOSED MURDER—Officers Munson and Kelly, of the Sixth Ward, on Saturday night arrested a black fellow named James Hunter on a charge of striking his wife a violent blow on the head with a billet of wood and inflicting a wound which will in all probability cause her death. This outrage was done up Murderer's Alley, Orange Street, Five Points. The woman was conveyed to the hospital in a dying condition. Justice Osborn committed the accused to the Tombs to wait the result.

SHOCKING JUVENILE PROSTITUTION—Information was laid before Justice Drinker of shocking juvenile prostitution pursued at a den in 18 Anthony Street, Five Points. It appears that no less than a dozen girls from ten to sixteen years, who pretend to sell candies, fruit, peanuts, etc., have been sent out by the woman in charge of the resort at No. 18 Anthony Street, named Jane White, alias Horn, alias Cook. Officer Stewart, with the assistance of some policemen, took into custody all found in the house.

FEMALE HIGHWAY ROBBERS—Two black women by the names of Mary Fermon and Emeline Freeman were arrested last night by Officer Gardiner on a charge of knocking down a white woman called Margaret O'Neill, in Cow Bay, on the Five Points, and stealing from her person a shawl and bonnet, and were just making good their escape when caught by the above officer. Justice Drinker committed them both for trial.

So it is readily believable that the terrors and degeneracies of the Five Points were an actuality; that violence and murders and orgies were an hourly occurrence; that each street was a congestion of beggars, thieves and murderers, of harlots and degenerates; and that miscegenation and incest were only too common; that the sloth and the frenzy of drink was all that took them out of the horror of being what they were.

An old *Gazette* story that has to do with the Five Points, and that has often been transferred to other localities, is one that could easily have been true. It tells of an unkempt urchin running up to a policeman and beseeching him to make all haste up Cross Street, as two men were engaged there in a fierce fight.

"Oh, to the devil with them," was the answer, "they're always fighting up in that alley."

"But, please," faltered the boy, "my father is in the fight."

So the officer followed after the boy and came upon two men who were man-handling each other with much vigor. They gave no heed to the demand that they must keep the peace and the policeman drew his club and with a smart rap over each bellicose head knocked the two unconscious.

"There you are, boy," said the obliging officer. "Which is your father?"

And the boy whimpered: "That's what they were fighting about."

Conditions equally intolerable, but no worse, since such a thing was not quite possible, existed in unsavory rivalry to the Five Points along the water-front and continued to maintain for more than a quarter of a century after the Old Brewery had been demolished. The area running parallel with the lower East River was the worst hotbed of crime. Let us ramble along Water Street and its immediate vicinity with the *Gazette* reporter.

Almost within the shadows of the forest of mast and rigging that rise to the sky, almost within reach of the bowsprits that extend across South Street, we find ourselves in the midst of the lowest of dives and the most squalid of places that ever answered to the name of home. We are on Water Street and along both sides of the way for a comparatively short distance there are close to one hundred drinking and dancing places that also serve as boarding-houses for sailors. If this were a segregated infamy it would be bad enough. But side by side with these terrible dens, almost a part of them, in fact, are dwellings in which unfortunate children are being born and raised. Heaven knows how. Cherry Street is on a par with Water.

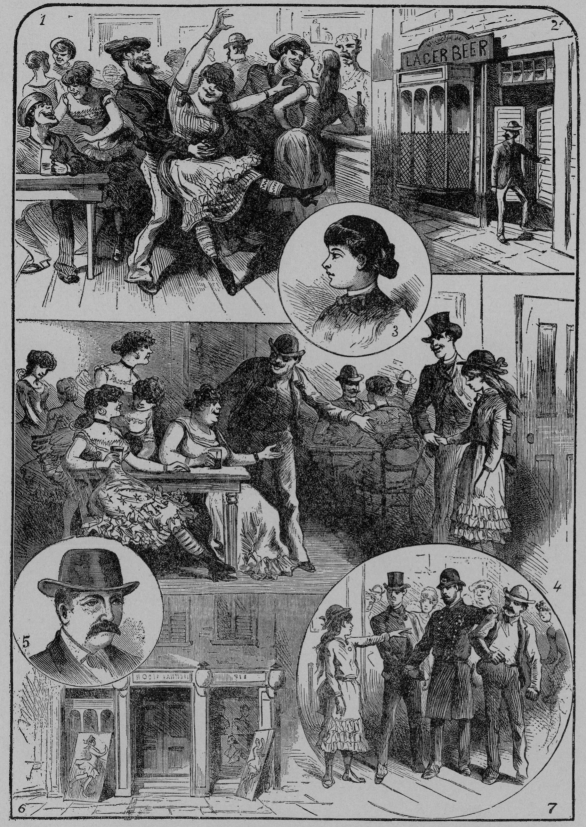

THE CHILD OF THE DIVES.

A SAMPLE OF THE UNUTTERABLE ABOMINATIONS BY WHICH THE LITTLE DAUGHTERS OF THE POOR ARE RAPIDLY FAMILIARIZED WITH VICE
AND DEBAUCHERY.

I.—A Sailor Dance-House on Cherry Street. II.—Exterior of Saloon 103 Cherry Street. III.—Kitty Cavanagh IV.—Interior of a Dive in Chatham Street V.—A Typical Diver.
VI.—Exterior of a Den on Chatham Street. VII.—Trappers Trapped.

SINS OF NEW YORK

Many of the houses here and the population, as well, subsist for one purpose alone, and that is to prey upon unwary Jack ashore. Over there is the unhealthy resort where Gallus Mag, one of the fiercest strumpets that ever existed, holds forth. Just around the corner is the pest-hole presided over by the "Queen of Cherry Street." The latter owes her sovereignty to the fact that she can drink more whiskey than any two men or any six women (this statement looks like discrimination) without showing it, while the Gallus one traces her cognomen to the fact that she supports her skirts with the aid of suspenders. She is an expert at biting off the ear of an opponent in a rough-and-tumble fight and has quite a collection of these trophies preserved in alcohol in a bottle which she keeps behind the bar.

Most of these places are nothing less than crimps where sailors are drugged and not only robbed, but shanghaied while still insensible. For years these desperadoes from Water Street have fastened on seamen as quickly as they left their ships and then through a system of advanced wages and exorbitant charges and "drinks for the house" have placed their dupes in debt. Once this fleecing was accomplished they were hustled on board some outbound ship while still intoxicated. Captains often had no other resource when it came time to make up their crews but to deal with these landsharks. Over one thousand girls between twelve and eighteen years of age were found in these places.

From out of this row of old gable-roofed houses, which were once the homes of fashionable New York in the days of the quiet Dutch burghers, now comes the twanging of cheap fiddles and of cracked pianos. Within we find ourselves in the company of a hard and polluted citizenry. The floors are covered with sand to make easy footing for the dancers. The places are illy lighted by swinging kerosene lamps or fluttering gas-jets. Cheap pictures of pugilists are usually the only adornment on the musty walls. Drunkenness and foul language is the least of the vices carried on in these houses of entertainment, and the rat and cockpits do not provide the most unwholesome of the entertainment.

And the vices practiced here are carried right into the houses used for living purposes. Rotten floors, oozing walls, crazy stairways, broken windows, sickening stenches, vermin everywhere; flickering tallow candles or musty kerosene lamps lend the only lighting. Paint, fresh air, water, are undesired luxuries. Hydrants are in the yards which are filled with decaying refuse and the halls are choked with rubbage. Even the cellars are populated, cellars whose ceilings are sometimes only six inches above the walk and whose floors give and splash under your feet. Women and men and children sleep indiscriminately.

One welfare investigator tells of finding one room divided up by an imaginary line for the accommodations of two families. One of the fami-

[288]

lies admitted that there was overcrowding, but that things would not be so bad if the family in the other corner did not keep boarders.

Mother Glump's five-cent lodging-house on Cherry Street, which was merely one of a number, offered no other sleeping accommodations than mattresses tossed on the floor and all in the same room. There were no restrictions as to sex, but Mother Glump never allowed more than three occupants to the same mattress at one time. Her lodgers came in drunk and so soon as one staggered out another staggered in.

Let us hurry away from these altogether degrading surroundings. A too intimate survey means a peep into such places as Gotham Court, a Cherry Street tenement that almost rivaled the Old Brewery in the degradations it housed—one of the main city sewers seeped into its area and during the cholera epidemic of the Seventies the deaths were so numerous the city had good cause to be horrified; it is a known fact that infants were gnawed to death here by rats.

The one dance hall that stood out as sumptuous in comparison to its rookery rivals, and that was only rivaled by the Kit Burns resort for unmitigated corruption, was that presided over by John Allen. In 1868 his fine brick building stood out like a palace over the other mean dens along Water Street. Allen is said to have been a student in the Union Theological Seminary and was educated for a sacred calling.* He had blood relations in the ministry and Bibles and religious papers were often conspicuous through his establishment. The female inmates were uniformed in scarlet and bright-colored dresses, and red-topped boots with ankle bells were part of their uniform.

In 1868 Allen's, Burns' and other of the Water Street places of ill-fame gained much newspaper space when an invasion by religious fanatics was supposed to have brought about a wholesale conversion of the district, so that even Allen's was turned into a place of prayer. Investigations by the New York *Times* and the New York *World* exploded most of these stories and the section continued a moral and physical pestilence for quite a few years after.

"It was not prayers," says the *Gazette,* "that finally wiped out sin along the water-front. Education, years of hard work and tolerance were the corrective. The Seaman's Exchange, which was established in 1872, did much to provide relief through its conveniences in the way of savings banks and reading rooms. Bethels and homes for seamen provided clean and attractive quarters, and sanitary precau-

---

* From reliable sources I find that this mixture of religion and prostitution has little foundation but is largely romancing.

tions were introduced against scurvy, one of the worst afflictions of the sailor man."

And it was a man who had been born a thief, so the *Gazette* sagely pointed out, "who became a modern Jean Valjean in the saving of his own kind." It was a pretty low kind from which Jerry McAuley had sprung. His father had been a counterfeiter. He had been of the Catholic faith, if any. In his youth, Jerry McAuley had been a prize fighter in the Water Street dens and he had thieved on the river by night. He had committed enough crime, in his own words, to deserve prison a half-hundred times. Before his twentieth birthday he was sentenced to prison for a fifteen-year stretch. And in 1872, the same year The Seaman's Exchange came into existence, Jerry McAuley founded his Water Street Mission. Here none were so low that they sought in vain for a helping hand, even though it was a meal or a lodging without salvation that was sought.

While in prison he learned to read. One day before his release in the fifth year of his term he suddenly found himself praying and some vision came to him that caused him to cry out: "Oh! praise God!"

A guard came rushing to his cell to inquire what all the noise was about.

"I've found Christ," said McAuley.

"I'll report you," threatened the guard. And he took Jerry's number.

McAuley was pardoned after seven years and six months in jail. Once he was free he soon fell into more or less evil ways again. One of his occupations was the purchasing of smuggled goods with counterfeit money. During one of the transactions, and while in a very intoxicated condition, he fell overboard. The water sobered him, but he only reached shore after a mighty struggle. As he fainted away from exhaustion on the dock, he declares a voice came to him saying:

"Jerry, you have been saved for the last time."

He struggled valiantly to stay honest and then when he was on the verge of starvation a missionary took the coat from his own back and pawned it so that Jerry might eat. McAuley says he was so touched by the naturalness of this deed that he vowed to himself he would die first before he would sink back into a life of sin.

This was the story of Jerry McAuley, which the *Gazette* recounted in its report of his death, as it had been heard to fall from his own lips many times. It is said that none doubted the details who had it from his own lips. And it seems few, if any, doubted the sincerity of the man and the work to which he had consecrated his remaining years. He was only forty-five when he died from a severe hemorrhage

SINS OF NEW YORK

of the lungs. "It's all right," he said, pointing upward. He had done a lot of good in his way. The Sunday following his passing, the Broadway Tabernacle was crowded with unkempt and expensively dressed, shoulder to shoulder. And some of the most prominent of the clergy of the day paid homage to his memory and led in the singing, with tender pathos, Jerry McAuley's favorite chorus:

> We, too, must come to the river-side,
>   One by one, one by one;
> We're nearer to its brink each eventide,
>   One by one, one by one.

Though it may not be easy of belief at this day, the *Gazette* in no way exaggerated when it described the Bowery as an artery that was originally designed to be the main thoroughfare of the great city; even in Civil War days it was rated the second principal street. Bowerie Pathje (Bowery Road) came into existence in the days of Governor Stuyvesant, being cut through in 1652 from Chatham Square to Sunfish Creek, a stream that diverged from where is now Fourth Avenue and Thirty-fourth Street to the foot of East Twenty-fifth Street. According to the map of 1804, it was known as Bowery Lane up as far as Bullock (now Broome) Street, and above that it was known as the Road to Boston. In 1832, thirteen years before the *Gazette* printed its initial number, the first street-car line started running up the Bowery.

It began as a street of pleasure resorts as early as 1732 when James Sperry, a Swiss florist, purchased a part of the Bayard Farm, which was in the vicinity of Astor Place, and opened his Botanical Gardens in 1752. In 1803 it was renamed Vauxhall Gardens and a theatre was added to the dance hall and picnic park; it was for years the most popular resort in all the city. In 1826 Bull's Head Tavern, which had beeen built in 1756 and was for years the last hostelry in the city on the highroad to Boston, became the site of the Bowery Theatre. This structure (still in existence at this writing) was the most famous theatre for quite a few years. It was the first theatre to be illuminated with gas and the greatest actors of the day trod its boards. Seven years later, 1833, the Bowery Amphitheatre came into existence and later became the Stadt Theatre, a famous German playhouse. In 1864 it was enlarged by taking in the German Volks Garten and with a seating capacity of 3,500 it became the largest theatre in all the land, and it was here that Lohengrin and Tannhauser and other famous operas were first sung in America.

Even when the German beer gardens were at their height and the amber fluid flowed so freely that a four-horse dray from the brewery was pressed on a busy day

"GOLLY, MISSEY, BIZ IS GETTIN' GOOD."

THE MANIA FOR GETTING THEIR SHOES BLACKED WHICH HAS TAKEN POSSESSION OF THE BELLES OF THE BOWERY.

to supply the thirsty, even years before this, a corrupting flow of mixed nationalities was seeping in and changing the pleasant complexion of the Bowery. Around these "gartens," where the songs of the Fatherland were blended into lusty harmony by family parties who found carefree happiness in eating, drinking, flirting and the playing of cards and dominoes, the belles of the Bowery and the Bowery B'hoys and young would-be sports in long black frock coats had begun to crowd in with their own social and political club centers and dance halls and saloons. Gradually the wine stube and the kaffee haus, where the patron could nibble his küchen and sip his coffee until long after midnight, were being crowded out.

Some old landmarks, such as Doc. Oliffe's drugstore, and the jewelry-store of A. C. Benedict, where there was a clock that had been ticking continuously for well beyond a hundred years, the hat-stores of McCann and of Callahan, stuck it out even as the Bowery changed from a way of inviting recreation to one of rowdy recklessness and finally to such a drab and colorless street and one of such evil associations that, when it finally became the trading artery it now is, there was a strong attempt made to change its name.

But of the Bowery of which Harry Connor sang in Hoyt's play, "A Trip to Chinatown"—

> *The Bowery! The Bowery!*
> *They say such things and they do such things;*
> *The Bowery! The Bowery!*
> *I'll never go there any more.*

Starting from Chatham Square [Paul Prowler is taking this stroll in 1879] it almost seems as though every other building is occupied by a saloon or a cheap beer dive or free-and-easy.

Some room has been given over to the several theatres and the few respectable business concerns, but otherwise it is a place of cheap lodging-houses, oysters saloons, dime museums, pawn-shops, cheap clothing-stores, lottery-shops, shooting-galleries, and the like. The way to most of these places, even the lowest of the dens, is lighted by various colored devices in the form of transparencies. The museums have a frontage that is made up of gaudily painted figures on canvas which are supposed to represent the attractions within.

Let us invest a dime and peer inside one of these museums. They are nearly all the same. Giants, dwarfs, fat ladies, living skeletons, tattooed men. The midget is always "the smallest man in the world, weighs only ten pounds," and so on. There is the "expansionist," who can inflate his chest until he breaks a strap that has been bound about him; the Turtle Boy, who has nothing much in the way of legs; the Champion Egg-eater and the Dog-faced Boy, whose bark has a Celtic ring. Snake charmers, glass and fire eaters, sword swallowers. The Transparent Man, who looks as though his wife might have no trouble seeing through him; the Human

NEW YORK'S DEADLY DIVES—CHATHAM SQUARE MUSEUMS—"CURIOSITIES" THAT SERVE AS A BLIND FOR THIEVES AND PROSTITUTES—GO-AS-YOU-PLEASE FEMALE WALKING MATCHES THAT BRING THEIR PATRONS INTO THE CLUTCHES OF CRIMINALS.—[SKETCHED BY OUR OWN ARTISTS.—SEE PAGE 15.

THE BOWERY ELECTRIC GIRLS.
HOW THEY PLAY THE UMBRELLA TRICK ON THE GREEN COUNTRYMEN IN THE DIVES.

SINS OF NEW YORK

Pin-cushion, who allows you to stick needles and pins into him; the Human Anvil, who permits large stones to be broken on his chest; and the Claw-hammer Man, who drives tacks with his thumb and would be a handy person to have around the house. Most of them have small theatres as an adjunct where lurid dramas are enacted by third-rate ranting Thespians. Many of these museums, as well as some of the larger saloons, conduct walking matches between women.

Abandoned, frowsy females accost on every side as you make your way up from Chatham Square. And should they entice you within, certain of the resorts will fleece you in various ways; beware of the "umbrella trick." The umbrella stick is so charged with electricity you cannot loose your hold. While you are thus caught your watch and other valuables will disappear. Sporting men, crooks, gamblers, sailors, out-of-towners with a streak of degenerate curiosity, tramps, bar flies, bootblacks, newsboys, saunter along or in and out of the vile groggeries or places of diversion. The elevated railroad, which had started to rumble overhead only a few months ago, adds a dreadful racket to the pandemonium of noises.

It must have been a pretty low-down Bowery that Prowler visited, less than one hundred years after General George Washington, in 1785, followed along this very way with his patriots on the heels of the evacuating British troops. Several flashy saloons flourished for years after, which was shortly before Steve Brodie's place came into existence and well before Chuck Connors had even been heard about. Brodie got away with the claim, in 1886, that he had successfully made the jump from the Brooklyn Bridge, a feat for which he was lauded by the *Gazette*. Later the *Gazette* insisted that Steve never "took a chance," but that the Fox champion did and made it. Maybe he did, but no one remembers the name of the Fox champion to-day, while the name of Brodie still lives. Connors, after his fame as Mayor of Chinatown was on the wane, resided in his declining days in one of the flats next to the Gazette Building, and his landlord, who was Richard K. Fox, never had his agents go to the bother of trying to collect the rent.

Chinatown, at the time of Prowler's visits, had been in existence for more than forty years, so we are informed. It was during the Forties that the Chinese junk, *Key-Ying,* made the port of New York after a long sail and became an object of such curiosity that great crowds paid admission to look through this strange boat and get a close view of its odd yellow-skinned crew. One day, during a big harbor fire, the ship was burned to the water's edge and some of its inmates drifted to Mott Street and formed the nucleus of the settlement, and the Mongolian population

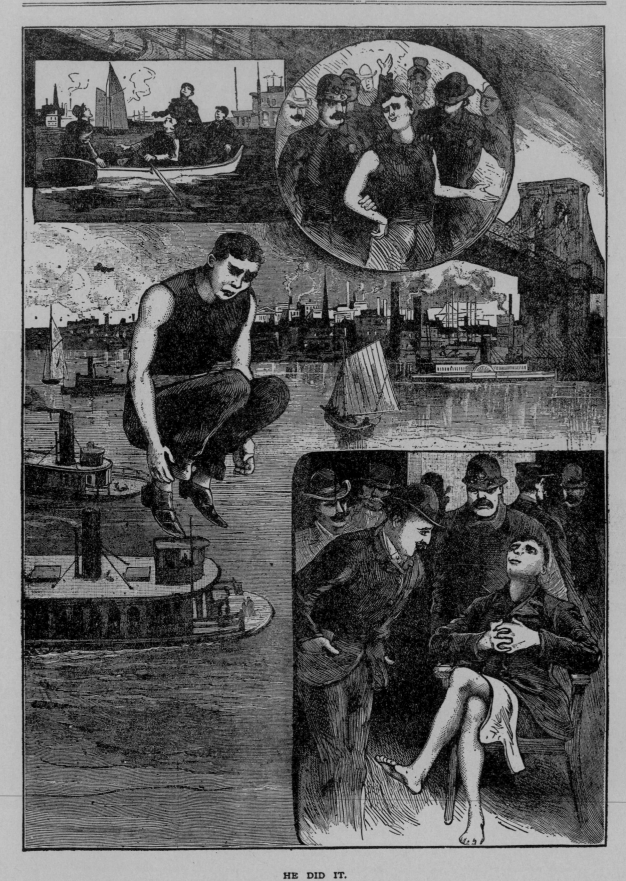

HE DID IT.

STEVE BRODIE, THE WELL-KNOWN NEW-YORK NEWSBOY, MAKES A FLYING LEAP FROM THE BIG BROOKLYN BRIDGE.

SLAVES TO A DEADLY INFATUATION.

OPIUM SMOKING—HOW AND WHERE ITS DEVOTEES "HIT THE PIPE" THAT LULLS THEM INTO THE OBLIVION OF DEATH.

spread to Pell and adjacent streets and then through the city with their laundries. "Smoking of opium and their dens thus became a new peril."

Not many years after Richard K. Fox, out of part of his *Gazette* profits, built a row of model flats far uptown and also over in Brooklyn, which were even equipped with bathtubs. And then his *Gazette,* in calling attention to the need of better housing conditions, had something to say in extenuation of the unbelievably wretched conditions that were to be found among the population of the wayfares that had outlet or that ran close to the Bowery when the series around which this article has been built was running in the pages of the pale pink periodical.

Until 1869 there was no foundling society in New York, nor even in the entire United States. Infanticide was common and new-born infants were often found under areaways or in ash barrels, sometimes floating along the docks. Then, in October, a woman whose heart belonged to the angels, and whose name is no more known than that she was called Sister Irene, had a most beautiful thought. Inside of the open doorway to 17 West 12th Street, she placed beneath a little gleaming light a curious tiny basket that had been softly lined. Late in the night and in the midst of a pouring rain a frightened woman found her way to the door with a bundle nestling under her arm. Tearfully and with one long, lingering kiss she placed the bundle into the cot and then hurried away. There was a sharp little wail and the inside door opened and a woman with a calm and gentle face reached out and the bundle was in her arms. Within a month forty-five babies had been left in the care of Sister Irene. Until then foundling mites were taken to the almshouse on Blackwell's Island where they were bottle-fed by aged paupers.

And then, after citing some further statistics, the *Gazette* touched off its moralizing editorial with the story of Mary Ellen.

Late in 1874, in a wretched East Side tenement a woman was found in the last stages of consumption by Mrs. Wheeler, a beloved social worker. She knew she was near the end and requested that Mrs. Wheeler should not concern herself over her last hours. But, if Mrs. Wheeler wanted to bring peace to her last hours she could do so by coming to the relief of a little girl who lived next door and who was being mistreated. She said:

"The little one's stepmother beats her, and I cannot die in peace while little Mary Ellen is being abused."

So Mrs. Wheeler took up the child's case with the Police Station, only to be informed by the captain that legally there was nothing that could be done unless positive evidence of assault was produced. The law held that parental authority was paramount and it was dangerous to interfere in this authority of the parent over the child. And the child could only be brought in under a legal order from the court. Mrs. Wheeler, not knowing where to turn, finally appealed to Henry Bergh, who consulted with Elbridge T. Gerry, counsel for a benevolent society which Mr. Bergh had sponsored some years previous. As Messrs. Bergh and Gerry agreed to assume all responsibilities, consent was gained to permit a test case.

A warrant was issued and the child was rushed into court and when the case was called Gerry announced that he was ready with his client. He had Mary Ellen rolled up in a blanket which he unrolled as he stood her on a table. A cry of indignation and pity went up through the room. There stood a child of six in rags insufficient to cover her starved and beaten little body, which was a mass of livid bruises and filth and vermin. A thousand witnesses could not have spoken more forcibly in the child's behalf.

No delay was lost in placing Mary Ellen in the custody of the Society of Prevention of Cruelty to Animals, of which Mr. Bergh was the president, and Mr. Gerry the legal advisor.

You see, while there was a Society of Prevention of Cruelty to Animals, there was no Society of Prevention of Cruelty to Children until the plight of little Mary Ellen was brought vividly to the public attention.